# TRANSFORMATIVE CONSTITUTIONALISM AND KENYA

## Law, Justice and Society in Africa

ISSN 3050-2829 (Print)
ISSN 3050-2837 (Online)

This new series welcomes interdisciplinary monographs and edited collections that rethink conventional approaches to contemporary legal issues in Africa. Innovative and scholarly books that challenge Eurocentric normative assumptions in the fields of law and society and socio-legal studies are of particular interest. Topics might include African-centred critical approaches to constitutionalism, property law, legal theory, law and humanities, human rights, transitional justice, environmental law or law and development.

**Series Editors**

Professor Ambreena Manji, Professor of Land Law and Development and Africa Dean at Cardiff University, manjial@cardiff.ac.uk

Professor Joel M. Modiri, Associate Professor and Head of the Department of Jurisprudence at the University of Pretoria, joel.modiri@up.ac.za

Preliminary enquiries and proposals from prospective authors are welcome. Please contact the Series Editors with an outline or download the proposal form at www.jamescurrey.com.

# TRANSFORMATIVE CONSTITUTIONALISM AND KENYA

## LAW-MAKING, POLITICAL PROCESS, AND THE STATE (2010–2025)

Gautam Bhatia

JAMES CURREY

First published 2025
James Currey

ISBN 978-1-84701-389-7

James Currey is an imprint of Boydell & Brewer Ltd
PO Box 9, Woodbridge Suffolk IP12 3DF (GB)
www.jamescurrey.com
and of
Boydell & Brewer Inc.
668 Mt Hope Avenue Rochester, NY 14620-2731 (US)
www.boydellandbrewer.com

Our Authorised Representative for product safety in the EU is Easy Access System Europe – Mustamäe tee 50, 10621 Tallinn, Estonia, gpsr.requests@easproject.com

British Library Cataloguing in Publication Data
A CIP record for this book is available from the British Library

*To the People of Kenya,*
*with gratitude and admiration*

# CONTENTS

# ACKNOWLEDGEMENTS

I AM grateful, before all else, to the community of Kenyan lawyers, law students, scholars, judges, and citizens who have accepted me as an interlocutor in an ongoing conversation about Kenyan constitutionalism. I hope that this book will do justice to their generosity.

Special thanks to: Waikwa Wanyoike, who initiated me into Kenyan constitutional law over long discussions about digital IDs and fundamental rights, and who has since been a wonderful friend and colleague; Walter Khobe, from whom I've learned so much, and who has been a constant source of encouragement; Ambreena Manji, whose scholarship has informed mine in ways too many to count, and who has believed in my work more than I have myself; and Joshua Malidzo, always a WhatsApp message away, brilliant counsel, brilliant friend, and fellow venter about the eccentricities of courts (if you know, you know!). Each of them also took the time out to read the whole – or parts – of the book, and their inputs were invaluable. Thank you once again.

I'm grateful to everyone who hosted me and spoke to me during my visit to Kenya in 2023. At Lake Bogoria and Nakuru: the Kabarak Law School, the Avid Readers Forum, John Ambani, Elisha Ongoya, Jared Gekombe, Lucianna Thuo, Willy Mutunga, and everybody else; in Nairobi: Justice Joel Ngugi, Jill Ghai and Yash Ghai, Emmanuel Ekiru, Muthomi Thiankolu, Jo Kahumbu, and so many others; a repeat thank you to Walter Khobe for showing me around the Supreme Court and its brilliant museum, and to Zakheem Rajan; to Ahmed Aidarus and the brilliant Prestige bookshop; and likewise, to Ubax Abdi and Cheche Books. A special shout-out to the Katiba Institute and my friends (both before and after we actually met in person) Ochiel Dudley and Evans Ogada. I know I'm forgetting someone, and I can only offer my apologies for that! Thanks, in addition, to the Jindal Global Law School, whose travel grant made this visit possible.

My thanks to Jacqueline Mitchell at Boydell & Brewer/James Currey for commissioning this book, and to Megan Milan who took it forward. I am grateful to an anonymous peer reviewer for their extremely detailed and deeply helpful comments on the first draft of the manuscript. I am also thankful to the production staff at Boydell & Brewer, including Rohais Landon and Henry Lafferty, as well as copyeditor Michael Wood and cover-designer Wayne

Kehoe, without whose efforts no book would ever actually reach the shelf, let alone your hands.

A book is always a conversation with all those who have come before. I am grateful to all the scholars – especially the Kenyan scholars – whose work has made mine possible. My tribute to them is the footnotes that line the pages of this book.

# INDEX OF CASES

## Kenyan Cases

*Abdalla Rhova Hiribae and Ors vs the Attorney General and Ors*, Civil Case No. 14 of 2010, decided on 4th February 2013 (High Court).

*Agnes Nanjala William v Jacob Petrus Nicholas Vandergoes,* MSA CA Civil Appeal No 127 of 2011 (UR) (Court of Appeal).

*Anthony Njenga Mbuti and Ors vs Attorney-General and Ors*, [2015] KEHC 6970 (KLR).

*Busia Sugar Industry Limited v Agriculture and Food Authority & 2 others* [2024] KEHC 1099.

*C.O.M. vs The Standard Group Ltd and Anr*, Petition 192 of 2011, decided on 5th April 2013 (High Court).

*Charles Muturi Macharia and Ors vs The Standard Group and Ors*, Petition 13 (E015) of 202, decided on 8th September 2023 (Supreme Court).

*David Ndii and Ors vs Attorney-General and Ors*, [2021] KEHC 9746 (KLR).

*Duncan Muriuki Kaguru v Baobab Beach Resort and Spa Ltd,* Petition No 223 of 2012, decided on 12th June 2013 (High Court).

*EG and Ors vs Attorney General and Ors*, Petition No. 150 of 2016, decided on 24th May 2019 (High Court).

*Eliud Karanja Matindi and Ors vs The President of the Republic of Kenya and Ors*, [2023] KEHC 19534 (KLR).

*Federation of Women Lawyers v Attorney-General*, Petition No 164B of 2016, decided on 14th May 2018 (High Court).

*Gatirau Peter Munya vs Dickson Mwenda Kithinji and Ors*, [2014] KESC 38 (KLR).

*In the Matter of Interim Independent Electoral Commission*, [2011] KESC 1 (KLR).

*In the Matter of the National Land Commission*, [2015] KESC 3 (KLR).

*In the Matter of the Principle of Gender Representation in the National Assembly and the Senate*, [2012] KESC 5 (KLR).

*In the Matter of the Speaker of the Senate and Anr*, [2013] KESC 7 (KLR).

*Isaac Ngugi v The Nairobi Hospital*, Petition No 407 of 2012, decided on 30th September 2013 (High Court).

*Isaka Wainaina vs Murito wa Indagara* (1922-23) Kenya Law Reports Vol. IX 102.

*Jacqueline Okuta and Anr vs The Hon Attorney-General and Ors*, Petition No. 397 of 2016, decided on 6th February 2017 (High Court).

*Jemimah Wambui Ikere vs Standard Group Ltd and Anr*, Petition No. 466 of 2012, decided on 18th December 2013 (High Court).

*John Harun Mwau and Ors vs IEBC and Ors*, [2017] KESC 54 (KLR).

*John Kabui Mwai and Ors vs Kenya National Examination Council and Ors*., Petition No. 15 of 2011, decided on 16th September 2011 (High Court).

*Joseph Ombogi Ogentoto vs Martha Bosibiri Ogentoto*, Petition No. 11 of 2020, decided on 27th January 2023 (Supreme Court).

*Katiba Institute and Ors vs The Director of Public Prosecutions and Ors*, HCCHRPET No E016 of 2023, decided on 18th March 2024 (High Court).

*Katiba Institute and Ors vs The Hon. Attorney General and Ors*, Constitutional Petition No. 548 of 2017, decided on 6th April 2018 (High Court).

*Kenya Airports Authority vs Mitu-Bell Welfare Society and Ors*, Civil Appeal No. 218 of 2014, decided on 1st July 2016 (Court of Appeal).

*Kenya Bus Services Ltds and Ors vs Attorney-General and Ors*, Misc Civil Suit No. 413 of 2005, decided on 10th June 2005 (High Court).

*Kiana Monique Arendse and Ors vs Meta Platforms Inc and Ors*, [2023] KEELRC 921 (KLR).

*Law Society of Kenya vs Betty Sungurua Nyabuto and Ors*, Petition 21 of 2010, decided on 20th January 2012 (High Court).

*LSK and 2 ors vs AG et al.* [2022] KEELRC 13324 (KLR).

*Mike Rubia and Anr vs Dr Moses Mwangi and Ors*, Petition No. 70 of 2012, decided on 26th August 2014 (High Court).

*Mitu-Bell Welfare Society vs Attorney-General and Ors*, Petition No. 164 of 2011, decided on 11th April 2013 (High Court).

*Mitu-Bell Welfare Society vs The Kenya Airports Authority*, [2021] KESC 34 (KLR).

*Mohamed Fugicha vs Methodist Church of Kenya*, [2016] KECA 273 (KLR).

*MW vs AN*, Matrimonial Cause Number, 20 of 2016, decided on 14th September 2021 (High Court).

*Mwangi Stephen Mureithi vs Hon. Daniel Toroitich Arap Moi*, Petition No. 625 of 2009, decided on 6th April 2011 (High Court).

*Mwangi Stephen Muriithi vs Hon. Daniel Toroitich Arap Moi*, [2023] KESC 61 (KLR).

*Nairobi Bottlers Ltd. vs Mark Ndumia Ndung'u*, Civil Appeal No. 99 of 2018, decided on 7th July 2023 (Court of Appeal).

*National Environment Management Authority vs Kelvin Musyoka* [2023] KECA 775 (KLR).

*NGO Coordination Board vs Eric Gitari and Ors*, [2023] KESC 17 (KLR).

*Okiya Omtatah Okoiti and Ors vs The Cabinet Secretary for the National Treasury and Planning and Ors*, [2023] KEHC 25656 (KLR).

*Okiyah Omtatah and Anr vs PSC and 73 Ors*, [2021] KEHC 464 (KLR).

*Raila Odinga and Anr vs Independent Electoral and Boundaries Commission and Ors*, [2017] KESC 42 (KLR).

*Raila Odinga and Ors vs Independent Electoral and Boundaries Commission and Ors*, [2013] KESC 6 (KLR).

*Raila Odinga and Ors vs William Ruto and Ors*, [2022] KESC 54 (KLR).

*Rose Wangui Mambo and Ors vs Limuru County Club and Ors*, Constitutional Petition Number 160 of 2013, decided on 7th March 2014 (High Court).

*Satrose Ayuma and Ors vs The Registered Trustees of the Kenya Railways Staff Retirement Benefits Scheme*, [2013] KEHC 6003 (KLR).
*Scoline Anyango Ojung'a vs Healthlink Matcare*, [2023] KEELRC 1607 (KLR).
*Sonia Kwamboka Rasugu vs Sandalwood Hotel and Resort Ltd and Anr*, Petition No. 156 of 2011, decided on 26th July 2013 (High Court).
*Speaker of the National Assembly of the Republic of Kenya & another v Senate of the Republic of Kenya & 12 others*, [2021] KECA 282 (KLR).
*Stephen Saitoti Kapaiku vs Cocacola Sabco Nairobi Bottlers Ltd*, Petition No. 338 of 2012, decided on 21st June 2013 (High Court).
*The Hon'ble Attorney General and Ors vs David Ndii and Ors*, [2022] KESC 8 (KLR).
*The Honourable Attorney-General vs David Ndii and Ors*, [2021] KECA 363 (KLR).
*The Institute for Social Accountability and Anr vs The National Assembly and Ors*, [2022] KESC 39 (KLR).
*The Institute for Social Accountability and Anr vs The National Assembly and Ors*, Petition No. 71 of 2013, decided on 20th February 2015 (High Court).
*Uhuru Muigai Kenyatta vs Nairobi Star Publications Ltd.,* Petition No. 187 of 2012, decided on 5th April 2013 (High Court).
*Wamwere and Ors vs Attorney General and Ors*, [2023] KESC 3 (KLR).
*William Musembi and Ors vs Moi Educational Centre Co Ltd and Ors*, [2021] KESC 50 (KLR).
*Zacharia Okoth Obado vs Edward Akong'o Oyugi and Ors*, [2014] KESC 22 (KLR).

## South African Cases

*AB vs Pridwin Preparatory School*, 2020 (9) BCLR 1029 (CC).
*Baleni and Ors vs Minister of Mineral Resources and Ors*, (2019) 2 SA 453 (GP).
*City of Johannesburg v Rand Properties (Pty) Ltd and Others*, 2007 (6) SA 417 (SCA).
*Daniels vs Scribante*, 2017 (8) BCLR 949 (CC).
*Dladla and Another v City of Johannesburg and Others*, [2017] ZACC 42.
*Governing Body of the Juma Musjid Primary School and Ors vs Essay N.O. and Ors*, 2011 (8) BCLR 761 (CC).
*Government of the Republic of South Africa vs Grootboom*, 2000 (11) BCLR 1169 (CC).
*Khumalo vs Holomisa*, 2002 (8) BCLR 771 (CC).
*Occupiers of 51 Olivia Road, Berea Township, and 197 Main Street, Johannesburg v City of Johannesburg and Others*, 2008 (3) SA 208 (CC).
*Port Elizabeth Municipality v Various Occupiers*, 2005 (1) SA 217 (CC).

## Indian Cases

*Bhim Singh vs Union of India*, (2010) 5 SCC 538.
*Indian Young Lawyers Association vs State of Kerala*, (2019) 11 SCC 1.

*Kaushal Kishor vs Union of India*, SLP No. 34629 of 2017, judgment dated 3rd January 2023 (Supreme Court).

*Kesavananda Bharati vs State of Kerala*, (1973) 4 SCC 225.

*Rojer Mathew vs South Indian Bank Ltd*, (2020) 6 SCC 1.

*Suhail Rashid Bhat vs State of Jammu and Kashmir*, PIL 24/2018, judgment dated 25th October 2019 (High Court of Jammu and Kashmir).

## Miscellaneous

*Barry M. Bowen v The Attorney General of Belize*, BZ 2009 SC 2 (Supreme Court of Belize).

BVerfGE 7, 198 (1958) (Lüth) (German Federal Constitutional Court).

*Case No. C-141/2019* (Constitutional Court of Colombia).

*The Civil Rights Cases*, 109 U.S. 3 (1883).

Constitutional Petition Nos. 99 and 100 of 2014, decided on 5th August 2015 (Supreme Court of Pakistan).

*Flagg Bros vs Brooks*, 436 U.S. 149 (1978) (Supreme Court of the United States).

*Maurice Tomlinson v TVJ and Ors*, [2020] JMCA Civ 52 (Court of Appeal of Jamaica).

*New York Times vs Sullivan*, 376 U.S. 254 (1964) (Supreme Court of the United States).

*Peter Gregory Obi and Ors vs Independent National Electoral Commission and Ors*, Petition No. CA/PEPC/03/2023 (Supreme Court of Nigeria).

*Sentencia Number T-494/1992* (Constitutional Court of Colombia).

*Southwest Case*, 1 BvervGE 14 (1951), Constitutional Court of Germany).

*Tumwesige Francis v Attorney General* (Constitutional Petition No. 36 of 2018) [2022] UGCC 5, decided on 2nd December 2022 (Ugandan Constitutional Court).

# INDEX OF STATUTES

(*Statutes are Kenyan statutes unless otherwise specified*)

Community Land Act, 2016.
Constituency Development Fund Act, 2013.
Constitution of California, 1849.
Constitution of Ecuador, 2008.
Constitution of India, 1949.
Constitution of Kenya, 1963.
Constitution of Kenya, 2010.
Constitution of Mexico, 1917.
Constitution of the Plurinational State of Bolivia, 2009.
Constitution of the Republic of South Africa, 1996.
Elections Act, 2011.
Federal Constitution of the Swiss Confederation, 1899.
French Constitution, 1848.
Interim Constitution of the Republic of South Africa, 1993.
Married Women's Property Act, 1882.
National Government Constituencies Development Fund Act, 2015.
Prevention of Illegal Eviction from and Unlawful Occupation of Land Act 19, 1998 ["PIE"] (South Africa).
Registered Land Act, 1963.
The Land (Group Representatives) Act, 1968.
The Matrimonial Property Act, 2013.
Trust Land Act, 1939.
Trust Land Act, 1968.

# 1

# Prologue

## A. 13th May 2021

'Unconstitutional, null and void.'

WITH THESE words – which would soon go down in national folklore – the High Court of Kenya brought an ambitious project of constitutional overhaul to a juddering halt.

The origins of the words lay four years in the past. The 2017 General Election had seen a close and bitter contest between the incumbent President Uhuru Kenyatta and his challenger Raila Odinga. The process had been so rife with irregularities that the Supreme Court of Kenya had taken the unprecedented step of declaring the election invalid and ordering a rerun. But a few weeks before the rerun, Raila Odinga stated that none of the reforms recommended by the Supreme Court had been implemented, and that he was, therefore, boycotting the second election. Kenyatta's re-election became a formality.

In office, President Kenyatta gradually moved towards political reconciliation. The public articulation of this was a famous handshake between the two erstwhile contenders, on the steps of Harambee House. The constitutional articulation was a proposed set of seventy-four amendments, collectively known as the Building Bridges Initiative (BBI) Bill, which would be presented to the public as a package deal for constitutional reform. From altering the structure of the executive to increasing the number of constituencies, from creating a presidentially appointed judicial ombudsman to police reform, the BBI Bill contained a motley set of far-reaching changes to the Constitution.

Critics of the BBI Bill charged Kenyatta and Odinga with making a bipartisan attempt to eviscerate the 2010 Constitution of Kenya. They pointed to its proposed expansion of executive offices as a way of distributing political spoils through successive election cycles. Supporters argued that this was a good thing, as it would break the 'winner-takes-all' nature of the executive presidency, which had been responsible for so much political violence in the past. Even as the process began to move through the gears of Kenya's complex 'popular initiative' method of constitutional amendment, a challenge was brought before the High Court, bringing the country to that fateful day of 13th May 2021, and the Court's verdict.

The history of a constitutional court – and indeed, of a constitution – is often told as a history of great moments, an arc of betrayal and redemption, a chronicle of cowardice and courage. In particular, there is a special romance imbued in moments of high political drama, where a constitutional court says 'no' to a powerful executive. The High Court's unanimous judgment striking down the BBI Bill had all the makings of such a moment. Here was a transformed court that had historically been perceived to be a branch of the executive, now acting in defence of a nascent constitutional order, and facing down a near-united political class that was perceived to be twisting the Constitution to suit its own partisan goals.

But it wasn't just the material and symbolic valence of the judgment – and its assertion of judicial independence under a new constitutional order – that mattered. There are other reasons why the High Court's 321 page-long judgment mattered. The question before the High Court was not new, nor was it unique to Kenya. For decades now, constitutional courts across the world have grappled with executive-dominated parliamentary supermajorities using amendment procedures to make extensive alterations to the constitutional order – often with a view to entrenching themselves in power, or cutting down other branches of the State to size. From India to Belize, from Malaysia to Tanzania, this has been a familiar battle, fought with familiar arguments. The BBI Case was the latest iteration of this battle.

While the contours of the battle are familiar, its specifics are deeply embedded in context. For this reason, the High Court's judgment moved between three levels of argument. It drew upon Kenyan constitutional and political history – in particular, a culture of 'hyper-amendments' to the 1963 Independence Constitution, facilitated by an 'Imperial Presidency'. It located the BBI Bill as a continuation of that contentious history. It drew upon comparative constitutional law to ask how other courts, in other countries, had attempted to answer the questions before it. It also drew upon concepts of political philosophy, including those of direct and representative democracy and transformative constitutionalism, to construct the analytical framework within which it could examine the dispute.

Integrating the particular, the comparative, and the philosophical into one web of public reason, the High Court provided a solution that was both a response grounded within the reality of the Kenyan situation and an entirely fresh perspective on the old problem of the nature of constitutional change. This solution was a new articulation of the five-decade-old doctrine of the 'basic structure', which sought to safeguard the core of a constitution from evisceration by political super-majorities or dominant executives.

The BBI Case is not the only occasion where the Kenyan courts have been called upon to address hoary questions about constitutionalism and power within a new constitutional order widely agreed to be 'transformative'. Since the advent of the 2010 Constitution, the catalogue of cases brought before the Kenyan judiciary could read like a 'greatest hits' collection in the annals of global constitutionalism: constitutional change, separation of powers, presidential election disputes, land rights, horizontality, and so much else.

In this book, I will consider five such case studies (including the BBI Case). In each of these cases, I will argue, the courts have drawn upon the particular, the comparative, and the philosophical, in order to craft answers that are both grounded in context, but also travel further and possess a more universal significance. My purpose, thus, from my standpoint as a comparativist and as an outsider, is to highlight the contribution of the Kenyan courts, under the 2010 constitutional dispensation, to an ongoing global conversation about constitutions and constitutionalism.

For this one must, of course, spell out the nature of the conversation. I proceed to do this in the next section.

## B. The Nature of the Conversation

Any project of comparative constitutional law – such as this one – must engage in a dialogue that moves between the specific and the general. Without sacrificing the nuances of the specific, for the conversation to be intelligible, we may begin by identifying, in the words of Ghai and Cottrell, 'a substantial common core of values and institutions' as the starting point for our conversation.[1]

For the purposes of this book, I identify four unifying frameworks as starting points. I set them out here, from the abstract to the concrete: *constitutionalism as a concept*, with a certain common minimum core; constitutionalism as it is effectuated through a set of national *public institutions* functioning within the contemporary, global market economy, throwing up a set of similar challenges that transcend nation-state boundaries; *commonwealth constitutionalism*, a shared heritage of British colonial and imperial heritage and responses to it; and *African constitutionalism*, which is informed by a set of shared colonial and post-colonial histories. These overlapping frameworks can be fruitful backdrops to the comparative constitutional conversation.

Let me briefly elaborate upon each of these.

1 Yash Ghai and Jill Cottrell, 'The State and Constitutionalism in Postcolonial Societies in Africa' in *Law's Ethical, Global and Theoretical Contexts: Essays in Honour of William Twining* (Upendra Baxi, Christopher McCrudden, and Abdul Paliwala (eds.), Cambridge University Press 2015) 165, 183. Ghai and Cottrell deploy this term in the context of a 'new' kind of constitutionalism that they discuss, but it is equally helpful as a starting point for the present enquiry as well.

First, there is *constitutionalism* as a concept. Put simply, when we refer to constitutionalism, we refer to the operation of 'norms (rules, principles or values) creating, structuring and possibly defining the limits of, government power or authority.'[2] In modern constitutionalism, of course, limits upon power are as integral as the creation and structuring of it. The word 'possibly' can be safely dispensed with.[3]

Thus, irrespective of specific histories, constitutionalism – as we understand it – is both shaped by and shapes power relations. It is a terrain upon which those power relations may be contested. As Githu Muigai – relying upon Ivo Duchacek – notes, a constitution is, in essence, a 'power map', in that it 'define[s] the boundaries of institutional formation and the parameters of institutional action, enabling governmental power while placing limits on its exercise.'[4] Thus – and by extension – 'the scope for institutional transformation is constituted by relations of domination, and these relations are partly structurally conditioned, partly politically negotiated.'[5]

In other words, while constitutions and constitutionalism do not exhaust or fully determine the domain of politics and the exercise of power in a society, constitutional design and practice do condition – in terms of enabling, facilitating, or constraining – how power is exercised and provide a vocabulary within which the debate can take place. They may contribute towards preserving existing power relations, or towards mitigating or transforming them (and different parts of a constitution could do either). As we shall see, the cases discussed in this book, in different ways, speak to the contestation of power relations upon constitutional terrain.

2 Will Waluchow and Dimitrios Kyritsis, 'Constitutionalism' in *The Stanford Encyclopaedia of Philosophy* (May 2023), available at <https://plato.stanford.edu/entries/constitutionalism/>, visited on 15 September 2024 (emphasis supplied).

3 Ibid.

4 Githu Muigai, *Power, Politics & Law: Dynamics of Constitutional Change in Kenya, 1887–2022* (Kabarak University Press 2022) 33, relying on Ivo D. Duchacek, *Power Maps: Comparative Politics of Constitutions* (Clio Books 1973). The language of 'power maps' is also found in Julius O. Ihonvbere, 'Politics of Constitutional Reform and Democratisation in Africa' in *Dynamics and Policy Implications of the Global Reforms at the end of the Second Millennium* (Takumbi Lumumba-Kasongo (ed.), Brill 2000) 9, 14; Paul T. Zeleza, 'The Protracted Transition to the Second Republic in Kenya' in *Kenya: The Struggle for a New Constitutional Order* (Godwin R. Murunga, Duncan Okello, and Anders Sjögren (eds.), Zed Books 2014) 17, 36; Makau wa Mutua, *Kenya's Quest for Democracy: Taming Leviathan* (Lynne Rienner Publishers 2008) 263.

5 Godwin R. Murunga, Duncan Okello, and Anders Sjogren, 'Towards a New Constitutional Order in Kenya: Introduction' in *Kenya: The Struggle for a New Constitutional Order*, *supra*, 1.

Secondly, upon this terrain of contestation, at a more concrete level, a common set of public institutions and the existence of a global market economy throw up similar kinds of constitutional struggles. With respect to the former, for example, and while allowing for deep contextual differences, most constitutions – at the very least – divide power in some manner between the executive, the legislature, and the judiciary, with some degree of separation between them.[6] Battles over the dispersion of power, the demarcation of terrain, and the appropriate boundaries between the wings of State, are a part of the common heritage of constitutionalism. These include, for example, problems around a 'drift' towards concentration of power in the hands of the executive, something that has been noticed in both presidential and parliamentary systems.[7] The question of whether and to what extent a constitution should prevent such a drift thus has global salience.

With respect to the latter, at the level of the political economy, there is an underlying tension between constitutional bills of rights (especially in more contemporary constitutions that make socio-economic rights enforceable) and the global market society. Not only does the enforcement of certain rights run up against the 'logic' of the market,[8] but also, this logic is based upon a separation of public and private spheres, with constitutional rights and norms deemed applicable only to the former. To what extent should a constitution interrogate the classic division between the public and the private, and address institutionally mediated private power? In their text, in their design, and in their jurisprudence, different constitutions have answered these questions differently, but they have been compelled to provide *an* answer (or, at least, something by way of an answer).

As we shall see, the five cases discussed in this book engage with either the structural/institutional question, or the political economy question.

The third and fourth frameworks of conversation are more context-specific. Along with many other countries, Kenya belongs to a loose grouping known as the 'Commonwealth', i.e., territories formerly under the control of the British Empire. Although geographically dispersed, commonwealth countries have a few overlapping features that are relevant for our purposes. First, of course, is a common language. For a variety of reasons, in most commonwealth nations, English is a predominant 'official' language, and often the language of law and

6 Most modern constitutions, including Kenya's, also establish independent fourth branch institutions.

7 See e.g. Arthur M. Schlesinger Jr, *The Imperial Presidency* (Houghton Mifflin 1973). While the provenance of the term is US-American, it now enjoys global purchase; see e.g. Githu Muigai, *Power, Politics & Law*, *supra*, 194; Murunga et al., 'Introduction', *supra*.

8 See the discussion in Amy Kapczyinski, 'The Right to Medicines in an Age of Neoliberalism' (2019) 10(1) *Humanity Journal* 79.

the courts. At a more concrete level, that leads to a shared substantive *legal* language and a shared legal vocabulary. This is more than mere happenstance. British rule was marked by legal enactments in one colony, which would then be transplanted to another colony, without regard for local context in either. For example, the Indian Penal Code of 1860 was transplanted to the colonies of Uganda and Kenya, among others.[9] And when the British were looking for a legal framework for expropriating land for the railways in the early days of the East Africa Protectorate, it was the Indian Land Acquisition Act of 1894 that they adopted.[10]

At a deeper level, however, and perhaps of greater significance for this book, is that colonial rule bequeathed to its myriad successor nation-states a shared set of constitutional institutions and institutional pathologies. In his analysis of colonial constitutional history in Kenya, for example, Githu Muigai argues that colonial constitutionalism was characterised by two features. First, even as the British gradually conceded to local demands for representation under pressure, they ensured that representative bodies would always be subject to the control of the colonial executive. Right from the beginning, 'the legislative mandate of the LegCo [Legislative Council] was subject to a veto power held by the Governor.'[11] While the form of control evolved with time, the basic principle – 'the legislature as subordinate to the executive and the colonial government as subordinate to the imperial Government'[12] – remained.

And secondly, constitutional arrangements were defined by their impermanence, and by their being subordinate to 'administrative, and later, political imperatives'[13] rather than constituting a normative framework establishing the boundaries of administration and politics. Muigai goes on to trace a direct line between these two pillars of colonial constitutionalism, and the trajectory

9 This included a transplant of British prejudices as well, with the notorious 'section 377' outlawing same-sex relations under the euphemistic language of 'carnal intercourse against the order of nature'. Struggles to overcome this legacy have been waged in the post-colonies, successfully in some instances, and not yet successful in others. See the concluding chapter to this book.

10 Ben Ole Koissaba, 'Elusive Justice: The Masaai Contestation of Land Appropriation in Kenya: A Historical and Contemporary Perspective' in *Kenya After 50: Reconfiguring Historical, Political, and Policy Milestones* (Michael Mwenda Kithinji, Mickie Mwanzia Koster and Jerono P. Rotich (eds.), Palgrave MacMillan 2016) 188, 192.

11 Githu Muigai, *Power, Politics & Law*, *supra*, 57. Of course, African representation in the legislature did not come until much after their establishment, such as occurred in 1944 in Kenya, for example.

12 Ibid., 61.

13 Ibid., 53.

of constitutionalism in the Kenyan post-colony under its 1963 Independence Constitution.[14]

It can immediately be seen that Muigai's story is not unique to Kenya. In his comparative study of legislatures in Kenya and Zambia, Ken Opalo observes that both colonies experienced the subordination of legislative institutions to the executive in similar ways. The governor was the 'embodiment of metropolitan authority',[15] and the Colonial Office at Whitehall retained the power to veto any legislation that arose out of the respective LegCos.

Nor were these structural features limited to the African continent. Unsurprisingly, Muigai's two pillars are equally characteristic of colonial constitutionalism in India, whether it was the subordination of grudgingly conceded representative bodies to the Imperial Viceroy, or the constitutionalisation of separate, communal electorates as an instrument of entrenching imperial rule. While it is a subject of some debate to what extent these pathologies persisted in Indian constitutionalism after Independence, it is perhaps safe to argue constitutionalism in the Commonwealth post-colonies is, at the very least, informed by an overlapping set of institutional pathologies inherited from similar constitutional arrangements, which were initially imagined as vehicles for the entrenchment and perpetuation of British Imperial rule.

This is not to say, of course, that post-colonial trajectories were identical. As Opalo notes, former British colonies saw 'legislatures with varied institutional forms' depending on the timing of their colonisation, and local demographic and economic realities.[16] These nuances, therefore, are an important part of the comparative conversation.

It is also important to note that Muigai's two pillars are not exhaustive. There are other – subtler – ways in which colonialism left its mark on post-colonial constitutional debates and structures, which have striking similarities across countries. With economic wealth having been drained from colonies to the metropolis for decades, the moment of independence saw new national governments faced with immense challenges on questions of poverty, illiteracy, and industrial development. It is therefore unsurprising that the debates around the structure of the state and, in particular, on the question of the devolution of power, were inflected by a belief that only a strong, centralised government could bring about the necessary economic and social transformation that was

14 See also Makau wa Mutua, 'Justice under Siege: The Rule of Law and Judicial Subservience in Kenya (2001) 23 *Human Rights Quarterly* 96.

15 Ken Ochieng' Opalo, *Legislative Development in Africa: Politics and Postcolonial Legacies* (Cambridge University Press 2019) 101. Opalo also points out differences in individual trajectories (for example, significantly greater racialisation and settler dominance in Zambia).

16 Ibid., 130.

needed in the moment.[17] One can therefore see a similar tone in the constitutional debates around the issue of federalism in different countries, which share a common past as erstwhile colonies of the British Empire.[18] Here, then, is another space for fruitful conversations across borders.

And fourthly, Kenyan constitutionalism is situated within and in conversation with a broader set of norms and practices that Berihun Gebeye calls 'African constitutionalism'.[19] While acknowledging the diversity and plurality of histories (political, social, and legal) within the African continent, Gebeye nevertheless draws upon Ali Mazrui's idea of the 'triple heritage'[20] to argue for an understanding of African constitutionalism that is best understood as a 'syncretic' inheritance of pre-colonial, colonial, and post-colonial histories. These have enough overlapping features to make a *theory* of African constitutionalism a useful and coherent enterprise: 'Past constitutional experiences along with present constitutional realities make constitutionalism in postcolonial Africa a blend of constitutional ideas, textures, and meanings that transcend both legal centralists and legal pluralist accounts.'[21] Gebeye locates these overlapping features within 'the continuous legal syncretic processes of negation and affirmation of liberal constitutionalism on the one hand, and the rejection, accommodation, and tolerance of customary laws and traditional authorities on the other.'[22]

To take a specific example that we have briefly flagged above, while considering the issue of federalism (one of his three case studies), Gebeye points out how the arbitrary colonial drawing of national boundaries created a set of

17 For an insider's articulation of this argument, see Tom Mboya, *Freedom and After* (East African Educational Publishers 1963) 88.

18 Compare, for example, the political economy imperatives that led to a 'skewed' federal structure in the Indian Constitution, heavily biased towards the centre (Louise Tillin, 'Building a National Economy: Origins of Centralised Federalism in India' (2021) 51(2) *The Journal of Federalism* 161), with the rhetoric around economic development that was used to justify the dismantling of the federal provisions in the 1963 Independence Constitution of Kenya (Robert M. Maxon, 'The Demise and Rise of *Majimbo* in Independent Kenya' in *Kenya After 50: Reconfiguring Historical, Political, and Policy Milestones*, *supra*, 19, 26.)

19 Berihun A. Gebeye, *A Theory of African Constitutionalism* (Oxford University Press 2021).

20 Ali A. Mazrui, *The Africans: A Triple Heritage* (Little Brown & Co. 1986). See also *Africa within the World: Beyond Dispossession and Dependence* (Adebayo Adedeji ed., Zed Books 1994); Makau wa Mutua, *Kenya's Quest for Democracy*, *supra*, 33.

21 Gebeye, *A Theory of African Constitutionalism*, *supra*, 179.

22 Ibid., 207. For a similar pan-African historical account, see Charles O. Oyaya and Nana K. Poku, *The Making of the Constitution of Kenya: A Century of Struggle and the Future of Constitutionalism* (Routledge 2018) 26–27.

ethnically heterogenous societies, the nature of which, in turn, has provided a certain common valence to debates around federalism in African constitutionalism. These debates have been conducted within a specific register of group rights *versus* national integration, of the benefits of devolution *versus* the creation of ethnic enclaves.[23] Gebeye draws similar comparisons when considering the fate of the political executive, and of women's constitutional rights and claw-back clauses in post-colonial African Constitutions.

To Gebeye's analysis, we can also add Ihonvbere's insight that many post-colonial African constitutions have followed a similar political trajectory. To begin with, 'African petty-bourgeois elements inherited the colonial structures and found them rather comfortable having in many instances, been part of the colonial state before independence.'[24] This led to the reshaping of colonially inherited constitutions (in the case of the commonwealth, the Lancaster House Constitutions)[25] into vehicles of personalised rule, often in the shape of an imperial presidency.[26] This, in turn, gave way to a new wave of democratisation starting in the mid-1990s, where participatory processes led to constitutions becoming 'the *tabula rasa* on which new patterns of power, alternative political arrangements, the divisions and defining of power, rights

[23] Gebeye, *A Theory of African Constitutionalism*, *supra*, 260–265. See also Mutua, *Kenya's Quest for Democracy*, *supra*, 41. While Gebeye does not look at Kenya in one of his examples, as Maxon shows, the Kenyan debate around federalism has been conducted in strikingly similar terms. See Maxon, 'The Demise and Rise of *Majimbo* in Independent Kenya', *supra*. For a comparative study along the same lines, that does look at Kenya as one of its examples, see Mai Hassan, 'Federalism and Devolution' in *The Routledge Handbook of Democratization in Africa* (Gabrielle Lynch and Peter VonDoepp (eds.), Routledge 2020) 91.

[24] Ihonvbere, 'Politics of Constitutional Reform and Democracy in Africa', *supra*, 16. See also Issa G. Shivji, *Accumulation in an African Periphery: A Theoretical Framework* (Mkuki na Nyota Publishers 2009) 15: 'the colonial state was a despotic state, a metropolitan police and military outpost, in which powers were concentrated and centralized, where law was an unmediated instrument of force, and where administrative fiat was more a rule, than the rule of law.'

[25] This is not limited to erstwhile British colonies. See e.g. J.B. Ojwang, 'The Nature and Scope of the Executive Power in English and French-Speaking Africa: A Comparative Perspective' (1980) 13 *Verfassung und Recht in Ubersee* 319.

[26] B.O. Nwabueze, *Presidentialism in Commonwealth Africa* (St Martin's Press 1974); Yash Pal Ghai, 'Chimeras of Constitutionalism: State, Economy, and Society in Africa,' Unpublished Paper, University of Pretoria, available at < https://www.up.ac.za/media/shared/Legacy/sitefiles/file/47/15338/chimera_of_constitutionalism_ygl.pdf>, visited on 15 September 2024. See also Shivji, *Accumulation in an African Periphery*, *supra*, 7–8: 'Liberal constitutional orders imposed by the departing colonial powers did not survive as the underlying logic of the colonial despotic state reasserted itself.'

and obligations is being written by the ruled and the rulers.'[27] Thus, when – in the BBI Judgment – the High Court noted that one of the tasks of the 2010 Constitution of Kenya was to contain the erstwhile 'Imperial Presidency', the judges were tapping into a conversation not just about Kenyan political and constitutional history, but a broader conversation about the trajectories of post-colonial African constitutionalism.[28]

The discussion above should make clear that these four frameworks do not operate in silos. A specific constitutional dispute can be understood in terms of each of the frameworks. Indeed, the very point of a comparative constitutional conversation is plurality. For example, Chapter Three of this book will consider the constitutional challenge to the Constituency Development Fund (CDF) scheme. As the analysis will show, the case can be understood in the context of constitutionalism as a terrain of contestation between different axes of public power (first framework: constitutionalism as a concept); a battle between the legislature and the executive, and between the two levels of government in a devolved constitution (second framework: public institutions); the continuing pathology of colonial constitutionalism's subordination of the legislature to the executive (third framework: commonwealth constitutionalism); and a specific contemporary African constitutional history of imperial presidencies and the struggle of legislators to perform their representative functions in an environment of patronage and clientelism (African constitutionalism).

Finally, I do not claim that these four frameworks are exhaustive of the comparative constitutional conversation. I do believe, however, that they constitute a useful starting point for approaching Kenyan constitutional jurisprudence in a comparative context. As we shall see in the succeeding chapters of this book, each of these dimensions is implicated, to some degree, in the judgments that have been selected for study – as in the example above. Taken together, I believe they will help us to move between the general and the particular, as we engage with these judgments, and with the evolution of contemporary Kenyan constitutional doctrine.

## C. Transformative Constitutionalism

It is common consensus among both scholars and judges that the Kenyan Constitution is 'transformative' in character.[29] While transformative

27 Ihonvbere, 'Politics of Constitutional Reform and Democracy in Africa', *supra*, 14.

28 For a comparative study of the struggles to rein in executive power in multiple African countries, see Landry Signe, 'Executive Power and Horizontal Accountability' in *The Routledge Handbook of Democratization in Africa*, *supra*, 117.

29 While common, it is by no means uniform. For example, Makau Mutua calls the 2004 Draft Bomas Constitution 'a centrist liberal Constitution laced with illiberalism

constitutionalism is a helpful framework within which to situate the succeeding chapters of this book, by way of a beginning, the phrase merits some unpacking.

The term 'transformative constitutionalism' was famously coined by Karl Klare, in reference to the South African constitution.[30] While literature on transformative constitutionalism is diverse and varied, it is often imagined as a 'bridge' from an unjust, inegalitarian, and unfree past to a future founded on values of democracy and equality.[31] Or, to put it in the more lyrical words of Yvonne Adhiambo Owuor, it is to walk the space between the past and the present, so that the future could be shared.'[32]

While the constitution is meant to be the vehicle of such transformation, the nature of the desired transformation can be of different types. A constitution could be transformative in a bare political sense, as with constitutions drafted immediately on a nation's gaining independence, which transfer political power from an alien, colonial ruler, to a democratic government of the people (and, by extension, transform the people from subjects to citizens). A constitution could be transformative in a *comprehensive* sense as well, i.e., by seeking to transform social structures and institutions in a democratic and egalitarian direction.[33] To these two iterations, let me here add a third: a constitution could be transformative in a *deep* sense, i.e., it could seek to rewrite the existing 'power map' altogether and radically alter how constitutionalism engages with power relations.

Transformative constitutionalism in the deep sense, naturally, overlaps with political and comprehensive transformation; that is, deep transformation is impossible in the absence of either. Deep transformation, however, goes beyond political and comprehensive transformation in that it is not limited to a particular set of political or social institutions, but asks how constitutionalism relates to the question of power itself. For example, is the dominant purpose of a constitution to enable or facilitate state power, in service of a vision of national development and transformation, led from the centre (as was the case

---

and patriarchy', while nonetheless being a 'vast improvement' on the previous Constitution. Mutua, *Kenya's Quest for Democracy, supra*, 176. Mutua's book was written in 2008, but the argument, presumably, would not change very much, as some of the objectionable provisions around – for example – abortion, were retained in the 2010 Constitution.

30 Karl E. Klare, 'Legal Culture and Transformative Constitutionalism' (1998) 14(1) *South African Journal on Human Rights* 146.

31 Chapter XV of the Interim Constitution of the Republic of South Africa; Etienne Mureinik, 'A Bridge to Where? Introducing the Interim Bill of Rights' (1994) 10(1) *South African Journal on Human Rights* 31.

32 Yvonne Adhiambo Owuor, *The Dragonfly Sea* (Knopf 2019) 154.

33 For this two-pronged typology, see Gautam Bhatia, *The Transformative Constitution: A Radical Biography in Nine Acts* (HarperCollins India 2019).

with many of the early, post-colonial constitutions)? Or is it to disperse and contain power, in pursuit of a more plural set of goals?[34] Of course, constitutions are complex documents with complex relationships with power, and this simple schematic may not always capture that complexity. It is nonetheless a useful heuristic for considering the many ways in which a constitution may be transformative (or not). As I take up specific case studies in the succeeding chapters, its utility, I hope, will become evident.

With this framework in place, let us ask the following question about the 2010 Constitution of Kenya (henceforth, 2010 Constitution), 'widely acknowledged as the most radical constitution in Africa'[35]: transformative with respect to *what*? The answer, I suggest, lies in excavating two sets of interrelated histories.

The first, of course, is the history of colonialism. I have indicated above a few salient features of colonial constitutionalism, such as the subordination of representative and all other popular institutions to an imperial executive, servicing imperial interests. In addition, substantively, colonial constitutionalism was characterised by *exclusion*, *racialisation*, *repression*, and *dispossession*[36]: exclusion of the African population from participation in political, economic, social, and cultural life on equal terms with the settlers (where these existed); racialised governance that treated colonial subjects not as individuals but as undifferentiated members of ethnic or 'tribal' groups, and treated groups as the units of governance;[37] repression through laws that denied political

34 Note that both purposes could be argued to be 'transformative' in the political and comprehensive senses. This is why thinking about transformation in the deep sense is a useful addition to political and comprehensive transformative constitutionalism.

35 Ghai and Cottrell, 'The State and Constitutionalism in Postcolonial Societies in Africa', *supra*, 185.

36 This is a summary of what Oyaya and Poku call the 'four pillars' of the colonial constitutional order. See Oyaya and Poku, *The Making of the Constitution of Kenya, supra*, 38.

37 This was especially true in Kenya, where the ban on national political associations set the colony down a track of ethnically mediated politics *via* the institution of the Local Native Council (LNC) from the very beginning. This had profound effects on the post-colonial political order, and continues to be at the heart of many of the constitutional issues discussed in this book. See e.g. the discussion in Constitution of Kenya Review Commission (CKRC), *The Final Report of the Constitution of Kenya Review Commission* (2005) 25; Opalo, *Legislative Development in Africa, supra*, 107, 123–125; Gabrielle Lynch, 'The Fruits of Perception: "Ethnic Politics" and the Case of Kenya's Constitutional Referendum' (2006) 65(2) *African Studies* 233, 252. Another issue with resonances in the present was British-engineered ethnic gerrymandering in the lead-up to Independence, with a view to ensuring a strong moderate/loyal presence in the legislature. As Maxon noted in 2009 – in the build-up to the new Constitution – 'the ethnic based electoral system, often at odds with concepts of majority rule and democratic governance, has continued to characterize Kenya down to the present. It was embedded in the system of constituencies created for the self-government election in

activity, and subjected basic civil rights – including the rights to life and personal liberty – to executive decree and the ideology of 'order'; and dispossession from land, including the conversion of self-sufficient communities into tenants of the Crown on their own land, or a proletarian underclass dependent upon the market for survival. We shall study some of the specifics of colonial constitutionalism in succeeding chapters.

What, then, happened at the moment of independence, and the passage of the independent Kenya's first Constitution? It is, by now, commonly accepted that other than accomplish a bare transfer of political power, Kenya's constitution of 1963 (the Independence Constitution) was marked by two features: first, a 'retention of the fundamental pillars of the antecedent [colonial] State';[38] and secondly, a silence on the social question (i.e., questions around the colonial political economy, land, equality, and redistribution).[39] For example, in the context of land, Ambreena Manji observes that '[the approach to land under the Independence Constitution] remained rooted in what Atieno-Odhiambo (1987) has described as Kenya's "ideology of order", which has held political order as the highest priority, and which was not overturned by but in fact survived the democratic transition.'[40]

In these two important senses, therefore, the Independence Constitution was more conservative than transformative in its relationship with the past colonial constitutional order. However, that is not all there is to the story. While in many ways the Independence Constitution 'institutionalised and entrenched' the colonial political legacy, Okoth-Ogendo also points out that 'like many of its Westminster predecessors, it showed extreme sensitivity to the compromise nature of African politics prior to independence … it thus impos[ed] on the new central government severe limitations on its exercise of the powers inherited under the administrative legacy.'[41] In the Kenyan context, similar to the fate of other British colonies upon Independence, this took the

---

1963 and really never changed.' Robert Maxon, 'Constitution-Making in Contemporary Kenya: Lessons from the 20th Century' (2009) 1(1) *Kenya Studies Review* 11, 28.

38 Muigai, *Power, Politics and Law*, *supra*, 188.

39 See e.g. Mutua, *Kenya's Quest for Democracy*, *supra*, 57–58.

40 Ambreena Manji, *The Struggle for Land and Justice in Kenya* (James Currey 2021) 14. Manji focuses, in particular, on independence-era decisions to entrench the *commodification* of land, following on from colonial programs such as the Swynnerton Plan. See also the essays in *Decolonization and Independence in Kenya, 1940–93* (B.A. Ogot and W.R. Ochieng (eds.), James Currey 1995), and Bruce Berman, *Control and Crisis in Colonial Kenya: The Dialectic of Domination* (Eastern African Studies 1991). We shall consider this in greater detail in Chapter Four.

41 H.W.O. Okoth-Ogendo, 'The Politics of Constitutional Change Since Independence, 1963–69,' (1972) 71(282) *African Affairs* 9, 14; see also Yash Pal Ghai and J.P. McAuslan, *Public Law and Political Change in Kenya: A Study of the Legal Framework of Government from Colonial Times to the Present* (Oxford University Press 1970).

form of a parliamentary system of government, a 'neo-Nigerian'[42] judicially enforceable bill of rights, and – because of certain specific political imperatives at the time of independence[43] – a federal polity ('majimbo').[44] In a bare political sense, therefore,[45] when it came to institutional arrangements, there were elements of transformation in the Independence Constitution.

These arrangements, however, did not last. The trajectory of the Independence Constitution was characterised by a culture of 'hyper-amendments', initiated with the goal of preserving existing power relationships and resolving political problems through the centralisation of power.[46] Very shortly after independence, Jomo Kenyatta used his political dominance to convert Kenya into a presidential system (albeit without the checks and balances that usually accompany classical presidential systems); dismantle *majimbo* and its bicameral protections;[47] subject the bill of rights to executive control through the recourse to administrative detention (among other things); take control over the bureaucracy and fourth branch institutions such as the Election Commission;[48] and destroy the political opposition. As noted immediately above, this was accomplished through a set of constitutional amendments.[49]

42 Stanley de Smith, *The New Commonwealth and its Constitutions* (Stevens and Sons 1964) 193. Cf. Jill Cottrell Ghai and Yash Ghai, 'The Contribution of the South African Constitution to Kenya's Constitution' in *Constitutional Triumphs, Constitutional Disappointments: A Critical Assessment of the 1996 South African Constitution's Local and International Influence* (Rosalind Dixon and Theunis Roux (eds.), Cambridge University Press 2018) 252, 258.

43 For an account of these imperatives – and the political contest between the KANU and the KADU parties, and the respective interests that they represented, along with colonial meddling, see Charles Hornsby, *Kenya: A History Since Independence* (I.B. Tauris 2012).

44 Ibid. The Final Report of the Constitution of Kenya Review Commission refers to parliamentary democracy and devolution as the 'two major themes or principles of the Independence Constitution'. *CKRC Final Report, supra*, 25. For an analysis of the constitutional arrangements, Ghai and McAuslan, *Public Law and Political Change in Kenya, supra*; Oyaya and Poku, *The Making of the Constitution of Kenya, supra*, 66.

45 See the beginning of this section.

46 Muigai, *Power, Politics and Law, supra*. Mutua, *Kenya's Quest for Democracy, supra*, 46. Oyaya and Poku, *The Making of the Constitution of Kenya, supra*, 26.

47 For an account of the dismantling of *majimbo*, see Maxon, 'The Demise and Rise of *Majimbo* in Independent Kenya', *supra*.

48 For a discussion, see *In the Matter of the Interim Independent Electoral Commission, Constitutional Application* [2011] KESC 1 (KLR) para 59.

49 For a summary of the eleven amendments between 1964 and 1969, see Oyaya and Poku, *The Making of the Constitution of Kenya, supra*, 82–83; Ben Sihanya, 'Reconstructing the Kenyan Constitution and State, 1963–2010: Lessons from German and American Constitutionalism' (2010) 6(1) *Law Society of Kenya Journal* 1.

The effect of these amendments was the creation of what Branch and Cheeseman have called a '"centralised-bureaucratic" regime … marked by the retention of clientelism, the centralisation of power in an executive, the displacement of the party by a bureaucracy answerable to the head of state, and the downgrading of representative institutions.'[50]

In other words, through hyper-amendments, the Independence Constitution was transformed into a tool of consolidation of executive power,[51] creating – in Okoth-Ogendo's immortal turn of phrase – 'a constitution without constitutionalism.'[52] Christina Murray paints the following picture of Kenyan constitutionalism on the eve of the 2010 Constitution:

> The 1963 Constitution had been amended over the years to centralize power in the executive. Some of the most egregious provisions had been repealed in the early 1990s, but Parliament and the courts remained weak and the President retained enormous power … he appointed all members of the electoral commission which demarcated electoral districts, registered voters and ran elections … he had control over the judiciary with the independent power to appoint the Chief Justice; the power to identify all members of the Judicial Service Commission which selected other judges; and the power to set up and appoint members to a tribunal to remove judges from office. Virtually all other significant appointments … were in the gift of the President … Cabinet members were to be drawn from Parliament. This simply served to secure the President's power over MPs who aspired to Cabinet positions. And the President held the power to dissolve and prorogue Parliament … together with a powerful system of patronage and weak political parties, until very recently these provisions made Parliament readily subservient to the President.[53]

[50] Daniel Branch and Nicholas Cheeseman, 'The Politics of Control in Kenya: Understanding the Bureaucratic-Executive State, 1952–78' (2006) 33(107) *Review of African Political Economy* 11, 14; see also P. Anyang' Nyong'p, 'State and Society in Kenya: The Disintegration of the Nationalist Coalitions and the Rise of Presidential Authoritarianism 1963–78,' (1989) 88(351) *African Affairs* 229.

[51] Erik Kramon and Daniel N. Posner, 'Kenya's New Constitution' (2011) 22(2) *Journal of Democracy* 89, 90. See also Mutua, *Kenya's Quest for Democracy*, *supra*, 62.

[52] H.W.O. Okoth-Ogendo, 'Constitutions without Constitutionalism: An African Political Paradox' in *Constitutionalism and Democracy: Transitions in the Contemporary World* (Douglas Greenberg, Melanie B Oliviero and Stanley N. Katz (eds.), The American Council of Learned Societies 1993).

[53] Christina Murray, 'Kenya's 2010 Constitution' (2013) 61 *Neue Folge Jahrbuch des offentlichen Rechts* 747. See also the damning assessment of the *CKRC Final Report*, which stated that the extant constitutional regime encouraged the personalisation of

The 2010 Constitution was the culmination of almost two decades of social movements, nationwide public participation, incremental reform, political compromise, civil society pressure, civil society splits, progress and clawback on the bill of rights, failed backroom deals, defeated referendums, successful court challenges, failed court challenges, and – eventually – a successful referendum.[54] But above all else, the intensely participatory process that led to the crafting of the 2010 Constitution was characterised by two things: first, by a popular desire to address age-old issues that the Independence Constitution had either conspicuously failed to address or where it had entrenched colonial relations of power (land being the most important);[55] and *secondly*, by an effort to resolve a set of issues that were the *creation* of the Independence Constitution itself (as amended).[56] The most important among these – as noted above – was the checking – or constraining – of the Imperial Presidency. For example, as Diepeveen notes in her empirical study of the hearings that were conducted in the lead-up to the drafting of the Constitution:

> Suggestions to limit individuals' power within high politics were thus, unsurprisingly, common in the Mombasa hearings. While the historical roots of dissatisfaction were unique, those at the hearings in Mombasa commonly recommended implementing measures to check presidential and parliamentary power.[57]

---

power within the figure of the President – the exact opposite of constitutionalism. *CKRC Final Report*, *supra*, 36.

54 For a history, see Mutua, *Kenya's Quest for Democracy*, *supra*; Christina Murray, 'Making and Remaking Kenya's Constitution' in *Constitution Makers on Constitution Making* (Tom Ginsburg and Sumit Bisarya (eds.), Cambridge University Press 2022) 37; Jill Cottrell and Yash Ghai, 'Constitution Making and Democratisation in Kenya (2000–2005)' (2007) 14(1) *Democratisation* 1; Jacob M. Mati, 'Antinomies in the Struggle for the Transformation of the Kenyan Constitution (1990–2010)' (2013) 31(2) *Journal of Contemporary African Studies* 235. For the Constitution of Kenya Review Commission's own account of its role, see *CKRC Final Report*, *supra*, Ch. 4.

55 For an account of the Independence Constitution's entrenchment of colonial land relations, see e.g. *Essays on Land Law: The Reform Debate in Kenya* (Smokin Wanjala (ed.), University of Nairobi Press 2000).

56 The two most debated and contentious issues during the framing process(es) were the structure of the state and the question of devolution. See e.g. Beth E. Whitaker and Jason Giersh, 'Voting on a Constitution: Implications for Democracy in Kenya' (2009) 27(1) *Journal of Contemporary African Studies* 1. Whitaker and Giersch trace these debates back to the founding of the post-colonial Kenyan state.

57 Stephanie Diepeveen, '"The Kenyas we don't want": Popular Thought Over Constitutional Review in Kenya, 2002' (2010) 48(2) *Journal of Modern African Studies* 231, 240. In constitutional language, this is often called 'aversive constitutionalism': that is, constitutionalism that seeks to learn from the past by *avoiding* the mistakes of the past.

In other words, therefore, the 2010 Constitution was intended to be transformative both with respect to the continuing pathologies of the colonial constitutional order, which had not been addressed (and in some cases, been exacerbated) by the Independence Constitution; and also with respect to the pathologies of the post-colonial order, characterised by the Imperial Presidency and impunity under a 'Constitution without constitutionalism'.[58] Understanding the complex and entangled nature of these histories is crucial to understanding transformative constitutionalism under the 2010 Constitution.[59]

While we will engage with the specifics of individual constitutional provisions in the succeeding chapters, this introductory overview is meant to reiterate a key insight offered by Migai Akech. Akech points out that – for example – in examining the devolution provisions of the 2010 Constitution, in light of Kenya's fraught history with federalism, a true understanding of the issue is possible only by acknowledging the complex relationship between three sets of documents. These are the 2010 Constitution and its design of non-federal devolution, the Independence Constitution with its guarantees of *majimbo* (and, by extension, the colonial history that led up to its framing), *and* the hyper-amendments to the Independence Constitution which abolished *majimbo*.[60] This, of course, is a method of constitutional interpretation that applies across the board, and not just to the question of devolution, federalism, and *majimbo*.

A final point: we have, so far, considered the substantive character of the 2010 Constitution's commitment to transformation. The transformative story, however, would not be complete without highlighting the *process* through which the 2010 Constitution came into existence. Colonial constitutionalism

58 Rosalind Dixon and David Landau refer to this kind of constitutionalism as separate from transformative constitutionalism. They call it 'restorative constitutionalism'. I would suggest – and as I argue in some detail in Chapter Three, when discussing the CDF case – sometimes, restoration is best understood as an aspect of transformation. See David Landau and Rosalind Dixon, 'Restorative Constitutionalism' (2024) 81(2) *Washington and Lee Review* 455.

59 With respect to nomenclature, a distinction is sometimes drawn between the 1963 Independence Constitution, and the heavily altered and hyper-amended document that existed in 1969 (the 1969 Constitution), and which effectively (with a few other amendments) held the field until 2010. To avoid confusion, in this book I will refer to the '1963 Independence Constitution', with the context making clear whether it refers to the constitutional settlement *at* Independence, or the centralised, presidential constitutional framework that existed after 1969.

60 Migai Akech, 'Institutional Reform in the New Constitution of Kenya' (2010) *International Centre for Transitional Justice*. See also Mutua, *Kenya's Quest for Democracy*, *supra*, 43. For a history of *majimbosim*, see David Anderson, '"Yours in the Struggle for Majimbo." Nationalism and the Party Politics of Decolonization in Kenya, 1955–64' (2005) 40(3) *Journal of Contemporary History* 547.

was a top-down enterprise. Successive constitutional instruments were enacted at the instance of successive Governors of the Kenya Colony, and with a view to 'managing' the situation in the colony in order to continue serving imperial interests. Even the Independence Constitution was crafted through a series of negotiations at Lancaster House in London. The final text was drafted by the British Government, and presented to Kenyan leaders for their approval.[61] The exclusion of the Kenyan people then carried over into the post-colony, with the continued centralisation of power within the presidency, and the gradual choking off of various democratic avenues of participation (whether via opposition political parties, through fourth branch institutions such as independent commissions, or otherwise).

In stark contrast, the movement for a new constitutional order was initiated by civil society organisations in the 1990s, and in the two decades of struggle that culminated in the 2010 Constitution, its hallmark was *participation*.[62] Participation took different forms during different stages of the process. While the history of the constitution-making process is layered and complex, and we will discuss it in subsequent chapters, we can signpost some of its major elements here. It began with social movements agitating for reform in the early and mid-1990s. When it looked like the political elite would co-opt the process through the establishment of the state-driven Constitution of Kenya Review Commission (CKRC), there was the formation of a parallel, faith organisations-led civil society body called the Ufungamano Initiative.[63] In May 2001, under the leadership of Professor Yash Pal Ghai – who had accepted chairmanship of the CKRC on the explicit condition that he would be given a chance to bring the two bodies together – the CKRC and the Ufungamano Initiative merged, marking the *formal* entry of civil society organisations into the constitutional review process. Once the process was underway, there were nationwide public consultations facilitated by the Constituency Coordination Committees, under the auspices of the CKRC.

The CKRC produced its first constitutional draft in 2002. It was considered at the National Constitutional Conference (NCC) at Bomas, also chaired by Yash Pal Ghai. The deliberations at Bomas resulted in the finalisation of the 'Bomas Draft' Constitution. Meanwhile, however, a court judgment requiring a referendum as a pre-requisite for a new constitution effectively stalled the process, and allowed a government takeover (briefly discussed below).[64] The

61 See Oyaya and Poku, *The Making of the Constitution of Kenya*, *supra*.

62 Willy Mutunga, *Constitution Making from the Middle: Civil Society and Transition Politics in Kenya, 1992–1997* (SAREAT 1999).

63 For an account of some of this early history, see Bethuel A. Kiplagat et al., *Report of the Committee of Eminent Persons on the Constitution Review Process* (Government Printer 2006) 9–19.

64 Ibid., 19–37.

changed draft, which was heavily influenced by the government, and known as 'the Wako Draft' – after Attorney General Amos Wako – was put to the legally mandated referendum in 2005, and defeated. This temporarily halted the constitution-making process. The process was, however, restarted in the wake of the horrific post-election violence after the disputed presidential elections in 2007, and at least partly in response to it. Another constitutional draft – overseen by a Committee of Experts – which sought to resolve some of the contentious issues that had derailed the previous effort, was put to a referendum in 2010. This time it succeeded – resulting in the creation of the 2010 Constitution of Kenya.

As noted previously, we will consider elements of this history in greater detail, both below, and in subsequent chapters. For now, let us note that, in substantial part because of this history, public participation is central to the new constitutional vision. This is evident from the text of the 2010 Constitution. It is a part of the 'national values and principles of governance' enshrined in Article 10 of the Constitution,[65] and an integral component of the constitutional amendment chapter,[66] to take just two examples. Public participation as the fount of constitutional legitimacy, thus, is a critical component of defining transformative constitutionalism under the Kenyan constitutional order, and in interpreting the Kenyan Constitution in a transformative manner.

It is important not to overstate – or to romanticise – the point. The role of the political elite in tempering – or even stifling – public participation in the constitution-making process is an ongoing debate. Indeed – as we shall see – it was a debate that was at the heart of the famous BBI Case, discussed in Chapter Two. It is recorded history that right from the beginning, President Moi – and later in the process, President Kibaki and the opposition leader, Raila Odinga[67] – sought to co-opt and control popular aspirations for constitutional overhaul, and deployed substantial political and procedural legerdemain to do so.[68] As noted above, the Bomas Draft, itself a contentious and imperfect document, but which was nonetheless said to reflect popular views as elicited through nationwide public consultations, was not enacted. Instead, the top-down Wako Draft was brought in to replace it. The Wako

65 Article 10, Constitution of Kenya, 2010.

66 Articles 255–257, Constitution of Kenya, 2010, discussed in greater detail in Chapter Two.

67 There is, of course, an irony here, in that Raila Odinga had been a staunch opponent of President Moi for much of his twenty-four-year long tenure, and that the movement for a new constitution was closely linked to the popular desire to bring an end to Moi's rule. I thank the manuscript's peer reviewer for bringing this nuance to my attention.

68 Mutua, *Taming Leviathan*, *supra*.

Draft – arguably – went down to defeat in a referendum in part because of a split within the political class.[69]

Subsequently, the second round of this constitution-making – from 2007 to 2010 – was a more familiar, technocratic-driven process,[70] with mediated public participation,[71] a much heavier involvement of the political elite, and a final referendum. The fact that the 2010 Constitution retained a presidential system of government (contrary to a majority of views expressed during the public consultations of 2001–2002) perhaps reflects the limits of public participation in influencing the constitution-making process. Added to this is the fact that – as multiple scholars agree – the drafting of the Constitution was in tandem with regular politics and election cycles, with an overlap of the protagonists in both processes (especially party political leaders).[72] This meant that the articulation of – and opposition to – specific constitutional issues (such as the structure of the executive or devolution) ended up being less about disagreement over constitutional principles, and more about advocating personal political interests, decked up in constitutional language.[73] To take just one example, Raila Odinga switched from advocating for a parliamentary system to supporting a presidential system, at a point at which his

69 Ibid. For a comparison between the Independence Constitution, the Bomas Draft, and the Wako Draft, see Preston Chitere et al., 'Kenya Constitutional Documents: A Comparative Analysis (2006) 5 *CMI Reports*, IPAR Working Paper No. 7/2006, available at <https://www.cmi.no/publications/file/2367-kenya-constitutional-documents.pdf>, visited on 15th September 2024.

70 This is not necessarily a criticism: given the co-option of previous rounds by political leaders, and the tragic post-2007 election violence, making a technocratic Committee of Experts as the primary driver of the drafting process, subject to time-bound deadlines, was perhaps the only feasible way in which the process could be brought to completion. As events turned out, this was indeed how it happened.

71 This does not mean that public participation was absent, only that it was of a far more limited character than the wide-ranging participation under the CKRC in the early 2000s; despite this limited nature, the Committee of Experts received memoranda and suggestions from the public in their thousands. It is also important to note that after the publication of the draft Constitution, and before the ratifying referendum, there was a nationwide process of civic education. The significance of this history will become clear when we discuss the BBI case in the next chapter.

72 Oyaya and Poku point to how, after the first failed referendum, proposals to insulate the drafting body from immediate political imperatives by mandating that members of the drafting body could not hold political office for ten years after the framing of the Constitution, were swiftly shot down. Oyaya and Poku, *The Making of the Constitution of Kenya*, *supra*.

73 Muigai, *Power, Politics & Law*, *supra*; Mutua, *Taming Leviathan*, *supra*.

own chances of becoming president after the next round of elections appeared substantially high.[74]

With all those caveats in place, however, and without subscribing to the romanticist view that the 2010 Constitution sprung forth from the will of 'the People' like Athena, fully armed with its articles and its provisions, there is still space to acknowledge the fact that it was significantly *shaped* by democratic public participation, right from its beginnings as a civil society reform movement in the early 1990s, to the final, ratifying referendum in 2010. Consequently, public participation was – and remains – fundamental to its transformative character. As Oyaya and Poku sum up:

> The process started with a popular demand for constitutional reform followed by multi-stakeholder negotiations and agreements on the constitution review principles, objects and framework; extensive civic education and media campaigns; countrywide consultation on the views directly expressed by the people; drafting, public debate and expert audit of the Draft Constitution; broad based debate, consideration and adoption of the Draft Constitution by the National Constitutional Conference ('NCC'); and holding of a national referendum on the Proposed New Constitution of Kenya.[75]

The precise relationship between participation and transformative constitutionalism is, of course, contested, and will be an important part of the next chapter of this book.

Thus, in sum, an examination of the transformative nature of the 2010 Kenyan Constitution – and Kenyan constitutionalism – must be conducted along multiple historical tracks. The 2010 Constitution is not simply a response to the wounds of the colonial past; it is equally a response to the pathologies of the *post-colonial* past. It is transformative not merely in substance, but in process. It places public participation and democratic engagement at its heart, as opposed to the top-down, imposed constitutional settlements of colonial and post-colonial history: a two-arched bridge over *two* sets of troubled waters.

## D. The Judgments

The succeeding chapters – each of which analyses an important constitutional dispute – do not claim to present a comprehensive study of constitutional doctrine under the 2010 Constitution. Nor do they constitute a handbook,

74 Thus, ironically, reprising the colonial and post-colonial tendency of subordinating constitutional change to political imperatives and using the former as a vehicle for advancing the latter, rather than envisaging the Constitution as the framework within politics would take place.

75 Oyaya and Poku, *The Making of the Constitution of Kenya*, *supra*, 177.

or a guide, to the interpretation of the Constitution. In the first instance, the purpose of these judgments is to illuminate various intersecting strands that form the web of transformative constitutionalism in Kenya: that is, to discuss the meaning of Kenyan transformative constitutionalism, in a comparative context, through judgments that are its most striking exemplars. Let us call this the archetype method of selection. The judgments that I discuss are, in my view, some of the clearest archetypes of transformative constitutionalism, discussed within the four frameworks that I have outlined above.

What does this mean, in particular? In the section above we have unpacked at some length the idea of transformative constitutionalism, in the Kenyan context. A crystallised summary of this discussion is provided by Kithinji, Koster, and Rotich, in the following words:

> The new constitution therefore aimed at undoing the imperial presidency by creating clear separation of powers and facilitating checks and balances. In order to deal with the colossal maladies inherent in the old constitution, the new document utterly transformed the distribution and management of power. The most significant feature of the new constitution is the devolution of power to a network of counties, which replaced the powerful provincial administration and by extension diluted the powers of the president. Other features include parliamentary oversight of most presidential appointments and decisions; a senate to review parliamentary decisions; the creation of a Judicial Service Commission; a citizens' Bill of Rights; and a land commission. All of those changes, in their own way, add checks and balances to the centers of power, and serve to curb executive despotism, which had plagued Kenya since independence.[76]

The presidency; checks and balances; devolution; a bill of rights; independent commissions; land; the avoidance of executive despotism: these pillars of the 2010 Constitution and how they reinforce each other and uphold the architecture of transformative constitutionalism is what the rest of the book will examine.

Beyond this, my selection of judgments also follows the criteria outlined in the first two sections of this chapter. These are cases that address questions familiar to constitutional democracies and constitutional courts around the world, questions that implicate the four frames explained above: constitutions as power-maps; struggles around institutions, structures, and the political economy; a shared legacy – warts and all – of colonial commonwealth constitutionalism; and a shared understanding of African constitutionalism. These are judgments where the courts' analyses navigate the particular, the comparative,

76 Michael Mwenda Kithinji, Mickie Mwanzia Koster, and Jerono P. Rotich, 'Introduction' in *Kenya After 50*, *supra*, 13 (emphasis supplied).

and the philosophical, providing responses that are both specifically *Kenyan*, but also invaluable contributions to a global, constitutional conversation.

What, then, of the judgments themselves? In Chapter Two, I discuss the BBI Case, where the Kenyan courts were faced with the old-age problem of (alleged) constitutional evisceration in the guise of constitutional amendment. The High Court of Kenya resolved this problem by adopting the famous 'basic structure doctrine', but in a unique and innovative form: a variant of the doctrine which, grounded in comparative political process theory, deftly avoided the criticisms that have accompanied it over the last half-century of its existence. While the High Court's articulation of the basic structure doctrine did not entirely survive on appeal, another – fascinating – aspect of the judgment did: all three Courts – the High Court, the Court of Appeal, and the Supreme Court – relied upon constitutional history, and the aversion towards an imperial presidency, to strike down the BBI Bill on the basis that the President had illegally influenced a process that was meant only to be initiated by *the People*. In doing so, the Courts navigated between the concepts of representative and direct democracy, and the extent to which public participation in constitutional change was to be *mediated* through the institutions of the State. The BBI judgments have already become – and will continue to be – landmark interventions in the global conversation on constitutional change, constituent power, and the role of the People.

Chapter Three considers the CDF Case. In modern constitutional democracies, there are many ways in which legislatures are made subordinate to the executive. One – insidious – way is a 'constituency fund', which turns individual legislators into executive and administrative functionaries, and – in devolved or federal constitutions – also ends up bypassing more localised government structures. These funds have popped up in countries as diverse as India, the Philippines, and Papua New Guinea, and were the subject of an (unsuccessful) constitutional challenge in India in 2011. In the CDF Case, the Supreme Court of Kenya deployed a classical version of the separation of powers theory – but informed by the specific histories of legislative subordination to the executive – to hold the Constituency Development Fund (CFD) unconstitutional. I will argue that the court's deployment of separation of powers – and its focus on the representative, legislative, and oversight roles of legislators – demonstrates how, in certain contexts, transformative constitutionalism involves a return to the basics, and a reiteration – or, in the words of Dixon and Landau, a 'restoration' – of certain principles that have been distorted over time.

Chapter Four considers a constitutional issue that has arisen across post-colonial societies, where skewed and unequal land distribution patterns, caused by colonialism, and entrenched by the post-colonial order, create tremendous precarity and suffering. As most modern constitutions guarantee the protection of private property, and refuse to impose constitutional obligations on private parties, constitutional courts have struggled with finding a 'balance' between the rights to housing and shelter and the right to property – primarily in the context of planned or threatened evictions. In a set of two cases – Mitu Bell and William Musembi – the Supreme Court of Kenya opened up radical possibilities within existing jurisprudence. It did so by holding, first, that under the Kenyan Constitution *all* land (in the last instance) belonged to the People (a departure from the old common-law concept of 'Crown lands', which had far too often found its way into post-colonial constitutions). Thus, every citizen had a legal *interest* in land, even though they may not have title to it. And secondly, the court held that substantive due process obligations, before an eviction could be carried out, applied with equal force to private landowners, as they did to the State. While the cases did not take these ideas to their logical conclusion, they did create a space for a more equitable – and egalitarian – jurisprudence of housing rights and evictions than has been seen so far.

Chapter Five considers the issue of private power. The public/private divide has been one of the organising principles of modern constitutionalism. Its long shadow continues to affect contemporary constitutional jurisprudence, even where constitutions explicitly provide for the horizontal application of rights. Despite a radical horizontal rights provision that applies the bill of rights to private parties *without* qualification, Kenyan constitutional jurisprudence, in general, has followed this trend. There is, however, one notable exception: Rose Wangui Mambo, where the High Court held the constitutional right to non-discrimination applicable to a private club, and engaged in a detailed analysis of how historical, private structures of power create patterns of discrimination that a constitution is bound to address. At a time when constitutional courts from South Africa to India to Jamaica are attempting to craft a conceptually and practically persuasive theory of horizontality, the High Court's analysis provides the beginning of an answer.

Chapter Six – the final substantive chapter – considers one of the most controversial cases in the Kenyan constitutional context: the presidential election petition. Responding to a painful history of post-election violence, the Kenyan Constitution attempts to *constitutionalise* any such dispute, by placing a duty and an obligation upon the Kenyan Supreme Court to decide legal challenges to a presidential election. Strict timelines ensure that the court cannot evade the dispute and hope for the controversy to die down. It must *decide*, one way or another. This, it should be obvious, is a path fraught with peril. A constitutional mandate upon a court to decide the most bitterly contested political contest in the land – i.e., to effectively decide the presidency – gives the 'judicialization of politics' a whole new meaning. As the record shows, it is something that has met with mixed success across the African continent. The chapter will consider the challenge to the 2022 Presidential Election, and the Supreme Court's attempts to lay down case-agnostic doctrines on burdens of proof and standards of evidence, which would allow it to navigate the political thicket without having its feet stung by the nettles of political partisanship. The court's efforts are particularly important as part of the ongoing global conversation about the constitutionalisation of polarising political disputes, in a manner that both preserves the judiciary and the rule of law, and also avoids political violence.

## E. Positionality

Finally, a word about positionality. I am an outsider, and write from the perspective of an outsider – although, I hope, an engaged one! It is therefore important to clarify that this is not a book that seeks – or claims – to explain Kenyan constitutional law on its own terms, or set itself up as an authoritative exposition either on Kenyan constitutional law and history, or even on the specific judgments discussed in succeeding chapters. As an Indian comparative constitutional lawyer writing about the Kenyan Constitution, I operate under both epistemic as well as affective limitations. This book, then, is not meant to compare with analyses of Kenyan constitutional law and constitutionalism written by Kenyans, of which there is no shortage.

The aim of this book is more modest. It is a work of comparative constitutional law, which places contemporary Kenyan constitutionalism at its heart. It asks what the ongoing, global constitutional conversation can learn from the Kenyan experience under its new order – and with humility, what perhaps it might be able to give back. The idea of writing this book occurred to me as, during my engagement with Kenyan constitutional law, I found myself increasingly struck by fresh and compelling answers to questions I had come across before, in different forms, and in different jurisdictions. This book is an attempt to systematise some of those impressions, and perhaps provide a proverbial bridge for future conversations. If this book can partially perform that task, then I will have succeeded.

# 2

# The People Are (Not) Silent: Constitutional Change and the BBI Case

*Silence was a mighty sound in its own right.*
*If you paid attention, you could separate its warps and wefts.*[1]

It is a story as old as it is familiar. The tides of change compel the political elite to accept, whether grudgingly or enthusiastically, a constitution that places significant constraints upon their power.[2] However, once the new settlement comes into force, they realise quickly that it is much more of an inconvenience than they had bargained for. The People – who were supposed to vanish after their ceremonial invocation in the Preamble – are invoking the constitution to make all sorts of claims against state power. The newly transformed courts are too often upholding these claims, and dealing serious setbacks to the government. The constitution is 'taming Leviathan'.[3]

Stung into action, the political class – in turn – devises various stratagems to tame the recalcitrant constitution, the contumelious courts, and the impudent People. The simplest method: use parliamentary super-majorities (easiest in countries dominated by a single party, often the party of the independence struggle) to change the constitution, and remove the provisions that are proving to be a thorn in the government's side. In small doses, this is often effective, and the political cost can be borne.[4] Equally often though, the government's vaulting ambition overleaps itself, and it becomes clear that what is dressed up as constitutional change is actually constitutional evisceration.

1 Okwiri Oduor, *Things They Lost* (Scribner 2022) 143.

2 Sometimes the political elite are themselves carried away in the moment, and end up framing a constitution that they soon come to regret. This was the story of land reforms and the first decade of constitutionalism in independent India. This was manifestly not the case with the Independence Constitution of Kenya, which – as we shall see – carried the seeds of its own evisceration in the manner that it was enacted.

3 Mutua, *Kenya's Quest for Democracy*, *supra*.

4 Although the newly minted provisions will inevitably be brought back to courts for interpretation, and the courts might not be too pleased about having their authority undermined in so blatant a fashion. Once again, the first decade of constitutionalism in independent India is instructive in this regard.

The stage is then set for the highest of political stakes to be played out in the courtroom. At what point does a constitutional amendment cease to be an 'amendment' and become, instead, an act of constitutional dismemberment? Who can adjudicate upon that distinction? And if it is constitutional dismemberment, can it be stopped? Who should stop it? The courts (granted final authority over constitutional interpretation)? Or the People (from whom all constituent power springs, at least in theory)? If it is the People, then who speaks for them, and how?

In the trajectory of constitutional democracies – especially democracies of the post-colony – battles over constitutional change have been among the most significant moments in political history: inflection points in the evolution of state power, constitutional governance, and the rule of law. But when, in 2018, the post-election 'handshake' between President Uhuru Kenyatta and Raila Odinga culminated in a proposed package of seventy-four amendments to the 2010 Constitution, some of which seemed to be tailored specifically towards ensuring a distribution of power between Kenya's five largest communities, the overwhelming feeling among Kenyans must have been one of *déjà vu.*

For more than a century, colonial and post-colonial regimes in Kenya had used the Constitution as a piece of executive fiat, altering, twisting, and mutilating it in service of preserving or expanding political power.[5] While one would scarcely expect colonial authorities to be champions of constitutional governance, it had taken President Jomo Kenyatta no more than five years after Independence to dismantle the Independence Constitution through successive amendments and replace it with the constitutional structures of an imperial Presidency.[6] It was this systematic devaluing of the Constitution – through 'hyper-amendments', among other devices – that led H.W.O. Okoth-Ogendo to coin the famous phrase 'constitutions without constitutionalism'.[7] And now, history was repeating itself yet again, under the innocuous moniker, the Building Bridges Initiative (BBI).

But this time, something was different. Unlike colonial constitutionalism (the constitutionalism of an alien conqueror) and unlike the Independence Constitution (a top-down imposition eviscerated by a top-down presidency), the 2010 Constitution was the culmination of a genuine and deep participatory process.[8] This process was engraved into the landscape of the Constitution, as

5 Muigai, *Power, Politics & Law*, *supra.*

6 Ibid. See also Ghai and McAuslan, *Public Law and Political Change in Kenya*, *supra.*

7 See *infra*, Ch. 1. Okoth-Ogendo, 'Constitutions without Constitutionalism', *supra.*

8 The exact nature of the process remains controversial (as discussed in the Introduction), and we will see how the controversy played out in the BBI Case over the course of this chapter.

we have seen in the previous chapter: from public participation as a national value under Article 10, to the explicit involvement of the People in constitutional change under Article 257. Constitutional overhaul would not be quite so easy at the third time of asking.

This chapter explores how, in the BBI Case, the Kenyan Courts brought the People back into the Constitution, and in doing so, made a series of fresh, fascinating contributions to age-old, global debates around constitutional change. In Section A, I begin with an overview of the BBI, how it came to Court, and the issues at the heart of the constitutional challenge to the BBI. I then contextualise the BBI Case within a broader political and constitutional history, both colonial and post-colonial, which was characterised by the concentration of power in the executive and the parallel exclusion of the People from meaningful participation in constitutional affairs. In placing the People at the heart of the constitutional process, I examine how the 2010 Constitution was transformative (in its drafting and in its design) with respect to both the colonial and the post-colonial constitutional orders that came before (Section B).

I then look at how this transformative history and design informed the courts' findings on two of the core issues in the BBI Case: the basic structure doctrine and the popular initiative for amending the Constitution. The High Court and the Court of Appeal agreed that the basic structure doctrine[9] – which prohibits constitutional amendments that 'damage or destroy' a constitution's 'basic structure'[10] – was applicable in Kenya. Both courts also agreed that the unique circumstances leading up to the framing of the Kenyan Constitution required that *if* the political elite did want to alter the basic structure, the only way to do so would be through re-creating the participatory process through which the 2010 Constitution was originally enacted. While the Supreme Court appeared to reject this position, I will argue that a close reading of the judgments reveals that a majority of the court effectively read it into the already-existing text of the Constitution: in other words, 'basic structure', but not by name (Section C).

A second, crucial finding – and on this, all three courts were agreed – was that the President could not initiate amendments to the Constitution *via* the 'popular initiative' route under Article 257. I will argue that the courts were faced with a constitutional silence. The Constitution neither explicitly prohibited nor permitted the President from initiating constitutional amendments under Article 257. The Kenyan courts, however, filled in this silence through a transformative reading of constitutional history, determining that one of the defining features of the 2010 Constitution was its aversion to the kind of executive concentration of power and imperial presidency that had blighted

9 As a judicial doctrine, basic structure originated in India in 1973, and has since been considered by a number of courts across the world, with mixed success.

10 We can also think of the basic structure in terms of constitutional 'identity'.

the life of the Independence Constitution. Consequently, the President was not allowed to influence a process of constitutional change that was meant for the People (Section D).

In sum, while the BBI Case left some questions open for future benches to decide, the judgment(s) made vital contributions to the jurisprudence on public participation in constitutional change. Equally importantly, they substantially vindicated the transformative nature of the 2010 Constitution in an early moment of crisis (Section E).

## A. Building Bridges, Breaking Constitutions?

In the introductory chapter, I set out the facts that led up to what was popularly called 'the BBI Amendment Bill' (or the BBI Bill, for short), which proposed a package of seventy-four constitutional amendments. For the purpose of this chapter, I will highlight a few salient features of this attempt to alter the Constitution of Kenya.

First, the background: there was little doubt that the BBI Bill was the culmination of the process that began with the handshake between President Kenyatta and Raila Odinga on the steps of the Harambee House. This then passed through the BBI Taskforce,[11] the report of a Steering Committee,[12] and, finally, a proposal for constitutional amendment that was crystallised into the bill.[13] It was a process that was driven by the two leaders.[14] Under the conceptual framework of Githu Muigai (discussed above) – who would appear in court in defence of the BBI Bill – this was arguably the latest in a long line of instances where constitutional amendment was driven by the imperatives of entrenching a settlement between the political elite.[15]

11 Presidential Task Force on Building Bridges to Unity, 'Building Bridges to a United Kenya: from a nation of blood ties to a nation of ideals' (23rd October 2019), available at <https://d2s5ggbxczybtf.cloudfront.net/bbireport.pdf>, visited on 15th September 2024.

12 Report of the Steering Committee on the Implementation of the Building Bridges to a United Kenya Taskforce Report' (October 2020), available at <https://nation.africa/resource/blob/2486392/88e5205129241296af3755acd99809c1/bbi-report-data.pdf>, visited on 15th September 2024.

13 The Constitution of Kenya (Amendment) Bill, 2020.

14 See e.g. the discussion in David Otieno Ngira, 'Some Passing Reflections on the Building Bridges Initiative' (2020) 5(1) *Kabarak Journal of Law and Ethics* 279, 285.

15 Note that there is nothing necessarily wrong with constitutional change entrenching a political settlement – in fact, it is often needed, especially in post-conflict societies. The problem tends to arise when politicians are able to use constitutional change to advance personal political projects and concentrate political power, rather than engage in politics *within* the constitutional framework. In the BBI Case, one of the contested questions was the precise relationship between constitutional change and politics.

Secondly, it was alleged that the substance of the BBI Bill laid bare its political imperatives. In its expansion of the executive branch and the cabinet, in its re-establishment of the position of Prime Minister and the addition of two deputy Prime Ministers, the Bill was explicitly designed (as noted above) to create a system for the distribution of political spoils among Kenya's largest communities.[16]

For the defenders of the BBI Bill, on the other hand, *this* was the point: it was meant to put an end to the winner-takes-all, ethnically mediated system of Kenyan elections, which had been responsible for so much violence in the past. This problem had not been fixed by the 2010 Constitution, as the last set of elections in 2017 showed.[17] There was a dispute, therefore, about the precise nature of the relationship between constitutional change and politics. Was the BBI Bill a cynical political power grab in the guise of constitutional reform, or was it a genuine attempt to leverage constitutional reform in order to take the edge off political violence?

Thirdly, this was not all there was to the BBI Bill. There were a total of seventy-four proposed amendments, which covered a range of diverse and seemingly unrelated constitutional issues: from executive expansion to increasing the number of constituencies, from the creation of a judicial ombudsperson to police reform. The BBI Bill lumped all these proposals into one legislative instrument, thus presenting to the county assemblies (who were required to pass it) and to the People (who were required to express their views in a referendum) a straight up-down vote on what was essentially a take-it-or-leave-it 'package deal'. Indeed – as the Court of Appeal would point out a few months later – some provisions (involving county funding, for example) seemed to have been included for no other reason than as 'sops' or 'sweeteners' to the county assemblies, pushing them to vote for constitutional change in exchange for immediate and tangible benefits.

And fourthly, there was the question of process. The 2010 Constitution prescribes two paths to amendment: the parliamentary route (Article 256) and the 'popular initiative route', or the route of 'Parliament and the People' (Article 257). The latter is a complex, ten-step process that begins with the collection of one million signatures, and then passes through multiple institutions: the Independent Electoral and Boundaries Commission (IEBC) for verification; the county assemblies and the National Assembly and the Senate

16 See e.g. Patrick K. Mbugua, 'Why BBI Will Not Promote Peace or Prevent Violence' *The Elephant* (20th November, 2020), available at <https://www.theelephant.info/analysis/2020/11/20/why-bbi-will-not-promote-peace-or-prevent-violence/>, visited on 15th September 2024.

17 For a crystallisation of some of these arguments, see the Amicus Brief of Professor Migai Akech in *The Hon'ble Attorney General and Ors vs David Ndii and Ors*, [2022] KESC 8 (KLR), on file with the author.

for a vote; and – in case either house of parliament rejects the proposal, or if it pertains to one of the 'entrenched subjects' set out in Article 255 (see below) – a referendum for ratification.

For the BBI Bill, the chosen path was Article 257. That raised a fundamental question: if Article 257 was a pathway for 'Parliament and the People' to amend the Constitution, could President Kenyatta be as deeply involved as he was? True, the 'formal' sponsors of the amendment were two parliamentarians, Dennis Waweru and Junet Mohamed. But from the moment of the 'handshake', everyone knew that this was a process *driven* by the President and Raila Odinga.[18] What, if anything, did this mean for the legitimacy of the 'popular initiative' that the BBI Bill was now going through?

The BBI Bill was winding its way through the long path of Article 257 (it had passed the county assemblies and both houses of parliament), when a coalition of individuals and civil society organisations brought constitutional challenges before the High Court of Kenya, kickstarting a legal battle that would last for a year and pass through a total of nineteen judges at the High Court, the Court of Appeal, and the Supreme Court.

The High Court's judgment identified seventeen separate issues for adjudication. Each of these is worthy of its own chronicle, but for the purposes of this chapter, I consider three issues, each of which has to do with the dynamics of constitutional change.

[18] A sentiment summed up by a Facebook post of a photo of President Kenyatta and Raila Odinga holding copies of the BBI Bill, with the caption: 'A rare photo of Junet Mohamed and his brother Dennis Waweru carrying the BBI document they initiated. I know they look like Null and Void but trust me, it is Junee and denno.' See: <https://www.facebook.com/snnyamao/photos/a-rare-photo-of-junet-mohamed-and-his-brother-dennis-waweru-carrying-the-bbi-doc/4294341890625532/?paipv=0&eav=AfawddlSaVXX-qETeXm0M3ORGwDwA2tM50vUbqII6liqBnN0Eb5m43rlwwbuEbw_8WA&_rdr>, visited on 15th September 2024.

'Null and void' is a sarcastic reference to the High Court's declaration of the BBI Bill to be 'unconstitutional, null and void'. After the High Court judgment, there were many memes of President Kenyatta and Raila Odinga, with captions such as 'Null and his brother Void'. See e.g. <https://twitter.com/search?q=null%20and%20his%20brother%20void&src=typed_query>, visited on 15th September 2024.

In his memoir, *In the House of the Interpreter*, Ngũgĩ wa Thiong'o traces the origins of this phrase in public consciousness back to 1957: to the African Elected Members Organization's (AEMO) strategy of non-cooperation with the Lyttelton Plan, and their declaration that the Plan – under which these eight members had been elected to the Legislative Council – was 'null and void'. Ngũgĩ – who was a student at the Alliance High School at the time – writes that 'the phrase *null and void* entered our student vocabulary immediately.' Ngũgĩ wa Thiong'o, *In the House of the Interpreter* (Vintage Books 2013) 106.

First, the petitioners argued that there were substantive limitations upon what counted as a 'constitutional amendment'. There was a distinction between *amending* the constitution and unmaking and remaking the constitutional order. Using the formal amending procedures to achieve what was, in effect, a complete overhaul of the constitution, was not permissible. To make this case, the Petitioners drew upon a venerable and controversial constitutional doctrine, which had originated as a theory in post-war Germany, and was judicially applied for the first time by the Indian Supreme Court in 1973: the basic structure doctrine.

Born out of a desire to stop parliamentary super-majorities from using their brute majority to eviscerate the constitution permanently (often with the goal of entrenching themselves in power), the basic structure doctrine held that the constitutional amendment procedure could not be used to 'damage or destroy' the constitution's basic structure. The basic structure, in turn, was understood as a set of core principles or values that gave the constitution its normative identity. Basic features were drawn *from* the text of the constitution, but not reducible to it. They stood above it, at a more abstract plane (examples taken from the Indian context include democracy, federalism, the separation of powers, the rule of law, and so on).

In the years since the articulation of the basic structure doctrine, it had travelled around the world: Asia, Latin America, and Africa. It had found a welcoming home in some constitutional courts, while others had barred their doors to it. And now, in a moment of high constitutional drama, it had come to Kenya, seeking admission. But did the doctrine have any applicability in a constitutional context where the People – who were the original authors of the constitution, at least in theory – were explicitly granted a role in the process of constitutional change under Article 257 through a mandatory referendum? That was the key question before the courts.

Secondly, the petitioners alleged that the popular initiative was irredeemably tainted by the handprints of President Uhuru Kenyatta. The entire purpose of the popular initiative – the clue was in the name – was that it provided a pathway for the People to be involved in the dynamics of constitutional change. And it did so by treating the People not merely as passive receptors of top-down change by limiting their participation to a ratifying referendum, but *throughout* the process: from the first stage of initiation and the collection of signatures, to participation at the county level, and, finally (if required), the referendum. Article 257 repudiated the old theory that constitutional change was the preserve of negotiations between the political elite. But if, now, the President was allowed to use his power and authority to set an Article 257 amendment in motion (whether directly or – as in this case – through proxies), the entire purpose would be defeated.

On the other hand, however, Article 257 nowhere expressly *barred* the President from initiating the process of amendment. The President, after all, was a citizen, with political rights. How, then, was the silence in Article 257 about the role of the President to be understood? That was another crucial question before the courts.

And thirdly, there was the framing of the referendum question itself. Were the People 'participating' in any meaningful way if they were presented with a 'package deal' of seventy-four amendments, in a take-it-or-leave it up-down referendum? What if an individual wanted to vote for police reform but against the expansion of the cabinet? For gender parity, but against the expansion of constituencies?[19] Was this not simply a way of forcing through sweeping constitutional change under an illusion of choice?

As with the question of presidential participation, there was a dispute about whether the Constitution was silent about how, precisely, a referendum question was to be framed, or put to the People; and if it was, what were the consequence of this silence.[20] Once again, then, the courts would be called upon to address constitutional ambiguity in a provision whose purpose was to let the People speak.

### B. The Past is a Foreign Country

As the constitutional challenge to the BBI Bill progressed through the High Court, the long shadow of the past loomed large over the hearings. History – always contestable, always contested – was at the heart of the constitutional dispute. How was the 2010 Constitution to be understood in light of the long history of constitutionalism in Kenya? In a certain sense, the battle over the BBI Bill was a battle over historical *meaning*: how was the past to be interpreted for the present and for the future?[21] More specifically, the question before the Court was: what role did 'the People' have in the processes of constitutional change?

[19] It might be argued that as some of these topics did not belong to the entrenched subjects set out under Article 255, for these topics, a referendum would not be needed at all, under Article 257. However, that is exactly the argument: it was the BBI Amendment Bill lumped them all together alongside proposals that *did* need a referendum, and then purported to subject the Bill, as a whole, to a referendum. I thank the manuscript's peer reviewer for bringing this point to my attention.

[20] Article 257 uses the word 'bill'. The question, therefore, was whether the word 'bill' in the singular already indicated the drafters' intention that all proposed amendments could be fitted into a single bill; or whether it could equally mean to signify that the word 'bill' in the singular referred to *one* proposed amendment.

[21] As Muthomi Thiankolu, one of the counsel challenging the BBI, argued in the Court of Appeal, what structure of incentives and disincentives would the verdict create, and how would future presidents handle the Constitution in view of the verdict?

Constitutions, in general, tend to begin with a ritual invocation of the People as the authors of the founding document.[22] Many constitutions, however, do not go beyond ritual. After the preamble, the People are swiftly shuffled off the constitutional stage, rarely to reappear in the document.[23] Roberto Gargarella therefore points to two forms of constitutional design: one, in which the People are present as constitutional agents, acting as an 'external' check upon the wings of State, through mechanisms such as a right to recall, instruments of instruction, referenda, and so on.[24] The second is a more limited constitutional vision, where the People's role is restricted to periodic elections. The checking of State power takes place *internally*, between the different wings of State (the legislature, the executive, and the judiciary).[25]

22 Interestingly, perhaps reflecting its origins in the Lancaster House negotiations (and not as the product of a Constituent Assembly), the Independence Constitution of 1963 *did not* begin with the titular line: 'We the People…'. This was specifically recognised by Constitution of Kenya Review Commission in its Final Report, as a general feature of post-Independence Constitutions in Africa, that were "given" by the metropolitan powers. *CKRC Final Report*, *supra*, 80.

23 This is often by design, and is a prominent feature of the post-colonial Constitutions of the mid-twentieth century, where constitutional framers were often driven by the vision of a developmental State. See e.g. Nazmul Islam, *Waiting for the People: The Idea of Democracy in Indian Anticolonial Thought* (Harvard University Press 2024) for a recent study in the context of the Indian Constitution.

24 See generally, Roberto Gargarella, *Latin American Constitutionalism 1810–2010: The Engine Room of the Constitution* (Oxford University Press 2013). For some representative examples of (newer) constitutions that envisage popular roles in one or more domains – constitutional change, law-making, and administrative action, see e.g. Article 240, Constitution of the Plurinational State of Bolivia, 2009 and Article 61(6), Constitution of Ecuador, 2008 (right to recall). For a brief discussion, see Jonas Wolff, 'New Constitutions and the Transformation of Democracy in Bolivia and Ecuador' in *New Constitutionalism in Latin America: Promises and Practices* (Almot Schilling-Vacaflor and Detlef Nolte (eds.), Routledge 2012) 183, 186; see also Article 1(3)(a), Constitution of California, 1849 (right to instruct); Articles 395(3) & 398, Constitution of Ecuador, 2008 (right to public participation). For the most recent interpretation of these clauses, see Sentencia No. 1149-19-JP/21, Constitutional Court of Ecuador. For a more overarching account of the tensions around public participation and constitutionalism in Latin America, see Cleide Calgaro, 'Latin American Constitutionalism: Comparative Law Study on Popular Participation for Urban Land Planning' (2023) 15(1) *Revista de Direito de Cidade* 237; Juan C. Herrera, 'Judicial Dialogue and Transformative Constitutionalism in Latin America: the Case of Indigenous Peoples and Afro-descendants' (2019) 43 *Revista Derecho del Estado* 191; Thea Riofrancos, *Resource Radicals: From Petro-Nationalism to Post-Extractivism in Ecuador* (Duke University Press 2020).

25 Gargarella, *Latin American Constitutionalism 1810–2010*, *supra*.

The Independence Constitution followed the latter model, setting out a classical scheme of separation of powers between the executive, legislature, and judiciary, within a federal (*majimbo*) and multi-party parliamentary democracy. As noted above, through a set of constitutional amendments (referred to as 'hyper-amendments' by the High Court in the BBI Case), this Constitution was swiftly transformed into an executive presidency. One hallmark of this transformation was the effective evisceration of multi-partyism (well before Kenya was *formally* turned into a one-party state through the constitutional amendment of 1981), and the 'centralisation and concentration of power in the state apparatus, notably in the upper levels of the bureaucracy and the major appointed executive positions from the cabinet on down'.[26]

Ground-level control was exercised by the Provincial Administration, which, contrary to the original design of the Independence Constitution – that had envisioned a decentralisation of the administration to the newly constituted Regional Authorities[27] – 'was restored to its former [colonial] status and placed directly under the Office of the President.'[28] This was a stark instance of colonial continuity, carrying on the pre-independence model where 'the executive was empowered by its control, via the chief native commissioner, of the provincial administration … enabl[ing] the executive to bypass the legislature when necessary.'[29] Indeed, as Opalo points out, the Provincial Administration frequently exercised authority under colonial era 'public order' laws, rendering 'colonial continuity' more than just a metaphor.[30]

In other words, therefore, a system of top-down governance (the President to the Provincial Administration, *via* the bureaucracy) further excluded popular involvement by eliminating the political party and the legislature,[31] as vehicles

26 Berman, *Control and Crisis in Colonial Kenya*, *supra*, 426.

27 Cherry Gertzel, 'The Provincial Administration in Kenya' (1966) 4(3) *Journal of Commonwealth Political Studies* 201. Gertzel notes how, during the colonial era, the Provincial Administration had been a 'powerful, sophisticated, and centralized machine through which the Governor administered by direct rule'. Ibid. By the end of 1965, this position had largely been restored, with the 'Administrative Officer rather than the party official … [being] the major link between the Executive and the people.' Ibid., 201–202. The role of the Chiefs was also maintained. Ibid., 204.

28 Ibid. Berman calls the colonial governance structure a form of 'prefectural administration': that is, top-down rule exercised indirectly through prefectural officials such as the native commissioners or chiefs.

29 Daniel Branch and Nicholas Cheeseman, 'The politics of control in Kenya: Understanding the bureaucratic-executive state, 1952–78' (2006) 107 *Review of African Political Economy* 11, 18.

30 Opalo, *Legislative Development in Africa*, *supra*, 144–145.

31 Interestingly, the marginalisation of the legislature in favour of a bureaucratic-executive-developmental state was a feature common to more than one post-colonial nation. Sandipto Dasgupta, for example, traces a similar ideology at work in the early

for popular aspirations.[32] As Tamarkin pithily summed it up, political stability in Kenya depended on 'the emasculation of the masses as a political factor'.[33] In sum, the entrenchment of the executive presidency and the exclusion of the People as constitutional agents were two sides of the same coin.[34]

It is hardly surprising, then, that the constitutional reform movement that began in the 1990s was heavily focused on the limitations of the executive presidency, as well as responding to President Moi's continued presence in office since 1978. This was reflected in the deliberations of the Constitution of Kenya Review Commission in its final report,[35] in the debates leading up to the defeated constitutional referendum of 2005, and in the run-up to the enactment of the 2010 Constitution.

To this end, the CKRC draft of 2002, and building upon it, the Bomas Draft Constitution, sought to replace the presidential system with a parliamentary system (there would still exist an elected President, but with limited

---

years of Indian Independence, where the legislature was seen as a legitimating body, but ultimately a junior partner in a developmental project that would be spearheaded by a strong executive, working through technocrats and the bureaucracy. See Sandipto Dasgupta, *Legalizing the Revolution: India and the Constitution of the Postcolony* (Cambridge University Press 2024).

32 Raymond Muhula and Stephen Ndegwa, 'Instrumentalism and constitution-making in Kenya' in *Kenya: The Struggle for a New Constitutional Order* (Murunga et al. (eds.), Zed Books 2014) 79, 91. The *CKRC Final Report* recorded feedback that the provincial administration system had turned out to be "the antithesis of people's right to govern themselves." *CKRC Final Report, supra*, 237.

33 Morcechai Tamarkin, 'The Roots of Political Stability in Kenya' (1978) 77(308) *African Affairs* 297, 300. In the words of Godwin Murunga and others, 'the architecture of power created by the pre-2010 constitution made the effective practice of <u>plural politics</u> impossible and prevented the country's transition from an imperial presidency to a constitutional democracy.' Murunga, Okello, and Sjogren, 'Towards a New Constitutional Order in Kenya', *supra*, 1 (emphasis supplied).

34 Okoth-Ogendo, 'The Politics of Constitutional Change Since Independence, 1963-69,'*supra*, 9.

35 As the Final Report noted, in strong terms: 'The democratic processes of the post-colonial era have not, therefore, promoted self-governance and the people of Kenya, in such circumstances, have failed to recover effective control over their social, political and economic destiny. The political system has not only reduced the people's sovereignty to a mere right to exercise their franchise at the elections every five years but the state, through its bureaucratic machine, has further subordinated society to itself and deprived the people of any real capacity to develop themselves.' Constitution of Kenya Review Commission (CKRC), *The Final Report of the Constitution of Kenya Review Commission* (2005) 61, available at <https://kenyalaw.org/kl/fileadmin/CommissionReports/The-Final-Report-of-the-Constitution-of-Kenya-Review-Commission-2005.pdf>, visited on 15th September 2024.

executive powers).[36] However, by 2009, for a set of reasons briefly flagged in the Prologue, political support for parliamentarianism had waned. When the Revised Harmonised Draft of the Committee of Experts was sent to the Parliamentary Select Committee, parliamentarianism was removed. The Committee of Experts was thus obliged to retain presidentialism, or risk a collapse of the entire process.[37]

However, despite the reintroduction of presidentialism, things had already travelled too far down the road for a reversion to an Imperial Presidency. Recall that every constitutional draft other than the Wako Draft had proposed a parliamentary system, with the Presidency stripped of meaningful executive power. The direction of travel, thus, was clear: and so, repeated attempts by politicians during the final 'harmonisation' stage to include language that would increase the power of this re-introduced Presidency were categorically rebuffed.[38] These included measures that would have given the president complete control over appointments and dismissals of cabinet members and officers of fourth branch institutions. The result of the process was a constitution where, despite the retention of *Presidentialism*, 'the president's power is nonetheless curtailed, and parliament's strengthened, through new rules governing the presidential appointment of cabinet ministers.'[39]

The aversion to an executive presidency was accompanied in parallel by a movement in favour of public participation as the bedrock of constitution-making. I have considered this in Chapter One in some detail, but to reiterate: the 2010 Constitution was the culmination of an intensely participatory process that had begun with a civil society reform movement. The drafting process in 2002 saw many rounds of civic education and public engagement, a more 'targeted' form of engagement between 2008 and 2009,[40] and finally a popular referendum that resulted in the 2010 Constitution.[41]

36 See e.g. the *CKRC Final Report*, noting the widespread popular support ('a large majority of people') for a parliamentary system, during the consultation process. *CKRC Final Report*, *supra*, 197.

37 For an account of the process, see e.g. Godwin R. Murunga, 'Elite Compromises and the Content of the 2010 Constitution' in *Kenya: The Struggle for a New Constitutional Order*, *supra*, 144, 158.

38 See the discussion in Oyaya and Poku, *The Making of the Constitution of Kenya*, *supra*, 194–195.

39 Kramon and Posner, 'Kenya's New Constitution', *supra*, 89, 97.

40 Christina Murray, 'Making and Remaking Kenya's Constitution' in *Constitution Makers on Constitution Making* (Tom Ginsburg and Sumit Bisarya (eds.), Cambridge University Press 2022).

41 As noted in the Introduction, this account is not meant to romanticise public participation, or to imply that the political elite were uninvolved with the process. See Muhula and Ndegwa, 'Incrementalism and Constitution-Making in Kenya', *supra*.

Steps on the way included, for example, the Constitution of Kenya Review Act's mandate to the CKRC to 'visit every constituency in Kenya to collect citizens' views and to disseminate the draft constitution widely among the public'.[42] As a result of this, the CKRC created 'an ambitious and extraordinarily successful process of public education and collected over 35000 submissions from the public'[43] as a precursor to publishing its first constitutional draft.

Subsequently, even after the defeated 2005 referendum, the second round of constitution-making did not sacrifice public participation. For example, during public engagement with the 2009 'harmonised draft', Christina Murray notes that 'over 39000 submissions were received, just over 25000 from individuals, 7737 from religious organisations, and 22 from political parties.'[44] It is important to note that the aversion to unchecked presidentialism was a key point that was not only articulated by opposition politicians, but also *arose out of* the participatory process, conducted across the length and breadth of Kenya, throughout the various stages of the constitution-making process.[45]

Another integral part of this history is the 2005 referendum itself, referred to above. As noted in the Prologue, the constitutional draft that was presented to the Kenyan public (the 'Wako Draft') was significantly different from the draft that had been finalised at the culmination of the Bomas Conference a year before ('the Bomas Draft'). Driven by the imperatives of the ruling political elite, it sought to bring back – in substantial part – the executive presidency.[46] As Whitaker and Giersch perceptively note, opposition to the Wako Draft centred on both *process* and *substance*. On process, it was argued that the 'people-driven' and consultative process that had produced the Bomas Draft had been negated due to the 'decision by parliament to alter the document before holding a referendum … essentially undermin[ing] the constitution-making power of the people'.[47] And secondly, on substance, the 'No' campaign

42 Alicia Bannon, 'Designing a Constitution-Drafting Process: Lessons from Kenya' (2007) 116 *The Yale Law Journal* 1824, 1831; see also Cottrell and Ghai, 'Constitution Making and Democratisation in Kenya (2000–2005)', *supra*, 1.

43 Murray, 'Making and Remaking Kenya's Constitution', *supra*, 43.

44 Ibid., 53.

45 Stephanie Diepeveen, '"The Kenyas we don't want": Popular Thought Over Constitutional Review in Kenya, 2002' (2010) 48(2) *Journal of Modern African Studies* 231.

46 See the detailed comparative discussion between the Independence Constitution, the Bomas Draft, and the Wako draft in Preston Chitere et al., 'Kenya Constitutional Documents: A Comparative Analysis' (2006) *IPAR Working Paper No. 7/2006*, available at <https://www.cmi.no/publications/file/2367-kenya-constitutional-documents.pdf>, visited on 15th September 2024.

47 Beth E. Whitaker and Jason Giersh, 'Voting on a Constitution: Implications for Democracy in Kenya' (2009) 27(1) *Journal of Contemporary African Studies* 1, 8. See also Gabrielle Lynch, 'The Fruits of Perception: "Ethnic Politics" and the Case of

focused on the Wako draft's decision to retain 'executive power in the hands of the president',[48] linking it – among other things – to a failure to improve the socio-economic conditions of the People. Indeed, in their detailed report analysing the constitution review process, which included wide-ranging public participation, the presidentially appointed Committee of Eminent Persons (the 'Kiplagat Committee') specifically linked these two issues – the process and the substance – and noted how they reinforced each other in the public opposition to the Wako Draft.[49]

In this context, the resounding defeat of the Wako Draft – other than being a referendum on the then-President Kibaki, who had thrown his weight behind the Draft – also reflects the phenomenon of 'aversive constitutionalism', which we discussed in the previous chapter: that is, aversion to both concentrated executive power, as well as to the continued marginalisation of the People as constitutional agents.

When considered in light of this history, the 2010 Constitution emerges as a transformative document, driven by two complementary impulses. The first was an impulse of *containment and constraint*: that is, constraining presidential power in order to avoid a repeat of the drift towards an imperial presidency. Secondly, and equally importantly, the 2010 Constitution did not seek to accomplish this only through an 'internal' system of checks and balances and by redistributing powers to other representative bodies (the National Assembly and the Senate). It sought to do so also by *bringing the People back in* as constitutional agents and constitutional actors.[50]

In the text and design of the 2010 Constitution, this is reflected in multiple places. Article 10 cites 'the participation of the people' as one of the 'national values and principles of governance ... [that] bind all State organs, State officers, public officers and all persons.'[51] In more specific terms, the Constitution provides for public participation at each level of constitutional governance: executive action, legislation, and constitutional change. For example, Article 118 requires Parliament to 'facilitate public participation and involvement in the legislative and other business of Parliament'.[52] Article 184 requires

Kenya's Constitutional Referendum' (2006) 65(2) *African Studies* 233, 240: 'questions of due process and the contested road to Wako became almost as integral to the political campaigns, as those regarding detail and implications of constitutional content.'

48 Whitaker and Giersh, 'Voting on a Constitution', *supra*, 13.

49 Kiplagat et al., *Report of the Committee of Eminent Persons on the Constitution Review Process, supra.*

50 See e.g. Yash Pal Ghai, 'Constitutions and constitutionalism: the fate of the 2010 Constitution' in *Kenya: The Struggle for a New Constitutional Order, supra*, 119, 125.

51 Article 10, Constitution of Kenya, 2010.

52 Article 118(1)(b), Constitution of Kenya, 2010. Article 196 has similar provisions for County Assemblies. Many of these provisions find an early echo in the CKRC Final Report, which contained an entire chapter on public participation.

legislation to provide for public participation by residents in the governance of urban areas and cities.[53] And, most significant for the purposes of this chapter is the popular initiative method for constitutional amendment, which has the People both as the initiators and the ratifiers of certain constitutional amendments.[54]

The key question in the BBI Case was how, in light of this constitutional history, the role of the People was to be understood in the context of sweeping constitutional change. It is to this question that we now turn.

## C. The Basic Structure

At the heart of the constitutional challenge to the BBI Bill was a simple argument. Every constitution contains the procedure for the amendment of its own provisions. But a constitution is more than simply the aggregate of all its provisions. As a statement of political vision and as a charter of principle for the nation, a constitution has a normative core,[55] an identity which makes it *this* constitution, and not any other.[56] In its famous judgment on gender representation in the National Assembly and the Senate, the Supreme Court of Kenya recognised this when it observed that in addition to specific provisions and safeguards, the 2010 Constitution was characterised by

> ... declarations of general principles and statements of policy. Such principles or policy declarations signify a value system, an ethos, a culture, or a political environment within which the citizens aspire to conduct their affairs and to interact among themselves and with their public institutions.[57]

53 Article 184(1)I, Constitution of Kenya, 2010.

54 Article 257, Constitution of Kenya, 2010. The vocabulary and method of the popular initiative is borrowed from the Swiss Constitution (albeit with suitable modifications), where popular initiative processes are available at both the federal level, and at the level of the cantons. See e.g. Article 139, Federal Constitution of the Swiss Confederation, 1899.

55 *Barry M. Bowen v The Attorney General of Belize*, BZ 2009 SC 2 (Supreme Court of Belize). In this case, the Supreme Court of Belize accepted the basic structure doctrine.

56 What the Constitutional Court of Germany called 'an inner unity' (*Southwest Case*, 1 BvervGE 14 (1951), Constitutional Court of Germany), and what the Supreme Court of Pakistan called 'an inherent integrity' (Constitutional Petition Nos. 99 and 100 of 2014 (Supreme Court of Pakistan), decided on 5th August 2015 per Sh. Azmat Saeed J, paragraph 55)). Both cases arose in the context of the basic structure.

57 *In the Matter of the Principle of Gender Representation in the National Assembly and the Senate* [2012] KESC 5 (KLR), para 54.

Call this normative core – or 'ethos' – the 'basic structure' of the constitution. Changing the basic structure, then, is not equivalent to an amendment of the constitution. It is, in effect, a replacement or a repeal, an alteration of the identity of the document into something else.[58] In other words, it is akin to rewriting the constitution itself. And this – or so the argument goes – is not contemplated by the 'formal' procedures of amendment.[59]

This argument was, for the first time, accepted by a constitutional court in 1973. At the peak of a political clash between parliament and judiciary, in *Kesavananda Bharati vs State of Kerala*, the Supreme Court of India held that the power to amend the constitution did not entail the power to 'damage or destroy' its basic structure.[60] It was the task of the judiciary to review amendments on the touchstone of the basic structure – and to strike them down if they were found wanting.

The judgment in *Kesavananda Bharati* has been debated around the world. Critiques of the judgment have focused on the indeterminacy of the basic features, and the arrogation by the judiciary of the ultimate power over constitutional change. In its defence, it is argued that historical experience has repeatedly shown how parliamentary super-majorities can be a threat to the constitutional order. In such a situation – and when a constitution contains no recourse available to the People – the judiciary is the only body that can preserve the constitutional order against parliamentary evisceration. In choosing to accept or reject the basic structure doctrine, courts in different countries have been persuaded by one or the other argument, often depending on the political context within those countries.

Did the doctrine of the basic structure have any role to play in Kenya? In a fascinating and wide-ranging judgment, the High Court of Kenya held that it did.[61] The High Court based its decision on a reading of history. There were two core ideas, it argued, underlying the 2010 Constitution. The first was a desire by the People to insulate the constitutional order they had given to themselves from the culture of 'hyper-amendments' that had allowed President Jomo Kenyatta to eviscerate the Independence Constitution within

58 See, for example, the judgment of the Constitutional Court of Colombia in *Case No. C-141/2019* (Col.), holding that an extension of the term limits of the President amounted to 'constitutional replacement', given the amount of power this would give the President over all *other* constitutional bodies.

59 See the discussion in Yaniv Roznai, *Unconstitutional Constitutional Amendments: The Limits of Amendment Powers* (Oxford University Press 2017); Richard Albert, 'Constitutional Amendment and Dismemberment' (2018) 43(1) *Yale Journal of International Law* 1.

60 *Kesavananda Bharati vs State of Kerala* (1973) 4 SCC 225 (Supreme Court of India).

61 *David Ndii and Ors vs Attorney-General and Ors*, [2021] KEHC 9746 (KLR).

half a decade.[62] Drawing upon this constitutional history, the High Court noted that it was clear that 'Kenyans intended to protect the Basic Structure of the Constitution they bequeathed to themselves in 2010 from destruction through gradual amendments.'[63]

So far, so familiar. This is the classic justification for the application of the basic structure doctrine, grounded within the specifics of Kenyan history. But in the BBI Case, however, the issue was a more nuanced one. As we have seen, one of the pillars of the 2010 constitutional order was the participation of the People as constitutional agents – including in the process of constitutional change. For this reason, unlike the Indian Constitution, the Kenyan Constitution's amendment provisions are not limited to parliamentary super-majorities. For a certain set of 'entrenched' provisions,[64] popular involvement through a referendum is mandatory. Furthermore, if the 'popular initiative' route is followed under Article 257 of the Constitution, the People are involved at multiple stages of the amendment process, right from the beginning.[65] In constitutional theory, these are referred to as 'two-tiered amendment procedures' (as opposed to, say, a single-tier method of parliamentary super-majorities for amending all provisions of the constitution).[66]

Could it therefore not be argued that insofar as Kenyans wanted to protect the basic structure of the Constitution from evisceration, they had provided the remedy *within* the Constitution? In order to amend any of the 'entrenched' clauses under Article 255, whether through the parliamentary route under Article 256, or the popular initiative route under Article 257, a referendum was mandatory. Thus – and this was the argument of the State – during the framing of the 2010 Constitution, the 'basic structure' had been explicitly identified under Article 255(1), *and* a process for amending it – which involved the People – had been set out under Articles 256 and 257. In other words, the problem before the Indian Supreme Court in 1973 – i.e., parliamentary super-majorities destroying the constitutional order – had been identified by the framers of the Kenyan Constitution, and accounted for *as a matter of constitutional design*.[67]

62 See e.g. the *CKRC Final Report*, *supra*, 73, noting that one of the issues that arose frequently during public hearings was: 'considering how quickly and fundamentally the independence Constitution was amended, how can we protect the new constitution from a similar fate?'

63 Ibid., para 469.

64 Article 255(1), Constitution of Kenya, 2010.

65 Under Article 257, the amendment process must begin with the collection of one million signatures of registered voters.

66 David Landau and Rosalind Dixon, 'Tiered Constitutional Design' (2018) 86 *George Washington Law Review* 438.

67 This argument was eventually accepted by two dissenting judges at the Court of Appeal. See below, and the discussion in Gautam Bhatia, 'The Hydra and the Sword:

This is a powerful argument. In responding to it, the High Court crafted a powerful and innovative response. It noted that a core idea underlying the 2010 Constitution was indeed the participation of the People as constitutional agents. But this participation was intended to be deeper and richer than a simple top-down referendum. Indeed, the referendum was only the final step of the participatory process. Drawing upon the constitutional history that we have discussed in the previous section, the High Court held that the Kenyan Constitution had been crafted through a participatory process that had gone through four sequential stages: civic education, public participation, debate in a constituent assembly, and the final, ratifying referendum.[68]

This, then, set up the last step in the High Court's argument: if the basic structure of the Kenyan Constitution was sought to be altered, it could only be done through a process that *re-created* the four sequential stages that had gone into the creation of the Constitution. As the Court noted:

> What we can glean from the insistence on these four processes in the history of our constitution-making is that Kenyans intended that the constitutional order that they so painstakingly made would only be fundamentally altered or re-made through a similarly informed and participatory process. It is clear that Kenyans intended that each of the four steps in constitution-making would be necessary before they denatured or replaced the social contract they bequeathed themselves in the form of Constitution of Kenya, 2010.[69]

In the language of constitutional theory, rewriting a constitution was an exercise of *primary constituent power*, equivalent to the creation of a new constitution, or the destruction of an old.[70] That primary constituent power – a power reserved to the sovereign People – was not reducible to a simple

---

Constitutional Amendments, Political Process, and the BBI Case in Kenya' (2024) *Global Constitutionalism*, forthcoming.

68 Unsurprisingly, this account of constitutional history was bitterly contested by the State, as well as by other parties, when it went up in appeal to the Court of Appeal and to the Supreme Court. See e.g. Amicus Brief of Professor Migai Akech in *The Hon'ble Attorney General and Ors vs David Ndii and Ors* (Supreme Court), *supra*, on file with the author, arguing that the political elite were deeply involved in the crafting of the 2010 Constitution, and responsible for its ultimate enactment.

69 *David Ndii* (High Court), *supra*, para 470.

70 Ibid., para 472. There is an ongoing debate in constitutional theory about the nature of 'constituent power' (including 'primary constituent power'), which I will not go into here. Interested readers may consult Joel I Colón-Rios, *Constituent Power and the Law* (Oxford University Press 2020); Roznai, *Unconstitutional Constitutional Amendments*, *supra*; Sergio Verdugo, 'Is it time to abandon the theory of constituent power?' (2023) 21(1) *International Journal of Constitutional Law* 14. Mariana Velasco-Rivera and Joel Colón-Rios, 'On the legal implications of a "permanent" constituent

referendum within existing constitutional structures. It would have to possess a depth and quality that, at the very least, approximated the conditions under which the Constitution was created in the first place.[71]

Through its judgment, the High Court sparked new life into the fifty-year-old basic structure debate. The High Court's vision of the basic structure was not – as it had always been argued hitherto – a judicial *veto* over constitutional amendments that violated the basic structure of the Constitution. In the Indian context – and in many other contexts – where the amendment process was limited to parliament, and where there was no history of public participation written into the constitutional text, there was arguably no alternative: there was a straight clash between parliament and the judiciary over guardianship of the constitutional order.

The High Court acknowledged, however, that the final decision on altering the basic structure – and thus, altering constitutional identity itself – belonged to the People, exercising their primary constituent power. But in a remarkable innovation, the High Court also identified the procedure through which primary constituent power could be exercised, a procedure that was faithful to the participatory nature through which the 2010 constitutional order had been painstakingly crafted.[72] This, again, was a departure from the classic position, which held the basic structure to be essentially *unamendable*, subject to change only by a wholly extra-constitutional process such as a revolution or a coup.

The High Court's judgment was taken in appeal to the Court of Appeal. By a 6-1 majority, the Court of Appeal affirmed the High Court on the point that the basic structure doctrine was applicable in Kenya, and by a 5-2 majority, it held that the basic structure doctrine limited the amendment power under Articles 255–257 of the Constitution. By a narrower 4-3 majority it also affirmed the High Court on the four-step sequential process, with President Musinga casting the deciding vote.[73]

---

power' (2023) 12(2) *Global Constitutionalism* 269; Andrew Arato, *The Adventures of Constituent Power: Beyond Revolutions?* (Cambridge University Press 2017).

71 There is some support for this in the CKRC Final Report, which recorded that during the public hearings, a strong view was expressed by the people that 'the new Constitution should only be amended in the same way that it is made.' *CKRC Final Report*, *supra*, 76 (emphasis supplied). Of course, the four-step process was not spelt out in the CKRC Report; that was the High Court's gloss on the words 'in the same way that it is made'.

72 There is, of course, an unresolved tension in that the method for exercising the primary constituent power to rewrite the Constitution was prescribed by a body whose own authority flows from the present constitutional order; but that is one of the many paradoxes inherent in constitutionalism.

73 *The Honourable Attorney-General vs David Ndii and Ors*, [2021] KECA 363 (KLR).

A study of the Court of Appeal's judgment reveals the first discordant notes in what had so far been a unified judicial approach. In dissenting on this point, Okwengu JA found persuasive the argument that the popular initiative was a 'citizen-driven process', and that the referendum made the People the 'ultimate determinant' on whether an amendment could be carried.[74] The fact that the framers of the Constitution had already entrenched certain provisions within the amendment chapter, and subjected them to this more rigorous, citizen-driven process (the 'two-tiered amendment structure'), indicated that the Constitution was meant to be 'self-sufficient' when it came to amendments.[75] Sichale JA, also in dissent, agreed, noting that the very structure of the amendment provisions reflected 'a conscious effort ... to ensure that we do not have hyper-amendments'.[76] There was, therefore, no need for an additional, external basic structure doctrine to accomplish this purpose.

The majority judgments had various responses to this argument. Perhaps the most direct response came through the judgment of Kiage JA. Kiage JA joined the High Court in questioning whether a referendum, by itself, was enough of a People-oriented safeguard, given how often referenda could be – and were – top-down initiatives that sought to impose a pre-determined package of choices upon voters. The existence of a referendum in Article 257, therefore, was not a complete substitute for the basic structure doctrine, or a complete answer to the problem that the basic structure doctrine had been invoked to solve. As he concluded, therefore, 'an effective bulwark against abusive constitutionalism therefore seems to me to be, on the authorities, one that entails more as opposed to less people involvement.'[77] It was this greater public involvement, both in terms of depth and extent, that the High Court's judgment had sought to secure.

The stage was thus set for the battle to move to the Supreme Court. It was there that the basic structure doctrine ran into choppy waters. A majority of the Supreme Court appeared to be persuaded by the State's argument that the 'balance' between rigidity and flexibility had already been struck in the text of the Kenyan Constitution. The fears of hyper-amendment had thus been addressed by constitutional design. According to the disposition of the court, by a 6-1 majority (with Justice Ibrahim dissenting), the Supreme Court rejected the applicability of the basic structure doctrine in Kenya.

However, a close reading of the judgments reveals a more complex story, where at least two judges – other than Justice Ibrahim – left open the possibility of reconsidering the applicability of the doctrine, should a suitable case of

74 Ibid., para 76 (Okwengu JA, dissenting).

75 Ibid., para 82 (Okwengu JA, dissenting).

76 Ibid., 37 (Sichale JA, dissenting).

77 Ibid., 96 (Kiage JA, concurring).

'constitutional evisceration' present itself to the court.[78] Indeed, a plurality of judges appeared to recognise – and accept – the conceptual distinction between constitutional amendment and constitutional dismemberment or repeal. They also appeared to accept the prospect of potential judicial intervention in cases of constitutional dismemberment masquerading as constitutional amendment. However, they refrained from calling it 'the basic structure doctrine' and applying judicial review to the BBI Bill. The reason for this was the court's view that the challengers to the BBI Bill had failed to demonstrate quite how it was a project of constitutional dismemberment. Indeed, they had spent very little time even attempting to do so. For at least a few of the judges of the Supreme Court, this made the rest of the argument about the basic structure doctrine and its applicability borderline academic.

What, then, *was* the court's finding on the amendment question? To understand that, let us consider the judgment of Chief Justice Koome, arguably the 'casting vote' on the issue. While not expressing a categorical view upon the basic structure doctrine, Koome CJ nonetheless found the four-step sequential process a persuasive account of the kind of deep public participation that had gone into the framing of the 2010 Constitution. However, for Koome CJ, this four-step process – other than the existence of a formal constituent assembly – had *already* been encoded into the text of the popular initiative under Article 257. As she noted:

> … in a case where the amendment process is multi-staged; involve multiple institutions; is time-consuming; engenders inclusivity and participation by the people in deliberations over the merits of the proposed amendments; and has down-stream veto by the people in the form of a referendum, there is no need for judicially-created implied limitations to amendment power through importation of the basic structure doctrine into a constitutional system before exhausting home grown mechanisms.[79]

In other words, the involvement of the People in a popular initiative was not restricted to the one million signatures that kick-started the process, or voting in the final ratifying referendum. Rather, civic education and public participation were baked into the institutional procedures under Article 257 such as – for example – the stage of ratification at the county assemblies, and especially at the stage of the referendum (interestingly, in its final report, the CKRC had specifically noted the peoples' view that constitutional amendment referendums ought only to be conducted after 'thorough awareness creation').[80]

78 For a closer, textual reading of the judgments of the Supreme Court, see Bhatia, 'The Hydra and the Sword', *supra*.

79 *David Ndii* (Supreme Court), *supra*, Koome CJ (concurring), para 205.

80 *CKRC Final Report*, *supra*, 75.

Recall, for a moment, Kiage JA's concern at the Court of Appeal about the inadequacy of referendums to foster genuine and deep public participation. We see strong echoes of this concern in Koome CJ's judgment. However, where Kiage JA found the answer to his concern in the basic structure doctrine and the four-step sequential process, Koome CJ found the same answer *within* the design of Article 257. In other words, while appearing to be formally rejected as a doctrine of the *basic structure*, the High Court's holding that sweeping constitutional change could only be accomplished through a process of deep and rich public participation was resurrected in Koome CJ's judgment, albeit through *constitutional interpretation*: a constitutionally entrenched vision of the basic structure, one might say![81]

What, then, of the future? After the failure of the BBI, and at the time of writing, the Kenyan political elite have not yet embarked upon another project of far-reaching constitutional change – although there have been loud noises.[82] If and when that happens, it will be fascinating to witness the constitutional debates that that will inevitably occasion, their intensity heightened by the fact that the Supreme Court's judgment leaves more questions open than it answers. Whatever the shape that the debates will take, though, the High Court's unique articulation of the basic structure doctrine – and Koome CJ's gloss of it as a doctrine of constitutional interpretation – stand as a landmark contribution to the global debates around constitutional change, the interaction between parliament and the courts, and the role of the People as agents of constitutional change under a democratic and participatory constitution.

## D. The Popular Initiative

But what of the popular initiative itself? While the debate around the basic structure captured the headlines, an equally crucial contest unfolded around the interpretation of Article 257 of the Constitution, and the role of President Kenyatta in orchestrating the BBI Bill as a 'popular initiative'.

The issue was simple. Could the President, through proxies or otherwise, play a substantive role in initiating the amendment process under Article 257 – an article that was expressly about amending the Constitution 'by

[81] It is important to note that even with respect to the entrenched subjects under Article 255(1), Koome CJ's doctrine might be sidestepped if the chosen route is *parliamentary* (under Article 256), instead of popular (under Article 257) – unless a future court holds – as observed in the paragraph above – that the referendum requirement itself carries within it a requirement of deep public participation, and not simply an up-down vote. This might be one to watch for the future!

[82] See e.g. Samwel Owino, 'MPs shocker for Ruto, Raila over Nadco Report' *The Nation* (12th October 2024), available at <https://nation.africa/kenya/news/politics/mps-shocker-for-ruto-raila-over-nadco-report-4792790#story>, visited on 29th October 2024.

the People and Parliament'?[83] The Petitioners argued that he could not: the purpose of Article 257 was to provide for a bottom-up method of constitutional amendment, and a space for the People in the processes of constitutional change. The popular initiative could not be understood in the absence of a constitutional history where, under the Independence Constitution, the People had been systematically and structurally excluded from participation, in the manner outlined previously in this chapter. For this reason, the purpose of Article 257 was to infuse an injection of direct democracy into a constitutional design otherwise committed to representative institutions. That entire purpose would be defeated if the President could *also* take recourse to Article 257, and throw the weight, prestige, and pulpit of the executive behind a constitutional amendment.

The state, on the other hand, argued that Article 257 nowhere expressly excluded the President from participating in the initiation of an amendment. On ascending to the office, the President did not stop being a private citizen. Just like any other private citizen, he retained his constitutionally guaranteed political rights, *inter alia*, to agitate and push for constitutional change. The state also argued there was a deeper, normative reason to not exclude the President from Article 257. Under the Kenyan system, a President might be at odds with the Parliament, especially if Parliament was under the control of an opposing party. The Parliament might then stymie much-needed efforts at constitutional reform, by blocking the parliamentary amendment route under Article 256. It was therefore necessary for the President to have an alternative route – one that could let him bypass Parliament, and go straight to the People. This route was Article 257.

In adjudicating the issue, the High Court was faced with a classic example of 'constitutional silence'.[84] Article 257 neither permitted nor prohibited the President from initiating an amendment *via* popular initiative. In the teeth of a constitutional silence, how was the High Court to proceed? Its judgment would have resonance beyond the issue at hand. As with every other constitution, the Kenyan Constitution too has its ambiguities and silences. These silences often have to do with the scope, limits, and boundaries of public power (especially executive power). How the High Court interpreted *this* silence, therefore, would impact how the Kenyan Constitution was interpreted *in general* with respect to presidential power.

To fill in the silence – to 'separate its warps and wefts'[85] – the High Court turned once again to history. And on this point, the historical record was

83 Article 255(3)(b), Constitution of Kenya, 2010.

84 For a more detailed and technical argument on this point, see the amicus brief submitted by the present author to the Supreme Court: Amicus Brief of Dr. Gautam Bhatia in *David Ndii* (Supreme Court), *supra*, on file with the author.

85 Oduor, *Things They Lost*, *supra*, 143.

straightforward: there could be no doubt that checking presidential power, and an aversion towards the imperial presidency, were the most widely accepted motivations behind the 2010 Constitution. Not only that, it was also accepted that checking presidential power could not be left solely to the other branches of the State, but would also have to be undertaken *by and through* public participation. These were the impulses that explained the existence of the direct democratic procedures found in Article 257. Thus, as the court noted:

> … a Popular Initiative being a process of participatory democracy that empowers the ordinary citizenry to propose constitutional amendment independent of the law making power of the governing body cannot be undertaken by the President or State Organs under any guise. It was inserted in the Constitution to give meaning to the principles of sovereignty based on historical past where the reservation of the power of amendment of the Constitution to the elite few was abused in order to satisfy their own interests.[86]

Consequently, the High Court held – and, on this, it was affirmed by overwhelming majorities at both the Court of Appeal and the Supreme Court – that interpretive silences would have to be interpreted in service of the Constitution's goal to prevent a second imperial presidency, and in favour of bottom-up public participation. In his judgment at the Court of Appeal, for example, President Musinga drew a conceptual distinction between representative and direct democracy, and eloquently defended an interpretation of Article 257 that would preserve space for the latter to remain meaningful, even within a structure of representative government.[87] In an interesting and complementary analysis, Kiage JA addressed the State's argument that a President stymied by a recalcitrant Parliament should have the change to take his or her reform proposals directly to the People. Kiage JA's analysis that the 2010 Constitution was a direct response to the pathologies of the Imperial Presidency demonstrated that the exclusion of the President from Article 257 was *by design*: the Constitution, as it was envisaged, *did not* intend for the President to be able to bypass Parliament and solicit direct popular approval for constitutional change.[88]

The Supreme Court agreed, with multiple judges noting Kenya's long and troubled history with the imperial presidency, and how the 2010 Constitution was meant to be a response to the multiple problems generated by such an imperial presidency. This explained Article 257's focus on direct democracy and popular involvement in constitutional change, and necessitated an interpretation that sharply distinguished between the People and *State organs*

86 *David Ndii* (High Court), *supra*, para 497.

87 *David Ndii* (Court of Appeal), *supra*, Musinga P (concurring), para 348.

88 Ibid., 53, 109.

(including – and especially – the Presidency). Article 257 embodied a carefully crafted balance between the representative and direct elements of democracy, informed by Kenya's history of presidential power and the exclusion of the People from meaningful constitutional governance. It was the court's task to preserve that balance by interpreting Article 257 in a way that would protect the role of the People, rather than leaving it vulnerable to co-option by a top-down, executive-driven process.

Thus, for all three courts, the silences in the Constitution spoke. They spoke of all the hard-won historical lessons against the concentration of executive power. Indeed, as Koome CJ specifically put the point at the Supreme Court, to *imply* the extension of presidential power where it was not *explicitly* granted would be contrary to the 'the overall tenor and ideology of the Constitution and its purposes'.[89] Thus, it was not simply about the textual interpretation of Article 257, but about a constitutional philosophy that would only authorise the wielding of executive power where the Constitution explicitly granted it – and not otherwise.[90]

The importance of this holding cannot be overstated. It was, ultimately, on grounds of non-compliance with Article 257 that the BBI Bill was struck down. President Kenyatta could not escape from the overwhelming evidence of his own fingerprints plastered all over the BBI Bill. And in excluding the President from Article 257, the Kenyan courts brought *the People back in*, as agents of constitutional change, preserving an island of direct democracy from being overwhelmed by the exercise of raw state power.[91]

## E. Conclusion: The Done and the Undone

*Who will free us except ourselves?*[92]

The BBI Case divided opinion among lawyers and scholars, especially on the basic structure doctrine. This is scarcely surprising. After all, the basic structure doctrine has been dividing opinion for fifty years! Doctrinal disagreements

89 *David Ndii* (Supreme Court) *supra*, Koome CJ (concurring), para 243.

90 Indeed, one of the specific recommendations of the CKRC Final Report – after setting out the express powers that should lie with the President – was that the President 'should enjoy such other powers as may be derived only from the Constitution'. *CKRC Final Report*, *supra*, 201. See also Ch. 3.

91 Interestingly, in its section on public participation, the Final Report of the Constitution of Kenya Review Commission had specifically warned of the chance to participate being 'hijacked by the elite if not very carefully planned.' *CKRC Final Report*, *supra*, 162. The BBI case shows how prescient the CKRC was – and how alert the Courts were as well, to the risk of elite capture inherent in public participation provisions.

92 Rebeka Njau, 'The Scar: a Tragedy' (1963) 8 *Transition* 23, 25.

aside, however, the BBI judgments did justice to the two-pronged transformative purpose of the 2010 Constitution: *to constrain the President, and to empower the People*. All three courts agreed upon the correct interpretation of Article 257, in light of constitutional history: that the purpose of the popular initiative was to let the people speak, and not to have them spoken for by the President.[93] And while the Supreme Court disagreed with the High Court and the Court of Appeal on the basic structure doctrine and the deep public participation involved in the four-step sequential process, a close reading of Chief Justice Koome's opinion reveals an endorsement of the latter, coupled with an attempt to bring the essence of the four-step process *within* the processes of popular constitutional change, rather than leave it outside of the Constitution. These are all valuable insights, not just for Kenyan constitutionalism, but for students of constitutional change, and the role of courts in relation to other political actors, across the world.

That said, however, the seven separate opinions issued by the Supreme Court create a certain degree of messiness when trying to discern what, precisely, was the Court's holding on the issue of the basic structure. And whether in Kenya or elsewhere, messiness tends to favour the executive: blurred boundaries can be pushed and unclear constitutional borders can be tested to see how much and how far they will yield. As far as constitutional change is concerned, the BBI judgments(s) are far more likely to be the first words, rather than the last words, on the subject.

And then there is the undone: the issue of the referendum question. Recall that the BBI Bill, with all its seventy-four amendments, was proposed to be presented to the People for an up-down vote.[94] These amendments ranged over subjects as diverse as judicial reform and county funding, the structure

[93] In a particularly fascinating opinion in the Court of Appeal, Tuiyott JA warned of more subtle attempts by the executive to influence a popular initiative, and how constitutional courts would need to be specifically alert in protecting the philosophy of direct democracy and public participation underlying Article 257, when the facts were not quite so clear or obvious as they were in the BBI Case. See *David Ndii* (Court of Appeal), *supra* (concurring opinion of Tuiyott JA), para 60: 'A State actor, who is otherwise barred from initiating a popular initiative, cannot originate a proposal for amendment then hire or sponsor a citizen to formulate it into a Bill and then collect signatures in support. In that instance, the promoter will simply be a surrogate of the State actor. That will not be a truly citizen-driven initiative as it will an enterprise of the State actor. There will be occasion therefore when it will be necessary to look beyond the person who formulates the draft Bill and collects the signatures to discover the hand behind the initiative, only in this way will the true intent of the popular initiative process be protected against manipulation.'

[94] As noted above, however, that there is an argument that had the process been completed as intended, only those amendments touching upon the entrenched subjects would have gone to a referendum (under Article 255), as an Article 257 referendum is not necessary if both Houses of Parliament pass the popular initiative.

of the executive and changes to the constituencies. They also contained what were clearly incentives – or, to use a less generous terms – 'sweeteners' – to help push through a package containing what might otherwise have been unpalatable provisions.

Was this stratagem simply another way of silencing the People, by forcing them into a single vote for a series of highly complex – and technically diverse – proposals, making it impossible for any genuine deliberation or engagement with the substance of the proposals? Scholarship around the world has repeatedly warned against the potential of referendums to 'flatten' layered and nuanced questions, and thus reduce the People to simply endorsing (or rejecting) by acclamation, proposals conceptualised and driven by the political elite.[95]

The High Court agreed. It noted that it would defeat the purpose of public participation entirely if seventy-four amendments were presented to the public as a 'package deal' in a straight up-down vote.[96] Instead, it held that every proposed amendment would have to be proposed via a separate bill, and voted on separately. Only then would the 'direct democracy' mandated by Article 257 have any genuine meaning[97]

The Court of Appeal rejected this holding by a wafer-thin majority, but did not propose an interpretive approach of its own. Most of the Court of Appeal judges agreed with Nambuye JA's observation that 'when a bill is limited to a single subject, it is easier for the public to more fully understand the impact of the enactment … it also prevents fraud upon the people by minimizing the possibility of promoters of the amendment hiding harmful proposals in the midst complex multi-subject measures that the common man might not be able to grasp and understand.'[98]

95 For a book-length treatment of the issue, see Stephen Tierney, *Constitutional Referendums: The Theory and Practice of Republican Deliberation* (Oxford University Press 2012).

96 This is a general point about the efficacy of referendums as barometers of the popular will, that has been made by constitutional courts elsewhere (in particular, in Latvia and Switzerland). See e.g. The Constitutional Court of the Republic of Lithuania, 'On Organising and Calling Referendums: Summary', available at <https://www.lrkt.lt/en/court-acts/search/170/ta859/summary>, visited on 15th September 2024.

97 *David Ndii* (High Court), *supra*.

98 *David Ndii* (Court of Appeal), *supra*, concurring opinion of Nambuye JA (para 128). See also paragraph 156 of the concurring opinion of Gatembu Kairu JA: '[the voter's] choice, in my view, is rendered nugatory, inoperative, and inconsequential if the voter is called upon to vote on an omnibus draft Bill, that contains a raft of numerous, diverse, and unrelated proposed amendments to the Constitution, in this case over 70 proposals of amendments, that cut across the entire spectrum of the Constitution.'

In his concurring opinion, Gatembu Kairu JA accepted a somewhat modulated 'unity of theme approach': that is, amendments broadly dealing with the same issue (e.g., police reforms) could be voted on together, in the interests of efficiency. However, an amendment bill could not lump together wholly unrelated constitutional changes into one ratifying vote.[99] What came out of the Court of Appeal, therefore, was an indeterminate position. The High Court's one-bill-per-amendment had been overruled, but nothing had replaced it. The constitutional landscape was ideal for clarification from the Supreme Court.

Indeed, the answer seemed logically inevitable. Once the Supreme Court held that the protection against constitutional evisceration lay *within* the contours of Article 257, specifically in a deep and rich form of public participation, an interpretation of Article 257 that would allow State organs to indirectly defeat public participation by a backdoor method could not be sustained. In other words, every clause of Article 257 would have to be interpreted so as to *deepen* public participation, and not to dilute it. And the framing of the referendum question(s) was inextricably linked to this interpretive issue.[100]

But instead, the Supreme Court refused to rule on the point, on the basis that as the High Court's decision had stopped the BBI process before it got to the referendum stage, the question was not yet ripe for adjudication.[101] The question remains open at the time of writing. One may lament this as a missed opportunity, but also recognise it as a contest not yet foreclosed, left open for a future constitutional battle. If there is one constant in all the battles over constitutional change, it is that the executive will always attempt to transform public participation provisions into ciphers, reducing an active and engaged citizenry into passive recipients of executive-driven amendments; and just as surely, the People will resist their exclusion and marginalisation.

It is in this context that the BBI judgements demonstrated the importance of the courts and of transformative constitutionalism, in ensuring that 'the People [are not] silent'.[102]

99 *David Ndii* (Court of Appeal), *supra*, concurring opinion of Gatembu Kairu JA, para 157.

100 In my view, the arguments for a 'unity of theme' approach would apply equally to an Article 255 referendum as they would to an Article 257 referendum, as both referendums flow from the common commitment to public participation that we have discussed in this chapter.

101 *David Ndii* (Supreme Court), *supra*.

102 The epigraph refers to Alexander Pushkin's famous play about state oppression, *Boris Gudunov*, which ends with the line: 'The People are silent.'

# 3

# Reviving Institutions: The CDF Case

IN THE previous chapter, we examined the role of the People as an external counterbalance to Presidential power, and as a check upon the Imperial Presidency. Classical constitutional theory, on the other hand, has always focused on what Gargarella labels a system of *internal* checks and balances: that is, the different institutions of the State checking and constraining each other.[1] This is the 'separation of powers': originally between the legislature, the executive, and the judiciary,[2] and, in recent times, a more complex distribution of public power involving fourth branch institutions such as independent commissions, and other bodies.[3]

The separation of powers has always been more ideal than reality.[4] To start with, in parliamentary systems, there is no clean-cut separation between the legislature and the executive. The latter is drawn from the former and while, in theory, is meant to be answerable to it, in practice, often dominates it. Besides, the complexity of modern governance can no longer sustain (if it ever could) the bright-line division between law-making (the legislature),

1 Gargarella, *Latin American Constitutionalism 1810–2010*, *supra*. In its earliest articulation in the US Federalist Papers, the belief was that tyranny could be prevented only if 'ambition' was made to counter-act 'ambition' and that, therefore, a constitution needed an elaborate set of veto points, at the instance of different actors. Constitutional philosophy has evolved a bit since then, but the underlying idea remains somewhat similar. See James Madison, 'The Federalist No. 47,' *The New York Packet* (1st February 1788), available at <https://avalon.law.yale.edu/18th_century/fed47.asp>, visited on 15th September 2024.

2 Baron de Montesquieu, *The Spirit of the Laws* (Colonial Press 1899); John Locke, *Two Treatises of Government* (Peter Laslett (ed.), Cambridge University Press 1970).

3 For a discussion, see Charles M. Fombad, 'The Role of Emerging Hybrid Institutions of Accountability in the Separation of Powers Scheme in Africa' in *Separation of Powers in African Constitutionalism* (Charles M. Fombad (ed.), Oxford University Press 2016); Tarunabh Khaitan, 'Guarantor Institutions' (2021) 16 *The Asian Journal of Comparative Law* S40. For a Kenyan case study see Walter K. Ochieng, 'The Independence, Accountability, and Effectiveness of Constitutional Commissions and Independent Offices in Kenya' (2019) 4(1) *Kabarak Journal of Law and Ethics* 135–163.

4 See e.g. Bruce Ackerman, 'The New Separation of Powers' (2000) 113(3) *The Harvard Law Review* 633.

implementation (the executive), and adjudication (the judiciary). This complexity has, in turn, seen a mid-twentieth-century drift towards greater executive power, whether in parliamentary systems (beyond their inherent tendency of executive domination), or presidential ones.[5] Courts have grappled with doctrines such as 'excessive delegation' (where the legislature passes vague laws, giving the executive so much discretion that the line between implementation and law-making dissolves), the executive abuse of temporary rule-by-decree powers, and so on.

While, on the one hand, there are questions about the utility of separation of powers theory in preventing executive concentration of power in modern democracies,[6] on the other hand, there are situations where the separation of powers is critiqued for playing a conservative role and hampering the project of transformative constitutionalism. As we shall see in the next chapter, this critique has some bite in the context of socio-economic rights adjudication, where judicial attempts to craft innovative remedies in order to make socio-economic rights effective are resisted on the grounds of the separation of powers.

How might a court engage with the intertwined conceptions of the separation of powers, executive dominance, and transformative constitutionalism? In this chapter, we will consider a case where the Supreme Court of Kenya was faced with exactly this issue, in a context that is familiar to students of comparative constitutionalism. At stake was the constitutionality of the Constituency Development Fund (CDF). The CDF is a variant of a legal device that is found in multiple countries.[7] Individual legislators are provided with funds (drawn from public money) to engage in 'development work' in their constituency.[8] This, however, immediately raises a set of important questions. Are not legislators 'representatives' of their constituents, and is not their job, therefore, to *represent* their electors in the legislative body, instead of engaging in administration and governance? Will such funds not provide an incumbent with a structural advantage unavailable to their opponent when the next election comes? If the funds are centrally allocated, how do they impact concerns around federalism and devolution in non-unitary countries? And so on.

5 For the *locus classicus* on the subject, which continues to trigger debate and conspiracy, see Arthur Schlesinger, *The Imperial Presidency* (Houghton Mifflin 1973).

6 For a discussion, see Jeremy Waldron, 'Separation of Powers in Thought and Practice' (2013) 54(2) *Boston College Law Review* 433.

7 Prominent examples include India, Zambia, Tanzania, Uganda, Ghana, and Papua New Guinea. For a comparative discussion, see Kevin Deveaux, 'UNODC and COPAC Pacific Regional Conference: Constituency Development Funds Conference Discussion Paper and Report' (2022), available at <https://www.unodc.org/roseap/uploads/documents/pacific/2023/CDF_conference_report.pdf>, visited on 15th September 2024.

8 The mechanism of allocation and distribution varies across countries.

In considering how the Kenyan Supreme Court answered these questions, I will begin by examining the history of the separation of powers, both in the colony and in the post-colony. While colonial constitutionalism saw the formal emergence of (partially) representative legislatures, its defining feature was the overriding dominance of the executive (separation of powers only in name). In Kenya, the Independence Constitution did seek to entrench separation of powers both through a parliamentary system and a federal structure (*majimbo*). However, within five years of Independence, that Constitution had been eviscerated by a set of hyper-amendments, and transformed into a top-down presidential system with minimal parliamentary checks (Section A).

For this reason – and as we have already seen, partially, in the previous chapter – constraining the Imperial Presidency was at the heart of the constitutional reform debates from the 1990s onwards. This was sought to be accomplished both through a stronger parliament (there was a consistent push towards a parliamentary system, which was ultimately rejected by the political elite) and a restoration of devolution (albeit not the relatively stronger federal structure in the original 1963 Constitution) (Section B).

The Supreme Court's consideration of the CDF must be examined in this context. In striking down the CDF, I will argue, the court reaffirmed the importance of adhering to constitutional principles (in this case, the separation of powers) over arguments of administrative convenience. It also drew from historical experience to forestall centralised political control over the mechanics of fiscal devolution. The court's judgment, in my view, demonstrates the application of transformative constitutionalism to issues of constitutional structure and design, and to the containment of power (Section C). And while the status of the CDF is itself in limbo (by the time the court considered the constitutionality of the law, it had already been 'updated' by fresh legislation), legal disputes brought to the courts in its aftermath demonstrate the continuing relevance of these issues (Section D). As with the BBI Case, therefore, the CDF Case heralds the beginnings of an enduring constitutional debate – and not the end of one.

## A. Executive Dominance under Colonial and Post-Colonial Constitutionalism

British colonialism – as we have observed previously in this book – had certain common features, no matter where it was violently exported to. The origins of colonial governance were autocratic (first military, and then civilian). Eventually, under pressure from the colony, the regime was forced to make a certain – very limited – space for a representative organ. These representative bodies were gradually expanded, in an attempt to contain and manage aspirations for self-government and independence from spilling over. This containment took the form of a repeated assertion of the superiority of the executive over the legislature. In Kenya – as Githu Muigai notes – the colonial structure was defined by two features: the dominance of the Governor over the Legislative Council (LegCo), and the dominance of the imperial metropolis (Britain) over the colony.[9] This, in effect, created a 'formal impression of, but hardly real separation of powers'.[10]

Executive dominance was asserted through a number of legal devices, variants of which were found across former British colonies. These include certain 'reserved subjects' for the Governor, which the legislative council was not allowed to touch. The Governor had emergency powers through which they could dissolve the legislative council, thus ensuring that – in a sense – the latter existed only on the sufferance of the executive. And even for non-emergency times, the Governor had general powers to make rules and regulations for the 'peace, order, and good government of the colony'[11] (language that has survived into many post-colonial constitutions):[12] a power akin to discretionary executive law-making.[13]

Separation of powers, thus, came stillborn to the colonies. Representative institutions were extracted from the colonial regime, often grudgingly, and as the result of a cynical policy of containment – not out of any commitment to representation and representative institutions. Not only was representation itself limited, but the institutions worked under a formally structural and dominant executive, with partial and revocable powers. As with other colonies, such was the landscape at the time of Kenyan Independence.

The Independence Constitution – as many have noted – was a conventionally 'liberal'[14] Constitution in the sense that its design was motivated by a distrust of power-holders, and therefore primarily sought to constrain what they could do with power.[15] Constitutional design responded to the concerns of

9 Muigai, *Power, Politics & Law*, *supra*, 61. See, *infra*, Ch. 1.

10 Ibid., 67.

11 A holdover from the autocratic period. As early as 1897, an order empowered 'the Commissioner to make Regulations (known as Queen's Regulations) on public administration, policing, and "generally for the peace, order and good government of the Protectorate."' Ibid., 56. This is, of course, law-making. In the early twentieth century, in Kenya, the Governor was formally divested of the power, and it was granted to the Legislative Council. That latter body itself, however, was scarcely independent in any genuine sense.

12 See e.g. the Governor's powers in certain 'Sixth Schedule Areas' under the Indian Constitution that replicate this colonial phrase.

13 The language 'peace, order, and good government' is not always used in reference to the executive, of course: Kenya's 1963 Constitution used it in reference to legislative powers.

14 *In the Matter of the Speaker of the Senate and Anr*, [2013] KESC 7 (KLR).

15 Muigai, *Power, Politics & Law*, *supra*, 186.

two major players in the drafting process: the British, who feared a loss of their assets and influence in the colony after their departure;[16] and the coalition of groups and individuals that constituted the Kenya African Democratic Union (KADU) party, who feared dominance by the organisationally superior, and more nationally popular, Kenya African National Union (KANU) party.[17]

To limit the scope of what KANU could accomplish once they came into government, the 1963 Constitution not only created the familiar multi-party Westminster parliamentary system (hence, no strong executive head as in presidential systems), but also as a federal structure with extensive devolved powers (*majimbo*), keeping in mind that KANU's coalition was not uniformly dominant across Kenya.[18] The regions were granted legislative, executive, administrative and financial powers (albeit over a limited set of functions). The central government retained 'substantial control over regional finances … [there was] established a single public service commission and [the Constitution] returned central control over the police force.'[19]

As Jaramogi Oginga Odinga – then of KANU, and later of the Opposition – notes in his autobiography, KANU accepted this arrangement with the express

16 As the immediate post-Independence trajectory of Kenya showed, the British need not have worried.

17 See *CKRC Final Report*, *supra*, 25, for an acknowledgment of this tension. As scholars have noted, many of the advocates of regionalism proposed it as a constitutional model not out of a normative commitment to federalism as a means of democratising power and accommodating diversity, but out of immediate fears of majority rule coming for the first time to the colony. These included the white settlers, going back to the 1950s. See e.g. Jaramogi Oginga Odinga, *Not Yet Uhuru* (Hienemann 1969) 170. Muigai perceptively notes that 'if devolution was somewhat a radical project in light of colonial constitutional history, political propaganda did not fail to link it with moderation, not least because white settlers had been associated with devolution schemes in the past.' Muigai, *Power, Politics & Law*, *supra*, 165. See also Okoth-Ogendo, 'The Politics of Constitutional Change Since Independence, 1963–69', *supra*, 9.

18 See the discussion in Anderson, '"Yours in the Struggle for Majimbo"', *supra*, 547.

19 For a discussion, see *CKRC Final Report*, *supra*, 26–27; Muigai, *Power, Politics & Law*, *supra*, 183. Note that while the initial Lancaster House Constitution (the 'Self-Government Constitution') contemplated public service commissions under the control of the regions, KANU's victory in the May 1963 elections allowed it to push strongly for altering this arrangement at the third Lancaster House Conference, shortly before Independence. The British government gave in to these demands and – along with lowering the threshold for constitutional amendments – 'opened the way for constitutional change that would soon lead to the demise of *majimbo*'. Maxon, 'The Demise and Rise of *Majimbo* in Independent Kenya', *supra*, 19, 23; see also Maxon, 'Constitution-Making in Contemporary Kenya', *supra*, 11, 16.

intention of amending it out of existence the moment they gained power.[20] In this they were true to their intention: within half a decade, the 1963 Constitution was unrecognisable. Gone was (effective) parliamentarianism and *majimbo*, and in its place there stood the executive presidency.[21]

For the purposes of this chapter, there are two sets of relevant amendments: amendments designed to achieve an 'accretion of power from parliament to the President',[22] and amendments designed to dismantle the federal structure and transform Kenya into a unitary state.[23]

The first set of amendments aimed to remove parliament as an effective check upon Presidential power. Some of these were explicit and unsubtle. The First Amendment, for example, simply abolished the post of the Prime Minister, and replaced it with an executive President.[24] The Fourth Amendment introduced disqualification provisions for National Assembly members who failed to attend Assembly sessions, but in granting the President the power to pardon offenders, provided the Executive with constitutionally sanctioned leverage.

Other amendments were, however, more subtle. Consider, for example, the Fifth Amendment, which stipulated that on resignation from his/her political party, a Member of Parliament would also lose their parliamentary seat, and would need to fight a by-election. In political terms, the amendment was designed to destroy the more left-wing faction led by Jaramogi Oginga Odinga, which had recently quit KANU. In effect, it triggered the 'Little General Election' of 1966 that led to Oginga Odinga's defeat,[25] and saw the further consolidation of KANU under Jomo Kenyatta.[26] But in constitutional terms, the bite of this Amendment lay in the fact that it severely restricted the possibility of intra-party dissent, which is a crucial check upon party leaderships and the executive: a legislator who fundamentally disagreed with the direction in which the leadership was taking their party, could only express their dissent

20 Oginga Odinga, *Not Yet Uhuru*, *supra*. Indeed, KANU had begun the process of undermining *majimbo* immediately after the May 1963 elections, including through simple inaction, such as 'delays in transfer of services and funds to the regions', as required by the self-government Constitution. See Maxon, 'The Demise and Rise of *Majimbo* in Independent Kenya', *supra*, 23.

21 *CKRC Final Report*, *supra*, 31; Maxon, 'The Demise and Rise of *Majimbo* in Independent Kenya', *supra*. It is perhaps an irony of history that Oginga Odinga's political career was itself a casualty of these amendments.

22 Okoth-Ogendo, 'The Politics of Constitutional Change Since Independence', *supra*, 29.

23 Ghai and McAuslan, *Public Law and Political Change in Kenya*, *supra*, 213–214.

24 Discussed in Okoth-Ogendo, 'The Politics of Constitutional Change Since Independence', *supra*.

25 Caused, in part, by a liberal dose of political repression and misuse of State power.

26 Charles Hornsby, *Kenya: A History Since Independence* (I.B. Tauris 2012) 161.

by leaving Parliament altogether, and having to fight another election. In other words, therefore, it facilitated a shift in power from the legislator *qua* representative in Parliament, to the party leadership/executive.[27]

The amendments abolishing the federal structure followed a similar pattern. Certain flaws in the design of the Independence Constitution, as highlighted above, allowed the centre to gut the regions through control over fiscal devolution, and effectively prevent them from functioning.[28] Following this, the Second Amendment abolished Regional Presidents, replacing them with 'Provincial Commissioners' who were appointed by the President, and therefore beholden to him. The Seventh Amendment formally completed the centralisation process by abolishing the Upper House (Senate), and replacing it with a unitary, one-chamber legislature. As Murunga notes, the effect of this was to 'shift … the axis of political action and debate to the centre'.[29]

Thus, what began as a *parliamentary* and *federal* constitutional arrangement was transformed – through formal amendments – into a *presidential* and *unitary* system.[30] This involved either the abolition or the degradation of *intermediary institutions* that would stand between the President and direct personal rule: in this case, the Parliament, the Senate, and the Regions. Henceforth, governance – as we have noted in the previous chapter – would be carried on by the President, through the bureaucracy and the 'regional commissioners' under direct presidential control, and by side-lining the legislative body. In

27 A decade and a half later, the Indian Constitution would enact an even harsher version of this rule, called the anti-defection law: the anti-defection law triggered disqualification not on resignation from the parliamentary party, but on the simple act of voting against the party whip. See the Tenth Schedule, Constitution of India, 1949. There is general agreement that the Tenth Schedule has failed to quell the problem of unprincipled 'defections' between parties, while also squelching intra-party dissent.

28 Anderson, 'Yours in the Struggle for *Majimbo*', *supra*, 562. For a general discussion of how distribution of finances played a key role in centralisation under the 1963 Constitution – including a discussion of amendments – see e.g. Attiya Warris, 'Kenya's fiscal accountability revisited: A review of the historical erosion of the country's fiscal Constitution from 1962 to 2010' in *Human Rights and Democratic Governance in Kenya: A post-2007 Appraisal* (Morris Kiwinda Mbondenyi et al. (eds).,PULP 2015) 301, 333.

29 Godwin R. Murunga, 'Elite compromises and the content of the 2010 Constitution' in *Kenya: The Struggle for a New Constitutional Order*, *supra*, 144, 148. See also the *CKRC Final Report*, *supra*, 196: 'The unilateralist, who characterises the powers of the presidency in the current Constitution, is a result of the whittling away of the safeguards by the 11 amendments that took place between 1964 and 1969. The effect of those amendments was to consolidate immense powers in the Presidency and form a potential loophole for abuse and misuse of power.'

30 For a complete analysis of the amendments, see Muigai, *Power, Politics & Law*, *supra*, Ch. 5; Okoth-Ogendo, 'The Politics of Constitutional Change since Independence', *supra*; *CKRC Final Report*, *supra*, 235.

many ways, this was a mirror image of colonial constitutionalism.[31] Branch and Cheeseman demonstrate the continuity:

> As the colonial period progressed, the executive retained much of its power in spite of the emergence of an independent legislative council. The executive was empowered by its control, via the chief native commissioner, of the provincial administration. This enabled the executive to bypass the legislature when necessary.[32]

The result of the amendments was to establish a similar structure. Thus, in the words of Okoth-Ogendo, 'in many respects this [constitutional order] was a reversion to the pre-1963 situation, based on a framework essentially colonial and authoritarian.'[33]

Of course, the system could be resisted. Even after KANU became the sole political party in the country (as a direct, effective result of these amendments), there were times when parliamentary backbench coalitions were able to challenge – and at times, even thwart – the President.[34] Indeed, as Opalo points out, the Kenyan parliament remained relatively 'means-independent' at least until 1975, and the primary forum for influencing policy debates (its degradation was incremental, and only accelerated in the 1980s, during the rule of President Moi).[35] There were also attempts at limited *administrative* decentralisation and delegation through the establishment – for example – of local authorities, during the 1980s.[36] But these were exceptions in what was

[31] For a detailed analysis of the provincial administration as an instrument of rule both in the colonial era, and under President Kenyatta, see Opalo, *Legislative Development in Africa, supra*, Ch. 5; see also the discussion in the *CKRC Final Report, supra*, 237–238.

[32] Daniel Branch and Nicholas Cheeseman, 'The Politics of Control in Kenya: Understanding the Bureaucratic-Executive State, 1952–78' (2006) 33(107) *Review of African Political Economy* 11, 18. See also Ch. 2.

[33] Okoth-Ogendo, 'The Politics of Constitutional Change Since Independence,' *supra*, 21. See also Maxon, 'The Demise and Rise of *Majimbo* in Independent Kenya', *supra*, 24, for a detailed comparison with colonial structures.

[34] Hornsby, *Kenya: A History Since Independence, supra*. For a historical analysis of the relative independence of the legislature in the early years, see Opalo, *Legislative Development in Africa, supra*, 118–119, 129, noting in particular that the retention of the provincial administration allowed Jomo Kenyatta to grant a measure of leeway to the legislature 'without fear of losing power'.

[35] Opalo, *Legislative Development in Africa, supra*, Ch. 5.

[36] Some of these measures are chronicled in the concurring opinion of Mutunga CJ in *In the Matter of the Speaker and the Senate and Anr, supra*, 176–182. Mutunga CJ noted how a number of these measures failed, in part, because of the continued 'dominance of the Provincial Administration and the Central Government'. Ibid., para 179.

overwhelmingly – and by design – a constitutional order dedicated towards securing unimpeded presidential power.[37]

A final impact of this – and this is directly relevant to the argument in this chapter – was a change in the understanding and articulation of the role of the legislator. As Parliament's legislative role waned with the centralising drift in the 1960s and 1970s, 'clientelism and constituency service … [became] the currency of legislative politics'.[38] Through appointments to parastatal boards (also a form of executive patronage), legislators gained access to State resources, which – in turn – were deployed into developmental projects. These then became an instrument through which the legislators could 'fend off challengers … [and] control their own political destinies'.[39] Indeed, scholars have noted how this both flowed from – and reinforced – the ethnicisation of politics, another persistent problem with its origins in the colonial era, and which had only worsened after independence.[40] Thus:

> local political dynamics [were] … concentrated on the activities of individual politicians, by developing and reinforcing an image of politicians as the direct assistants of local communities. In turn, MPs emerged as a key linkage between Kenyan citizens and their government, while local support and re-election became heavily dependent on an MPs local development record.[41]

When we think of the CDF, therefore, it is important to remember that the blurring of legislative and executive functions that it represents can be traced back to the centralising tendencies of the old regime. Constituency service as the role of the legislator was directly related to the legislative lack of power under an executive-dominated parliament.[42] This, then, brings us to the question of whether – and to what extent – the 2010 Constitution's transformative vision was tied up with reversing this centralising drift. It is to this that we now turn.

37 Tamarkin, 'The Roots of Political Stability in Kenya', *supra*, 297.

38 Opalo, *Legislative Development in Africa*, *supra*, 155.

39 Ibid.

40 See e.g. Lynch, 'The Fruits of Perception', *supra*, 233, 251–252; we will revisit this topic in the chapter on presidential election disputes. Its relevance to more than one locus of discussion shows, however, how the axes of transformative constitutionalism do not exist in isolated silos, but are interconnected.

41 Ibid., 252.

42 As the Constitution of Kenya Review Commission noted in its Final Report, one feature of the Independence Constitution – after Kenyatta's amendments – was the 'conflicts of interests and blurred lines of responsibility, diminishing, among others, the role of the Legislature and its ability to control or monitor the executive.' *CKRC Final Report*, *supra*, 31.

## B. Constitutional Design in the 2010 Constitution

Debates around containing Presidential power and devolution were central to the constitutional reform movement. They drew upon a decades-long legacy. They were also intertwined with each other. As Whitaker and Giersch note:

> Although the official constitutional review process did not start until the late 1990s, debates about the constitution in Kenya go back decades. Since before independence from Britain in 1963, Kenyans have argued about the best way to structure political institutions in a diverse society. The debate has focused especially on the vertical and horizontal divisions of power, that is, the extent to which power should be devolved to subnational units and the extent to which executive power should be kept in check. Other issues have also become contentious, but these core questions have been the underlying focus of constitutional debates in Kenya for years.[43]

I have discussed some of the debates around limiting executive power in some detail in the previous chapter, and will not retrace traversed ground here. As we have seen, during the public consultations organised by the CKRC, a clear consensus emerged for limiting Presidential power under the new constitutional order.[44] While public participation was one way of achieving this goal, it was equally clear that without strong, counterbalancing *representative* institutions, any new constitution would swiftly drift back into an imperial presidency. In fact, the Bomas Draft Constitution – an outcome of the CKRC's deliberative and participatory process – sought a return to a parliamentary and devolved system. This was not acceptable to the incumbent Kibaki government, which altered the draft constitution. The spirit of these changes is described by Murray:

> [The] executive arrangements were fundamentally altered with the Bomas proposal replaced by provisions which concentrated power in a President and which, in essence, created a hyper-presidential system. In addition, the draft had been meticulously edited to remove many of the checks on executive power that it had introduced. Second, the multilevel system of government supported by a Senate that was proposed by the Bomas draft, and that promised to disperse power and grant some autonomy to communities outside Nairobi, was largely undone. In the 'Proposed New Constitution' the Senate was removed and the powers of districts subject to national law.[45]

43 Whitaker and Giersh, 'Voting on a Constitution', *supra*, 1–2.
44 Diepeveen, '"The Kenyas we don't want"', *supra*, 231.
45 Murray, 'Kenya's 2010 Constitution', *supra*, 747.

In effect, this signalled a return to the executive-bureaucratic unitary state of the hyper-amended Independence Constitution. There was immediate and strong objection to this, both by civil society, as well as that faction of the political elite (led by Raila Odinga) who saw their own political futures thrown into jeopardy by the proposed changes. Odinga and his allies, thus, mounted a strong campaign against the ratification of the Wako draft, which accordingly went down to defeat in a referendum: a defeat caused, at least in part, due to concerns about the continuation of the Imperial Presidency and the centralisation of power.[46] Thus, as Murunga sums up the history:

> By March 2004, [the] contentious issues had narrowed to three: executive authority, the devolution of powers, and transitional and consequential arrangements. While one side preferred an executive president who was head of state and government and who in turn appointed a prime minister, others preferred a prime minister as head of government. While some wanted a government centralised in Nairobi, others preferred a devolved system in which regional governments enjoyed a modicum of control over regional resources. Eventually, the government rejected the Bomas process and walked out. They went on to rework the draft through a process led by Amos Wako, the attorney general, and presented what was known as the Wako draft at a referendum in 2005. The draft was roundly defeated.[47]

The disputed Presidential election of 2007, between President Kibaki and Raila Odinga, saw tragic, large-scale post-election violence, with more than a thousand deaths, and hundreds of thousands of people displaced. Its triggers were many, including electoral manipulation, grievances over land distribution going back to the colonial era, and the ethnically mediated winner-take-all nature of the elections under the existing constitution's presidential system.[48] As part of the externally mediated reconciliation process, President Kibaki and Raila Odinga agreed to kick-start a second constitutional drafting process.

At the second time of asking, the drafters attempted to keep the process on track by focusing attention on three core areas of disagreement, which had stymied Bomas. Unsurprisingly, and in tune with decades of history, the structure of government and the scope of executive power was the first – and

46 Whitaker and Giersch, 'Voting on a Constitution,' *supra*.

47 Murunga, 'Elite compromises and the content of the 2010 Constitution,' *supra*, 158.

48 See e.g. Office of the AU Panel of Eminent Legal Personalities, *Back from the Brink: The 2008 Mediation Process and Reforms in Kenya* (2008), available at <https://www.kofiannanfoundation.org/wp-content/uploads/2014/08/backFromBrink_web.pdf>, visited on 25th October 2024.

most intractable – issue. The scope and extent of devolution was the second. As Oyaya and Poku reiterate:

> the most contentious issues ... date back to the pre- and post-independence periods. These included such unresolved historical issues as the structure and system of government – unitary versus federal system and parliamentary versus presidential system; devolution of power; and marginalisation and social exclusion.[49]

Indeed, as Christina Murray notes, because it was devolution and the structure of government that 'had defined the main opposing positions taken at the failed referendum in 2005',[50] it was resolving these issues that the 2007 process – and the Committee of Experts – had to do on a priority basis.

Let us discuss the second issue (devolution) first. Much like the structure of the government, devolution had been at the forefront since the beginning of the constitutional reform movement. The start of the 1990s saw a revival of the long-moribund *majimbo* debate, which was now framed in the vocabulary of 'bring[ing] about balanced development in the country through a more equitable distribution of resources and government services'.[51] From these beginnings, *majimbo* turned into a (sometimes violent) political and electoral issue through the decade, now expanding to include 'historic land grievances, bitterness and opposition to "outsiders" occupying land in areas that should be reserved for the "indigenous" inhabitants, perceived favoritism toward certain ethnic communities in government employment combined with victimization of others, and a demand for an equitable division of resources and social services.'[52] Indeed, as Maxon notes, by 2005, the *principle* of devolution enjoyed a wide consensus, with the only question being about the nature of the form it would take under the new constitutional settlement.[53] This consensus was further entrenched by the fact that the successful campaign against the Wako draft (as noted above) had, as one of its major critiques, the argument that the draft did not 'go far enough in the direction of devolution,'[54] especially on key issues such as control over land. Devolution was, likewise, a key issue in the 2007 Presidential elections, including its tragic aftermath.

49 Oyaya and Poku, *The Making of the Constitution of Kenya*, *supra*, 138. See also Conrad Bosire, 'The Constitutional and Legal Framework of Devolved Government and its Relevance to Development in Kenya' in *Human Rights and Democratic Governance in Kenya*, *supra*, 211.

50 Murray, 'Making and Remaking Kenya's Constitution', *supra*, 37.

51 Maxon, 'The Demise and Rise of *Majimbo* in Independent Kenya', *supra*, 33.

52 Ibid., 37.

53 Ibid., 44.

54 Ibid.

This background made devolution – as a structural complement to containing the Imperial Presidency – an inevitability in the final constitutional settlement. Admittedly, fears of entrenching an 'ethnic democracy' – and a set of ethnic enclaves – prevented the 2010 Constitution from embracing a return to federalism in its 1963 *majimbo* form.[55] There was, however, a serious commitment to devolution that took the form of counties with their own elected governments, and the return of a bicameral legislature with a senate, for the purpose of articulating regional aspirations.[56] As the Supreme Court would note, in an early advisory opinion concerning the role of the Senate in scrutinising bills 'concerning' county governments, there was a clear belief at the time of the framing of the Constitution that 'a deconcentration of powers would not only give greater access to the social goods previously regulated centrally, but would also open up the scope for political self-fulfilment, through an enlarged scheme of actual participation in governance mechanisms by the people.'[57]

Secondly, on the issue of the structure of the executive, the 2007 violence had once again revealed the problems of

> ... the growing personalisation of power around the President. This gave rise to the view that it is essential for the ethnic group from which presidential candidates come to win the election to assure them of access to state resources and services. <u>It also led to a deliberate diminution of the authority and legitimacy of other oversight institutions that could check abuses of power and corruption</u>.[58]

The political imperatives of the contending parties – in particular, Raila Odinga, who now harboured presidential aspirations, and was therefore no longer as enamoured of a parliamentary system with a weak executive as he once had been – saw to it that the 2010 Constitution, ultimately, retained the presidential system.[59] However, for the reasons explained above, there was an equally strong imperative towards ensuring that Parliament could no longer be

55 Murray, 'Kenya's 2010 Constitution,' *supra*. Interestingly, in the course of the hearings before the Supreme Court in its famous Advisory Opinion No. 2 of 2013 (*Speaker of the Senate*, *supra*), counsel argued that in interpreting the Constitution, the people's choice to 'retrace' the federal path chosen under the 1963 Constitution, before it was dismantled, ought to be one of the considerations kept in mind. See para 16.

56 Murray, 'Kenya's 2010 Constitution,' *supra*.

57 Advisory Opinion No. 2 of 2013, *supra*, para 136. In his concurring opinion, Mutunga CJ noted that 'devolution was instrumental in mobilizing support for the Constitution in the referendum, because many people perceived its dispersal of economic and political power as an act of liberation.' Ibid., para 173.

58 Oyaya and Poku, *The Making of the Constitution of Kenya*, *supra*, 185.

59 The political imperatives are discussed in some detail in Kramon and Posner, 'Kenya's New Constitution', *supra*, 89.

subordinated to the Executive, to the point of degradation into a ceremonial body. Thus, for example, as we have previously seen, proposals to give the President powers to appoint and dismiss parliamentary ministers and fourth branch officials were specifically rejected by the Committee of Experts.[60]

But more than that, this goal of containment was sought to be accomplished through constitutional design. As Christina Murray – speaking from first-hand experience – notes, the intention of the drafters was to set out the powers and functions of each constitutional body with as much clarity and specificity as possible.[61] Ghai likewise affirms that the level of detail in the 2010 Constitution was meant to limit Presidential discretion by spelling out the roles, rights, and obligations of the institutions of government as concretely as possible.[62] A natural corollary of this, then, would be a constitutionalism that was less tolerant of the kind of 'blurring' that we have discussed in the previous section, where – for instance – legislative powerlessness turned legislators into mini-executive agents, holding on to their electoral base through a politics of clientelism and constituency service.

This yields an important insight. In a country where the separation of powers was – from the colonial beginnings – a matter of administrative convenience, subordinated to overriding executive power at the discretion of the executive, *separation of powers that is consciously embedded into the constitutional design* is a part of the transformative constitutional project. It seeks to accomplish this by creating a set of counterbalancing institutions to presidential power and clearly delineating the scope – as well as the *limitations* – of each of these bodies.

Naturally, a constitution only has to come into being for its scheme, design, and structure to be tested – especially by an executive looking to push the boundaries of its power at every opportunity. Indeed, as Murunga perceptively notes, the conflicted history of the drafting meant that 'these two provisions [presidential systems and devolution] have continued to sit uncomfortably

60 Oyaya and Poku, *The Making of the Constitution of Kenya*, *supra*, 185.

61 Murray, 'Kenya's 2010 Constitution,' *supra*. Or, in the words of John Osogo Ambani, the aim was to 'leave very little to chance'. J. Osogo Ambani, 'The Ghai in our Constitution' in *Furthering Constitutions, Birthing Peace: Liber amicorum Yash Pal Ghai* (Humphrey Sipalla and J Osogo Ambani (eds.), Strathmore University Press 2021) 173, 179.

62 'The powers of state institutions are prescribed with greater precision; the purposes for which powers may be exercised are specified; and rules are established to remove conflict of interests through codes of conduct and other mechanisms.' Ghai, 'Chimeras of Constitutionalism', *supra*, 5. See also the debate at the National Constitutional Conference during the first round of the drafting process, affirming this principle. *CKRC Final Report*, *supra*, 396–397.

together in the constitution, even during implementation.'[63] And right from 2010, the Kenyan Constitution has been a terrain of contestation between its centralising and decentralising impulses, with the executive working towards an entrenchment of the former, through various moves

> … such as rendering the transitional authority ineffective and seeking to exercise financial oversight and control over counties, including through the appointment and entrenching of executive powers in county commissioners. The unease generated by these provisions continues to fuel debate over the independence of the county governments, the role of the senate, and the implications of the new constitution for the wage bill.[64]

The same has been true for the relationship between the Executive and the Parliament as well. Notwithstanding the best intentions of the 2010 Constitution in setting out the powers and functions of the National Assembly, and restoring it to a position that is at least co-equal with to that of the Executive, in practice, a combination of inherited structures, weak political parties (that often continue to serve as vehicles for the ambitions of presidential aspirants),[65] and

63 Murunga, 'Elite compromises and the content of the 2010 Constitution', *supra*, 159. For a detailed, descriptive account of the structure of devolution under the 2010 Constitution, see Bosire, 'The Constitutional and Legal Framework of Devolved Government', *supra*.

64 Murunga, 'Elite compromises and the content of the 2010 Constitution', *supra*, 159. The 'transitional authority' mentioned in this paragraph is presumably a reference to the statutory Transition Authority, set up under the aegis of the Devolved Government Act of 2012, whose task was to oversee the transfers of functions and assets to the counties; however, this body was dissolved before it could complete its task.

For an account of the enduring influence of the 'provincial administration' down to the present day – specifically accomplished through executive control over the police and security – see Walter O. Oyugi and Jimmy O. Ochieng, 'The Politics of the Provincial Administration' in *The Oxford Handbook of Kenyan Politics* (Nic Cheeseman, Karuti Kanyinga and Gabrielle Lynch (eds.), Oxford University Press 2020) 221; see also Mai Hassan, 'Continuity Despite Change: Kenya's New Constitution and Executive Power' (2015) 22(4) *Democratization* 587; for a similar account of mixed trajectories of devolution under the 2010 Constitution, see Michelle D'Arcy, 'Devolution and County Government' in *The Oxford Handbook of Kenyan Politics*, *supra*, 251; for an analysis of the Presidential veto, Walter O. Khobe, 'Presidential Veto in the Law-Making process: The Case of Kenya's Amendatory Recommendations' (2023) 67(1) *Journal of African Law* 79.

65 See the reference in Lynch to 'briefcase political parties'. Lynch, 'The Fruits of Perception', *supra*, 254.

behind the scenes dealmaking (such as the BBI) has ensured the retention, in effect, of Executive and party-leader dominance over the Assembly.[66]

It is in this context that in the CDF Case, the Kenyan courts were faced with a stress-test of the new Constitution's vision of the separation of powers. It is to that judgment that we now turn.

## C. The CDF Judgment

In *The Institute for Social Accountability vs The National Assembly*, the issue before the Supreme Court was the constitutionality of the Constituency Development Fund Act of 2013 (CDF Act).[67] This legislation created a fund called the Constituency Development Fund, or the CDF. The CDF held up to 2.5% of national government revenue that was collected in that financial year. According to Section 22(1) of the Act, the purpose of the CDF was to fund 'community-based projects' for the benefit of a 'widespread cross-section of the inhabitants of a particular area'.[68] Oversight and monitoring of project implementation was given to a Constituency Development Fund Committee, with one committee for each constituency.[69] An overwhelming majority of the Committee – eight out of ten members – were to be appointed by the member of parliament for that constituency. The MP himself was an *ex officio* member of the Committee.[70]

The design of the CDF made it clear, therefore, that it was a fund for developmental projects, executed and implemented at the level of individual constituencies. Furthermore, the utilisation and administration of the fund, for all practical purposes, was under the control of the MP for that particular constituency.[71]

The High Court found the CDF Act – and the system of constituency development funds – to be unconstitutional.[72] On appeal, the judgment was partially upheld, and partially reversed, by the Court of Appeal. The case

66 See e.g., Jessica Musila and Gitungo Wamere, 'The Vulnerable Guardian Angel: Kenya's Parliament in the Post-2010 Constitution' in *Ten Years On: Assessing the Achievements of the Constitution of Kenya 2010* (Yash Pal Ghai, Emily Kinama, and Jill Cottrell Ghai (eds.), Katiba Institute 2021) 19.

67 *The Institute for Social Accountability and Anr vs The National Assembly and Ors*, [2022] KESC 39 (KLR).

68 Section 22(1), CDF Act 2013.

69 Section 31(3), CDF Act 2013.

70 Section 24(3), CDF Act 2013.

71 For an ironic description of the uses of the CDF to 'plant flowers on the roundabout and build one school', see Binyavanga Wainaina, 'I Hate Githeri' in *How To Write About Africa* (Hamish Hamilton 2022) 122, 124.

72 *The Institute for Social Accountability and Anr vs The National Assembly and Ors*, Petition No. 71 of 2013, decided on 20th February 2015 (High Court).

ultimately came before the Supreme Court of Kenya, which – like the High Court – held that the CDF Act was unconstitutional.

There were two core – and interrelated – features of the challenge before the Supreme Court: the *devolution* challenge and the *separation of powers* challenge. On the first, it was argued that the CDF Act effectively undermined devolution under the 2010 Constitution. It did so by creating a 'third level of government' in every constituency which – as a matter of fact – would end up competing with and, in some cases, usurping the functions of the devolved county governments. That these functions were to be performed under the control of MPs of the National Assembly essentially brought back centralisation through stealth. As a related point, it was argued that as the CDF Act impacted the functioning of county governments, under the constitutional scheme, the Bill needed to be passed by both the National Assembly and the Senate (whose role, as we have seen, is the articulation of regional aspirations under the devolved system of government).

Secondly, it was argued that MPs are members of the legislature, whose primary role is to represent their constituents in the processes of *law-making*, by crafting, deliberating on, and voting for bills in parliament. The CDF Act essentially granted to MPs control over the implementation and administration of developmental projects, which was an *executive* function. Thus, there was a clear violation of the separation of powers.

The Supreme Court began by considering the procedural issue. It held that, pursuant to a 2013 amendment, the constitutional basis of the CDF Act was Article 206(2) of the Constitution of Kenya. Article 206(2) authorises withdrawal of money from the Consolidated Fund. Furthermore, this money would be used to fund projects pertaining to 'infrastructural development, such as roads, health, agriculture and trade', all of which were within the domain of county governments.[73] Thus, the court held that there was a clear impact on 'the functioning of county governments'.[74] Therefore, Senate approval was mandatory for the passage of the CDF Act.[75] Notably, in doing so, the Supreme Court upheld the High Court, which had overruled the joint finding of the Speakers of the National Assembly and the Senate that the CDF (Amendment) Bill did not need to be considered by the Senate, as it did not impact county governance.[76]

Why is this important? It is important because had the court treated the determination of the speakers as dispositive, it would have authorised the marginalisation of the Senate through a simple stratagem: engineer collusion

73 *The Institute for Social Accountability and Anr vs The National Assembly and Ors* (Supreme Court) *supra*, para 63.

74 Ibid., para 64.

75 Ibid., para 72.

76 Ibid., para 75.

between the two speakers to 'misclassify' a bill as not concerning counties, and therefore, take the Senate out of the equation entirely. This is a stratagem that has a long history in battles over the scrutiny of 'money bills' in countries such as England, Ireland, and India.[77] It is a problem that is exacerbated where a constitution does not entrench – or guarantee – the independence of the Speaker from the executive or the ruling party (the Kenyan Constitution does not do so, allowing for what Musila and Wamere call the '*de facto* control by the President over the Speaker',[78] via the legislative party majority). In such a situation, devolution as a check upon centralised executive power *depends* upon judicial oversight of how speakers classify bills. The High Court and the Supreme Court reaffirmed that important position.[79]

Moving on to the substantive devolution challenge, the key issue – as we have noted – was whether the CDF Act was a backdoor way of granting to MPs the power to perform certain functions that were otherwise within the domain of the devolved governments.[80] The Supreme Court held that it was. It noted that the powers and functions of the National Assembly were spelt out under Article 95 of the Constitution. These were representation, legislation, oversight over national revenue and expenditure, and allocation of revenue

[77] See *Rojer Mathew vs South Indian Bank Ltd.*, (2020) 6 SCC 1 (Supreme Court of India), where – at the time of writing – the issue remains unresolved: there are multiple pending challenges to the decisions of the Speaker to classify bills as money bills, and therefore deprive the Indian Parliament's Upper House – the Council of States – from effective scrutiny. In England, there was a long-standing controversy over the 'tacking' of extraneous matters on to money bills in order to take away the House of Lords veto. The Constitution of Ireland also adopted the concept of Money Bills from the British Parliament Act of 1911, but in a bid to avoid exactly these sorts of difficulties, contained an elaborate mechanism where a committee comprising of members of both Houses, and headed by a High Court judge, would examine disputes over classification. In the 2023 Kenyan Finance Act challenges, the money bill issue was front and centre, and the subject of detailed adjudication by the High Court of Kenya. See *Okiya Omtatah Okoiti and Ors vs The Cabinet Secretary for the National Treasury and Planning and Ors*, [2023] KEHC 25656 (KLR).

[78] Musila and Wamere, 'The Vulnerable Guardian Angel,' *supra*, 20.

[79] In fact, this holding would be even more important in the case of mis-classification of money bills in Kenya, as there even the concurrence of the Speaker of the Senate is not required: the Speaker of the National Assembly, with the assistance of the Budgetary Committee, can make that determination. See *Speaker of the National Assembly of the Republic of Kenya & another v Senate of the Republic of Kenya & 12 others* [2021] KECA 282 (KLR), para 129. I thank the peer reviewer of the manuscript for bringing this nuance to my attention.

[80] It is important to note that, by the time the case came to the Supreme Court, the CDF Act under challenge had been replaced by fresh legislation specifying that the CDF could only be used for performing functions that came within the purview of the national government.

between the levels of government.[81] They evidently did not include 'the power to implement projects as a service delivery unit at the county level'.[82] The latter was an executive function, meant to be exercised at the county level. The executive authority of the county, in turn, was to be exercised through County Executive Committees under Article 179 of the Constitution. In essence, therefore, the CDF Act was a usurpation by the *National* Assembly of the executive functions of the *county* government. In the language of the court:

> … where a Member of the National Assembly is allowed to play a role related to functions vested in devolved units, then this will compromise the vertical division of powers between the national and county governments.[83]

This, however, was not a purely textual issue. The Court took care to spell out, as well, the normative commitments underlying the devolution project under the 2010 Constitution which – again – existed because of the specific experiences of service delivery under the old unitary and centralised state:

> Subsidiarity is the broad presumption that sub-national governments ought to be assigned those functions and powers which vitally affect the life of the inhabitants and allow the development of the country in accordance with local conditions of sub-national units, while matters of national importance concerning the country as a whole and overarching policy formulation are assigned to the national government.[84]

Consequently, as noted above, the national government was not authorised to 'usurp the mandate of the county governments'.[85]

Beyond the concerns around pure devolution, the Supreme Court advanced another argument for the unconstitutionality of the CDF, located at the intersection of the separation of powers. This concerned the creation of an effective

81 Interestingly, the court's gleaning of the principles underlying Article 95 echoed the CKRC Final Report, which specifically stated that the functions of legislators were meant to be 'representation, legislation, and oversight'. *CKRC Final Report, supra*, 186.

82 *The Institute for Social Accountability and Anr vs The National Assembly and Ors* (Supreme Court), *supra*, para 83.

83 Ibid., para 85.

84 Ibid., para 88.

85 Ibid., para 90. One important unarticulated premise of the judgment was that the CDF was a method of exercising centralised *fiscal* control over the counties. This was particularly poignant, as before Jomo Kenyatta had dismantled the *majimbo* constitution, he had begun by starving the regional assemblies of funds. A central pillar of making devolution meaningful, thus, would be to prevent a recurrence of fiscal dominance by the centre. See e.g. the concurring opinion of Mutunga CJ in Advisory Opinion No. 2 of 2013, *supra*, para 186.

'third level of government', whose unit was the constituency. The court made the crucial observation that in a democratic, electoral system, the purpose of a 'constituency' was to serve as an *electoral unit*: that is, a constituency elected an MP to represent a particular territorial unit in parliament. The *function* played by constituencies, therefore, was tied to the function of an MP, which was *legislative*, and not that of service delivery.[86] The CDF – as tied to a constituency – defeated the entire *raison d'etre* of constituencies themselves.

When we think back to the imperatives of a clear constitutional demarcation of powers and functions under the 2010 Constitution, the reasoning of the court immediately becomes legible. Indeed, the court was directly responding to the precise problem that we have discussed in the previous section where – under the old regime – legislative powerlessness fundamentally altered the *role* of legislators within the constitutional system, and created a cycle where one form of executive drift perpetuated another. In this sense, the court's emphasis on demarcation of powers and functions was – as we have noticed – both *restorative*[87] (in the sense of restoring the role of legislators in a parliamentary system, as envisioned in the 1963 Independence Constitution, prior to its mutilation) and *transformative* (transforming a system where the blurring of these roles resulted in increasing executive dominance).[88]

Furthermore, at a more tangible level, the issue of the CDF is one of those cases where we can understand the underlying justification for the court's conceptual argument, and the need for clear demarcation of powers and functions: that is, for the prevention of concentration of power at the level of the MP. If an MP is able to serve both as a legislator, but also as a controller of patronage, *via* the provision of developmental projects in their constituency, the prospects of an incumbency bias are clear. Separation of powers, in this context, is not merely a theoretical nicety, but deeply embedded within the 2010 Constitution's goal of using constitutional structure and design to avoid concentration of power.

This also serves as a good segue to move into the court's actual separation of powers analysis. The argument – as noted above – was straightforward: the CDF Act granted executive powers to legislators, and therefore violated the separation of powers. The response was also a familiar one: that the separation of powers was not a rigid concept, where the functions of various branches of government were kept hermetically sealed. Rather, the separation of powers was flexible, and meant to evolve and be responsive to the exigencies of good governance, as the circumstances required.

[86] *The Institute for Social Accountability and Anr vs The National Assembly and Ors* (Supreme Court), *supra*, para 92.

[87] Landau and Dixon, 'Restorative Constitutionalism', *supra*, 455; see *infra* Ch. 1.

[88] The clear demarcation of executive power within the Constitution was one of the significant demands that arose out of the CKRC consultation process, as recorded in its final report. See the *CKRC Final Report*, *supra*, 198.

As pointed out at the beginning of this chapter, there is little doubt that 'pure' separation of powers does not exist in modern democracies (and it is doubtful if it ever did). That does not, however, answer the question. The real question – as the court recognised – was what *form* the separation of powers was meant to take, in the specific context of Kenyan constitutional history, and the transformative goals of the 2010 Constitution.

The court's answer was simple: the purpose of the doctrine – and therefore its shape, scope, and limits – was to prevent the concentration of power:

> Kenyans having witnessed excesses of absolute power vested in the Executive branch which operated with abandon and riding roughshod over other state institutions sought to constrain and temper the exercise of public power. Citizens during the pre-2010 dispensation chose to respond to excesses of that legacy by explicitly dividing state power into three branches of government to preclude the exercise of arbitrary power.[89]

Notice, here, the focus on the *explicit* division of power that we have discussed above, as an essential element of the transformative project. Now, what did this mean at the level of constitutional doctrine? The Supreme Court articulated a two-pronged test to decide when the Kenyan vision of the separation of powers had been infringed. First, one would ask if one branch of government had trespassed upon the 'nucleus, core functions, or pre-eminent domain' of another branch of government. And the second question was whether, in doing so, the exercise of power by that branch threatened the 'values and principles' articulated in the Constitution.[90]

What, then, was the 'nucleus' or the 'core function' of the legislature, and what was the nature of legislative power under the 2010 Constitution? The court held that legislative power included *representation* (of the People, in parliament), *legislation* (that is, the core act of law-making), and *oversight* (of the executive).[91] On the other hand, the core function of the executive branch was implementation and administration.

From this perspective, the MP's effective control over the CDF through the power of appointments was fatal to the CDF Act. As the court noted, the MP was in a position to influence 'the selection, prioritization of projects, allocation of funds ... and also monitor the implementation of the projects'.[92] These were all core executive functions, and therefore:

89 *The Institute for Social Accountability and Anr vs The National Assembly and Ors* (Supreme Court), *supra*, para 116.

90 Ibid., para 118 (emphasis supplied).

91 Ibid., para 120. The court drew this from Article 95 of the Constitution of Kenya.

92 Ibid., para 124.

> … the Fund, as conceived under the CDF Act 2013, vested in the Legislature and its personnel – being the Members of the National Assembly – functions that typically fall within the nucleus, core function, or pre-eminent domain of the Executive branch.[93]

The first prong of the test was thus violated. What of the second prong? The court held that the 'checking' function at the heart of separation of powers doctrine would be defeated if power-holders were placed in positions where there was a conflict of interest. Under the CDF Act, however, this conflict of interest was clear. As noted above, the implementation of a CDF would often have a direct impact upon an MP's re-election prospects. How, then, could that same MP perform their oversight functions with respect to the fund, given that they had a personal stake in how the fund was used and implemented?[94] As the court observed:

> We, therefore, find that a Fund operating outside the strictures of separation of powers and the system of checks and balances would not be constrained given the absence of legislative oversight and therefore would be prone to be abused. In effect, a Fund that allows personnel from the Legislative branch to exercise executive powers is problematic from a constitutional lens. In the context of this case, we adopt the view that the constitutional scheme on separation of powers should be upheld given its implication for underlying constitutional values; that is, the maintenance of accountability and good governance. Were we to adopt a contrary approach, as urged by the respondents, <u>even for the best of policy reasons</u>, these constitutional values and principles will be eroded.[95]

Importantly, the court rejected arguments of administrative convenience or efficiency as grounds to override constitutional imperatives. That apart, there is also a clear link between the its reasoning and transformative constitutionalism. Recall – as we had discussed in the previous section – that under the old regime, legislative politics was articulated through clientelism and constituency service (often through control over para-statal boards). Under the CDF, while the executive was no longer directly involved, it still replicated the *form* of such politics. This was precisely what the 2010 Constitution had set out to transform, through its clear demarcation and separation of powers, and its vision of *restoring* the legislature to its proper role in a democracy.

For these reasons, the Supreme Court found the CDF Act to be unconstitutional. What is particularly fascinating about the judgment is how the

93 Ibid.

94 Ibid., para 127.

95 Ibid., para 129 (emphasis supplied).

court was confronted with exactly the same issues that had burdened Kenyan constitutional debates from before the time of Independence: the separation of powers between the executive and legislature and the structure of government ('horizontal' division of power), and devolution and decentralisation ('vertical' division of power). The CDF Case shows most clearly how these two issues are fundamentally interlinked, even though the debates may not have always reflected the overlaps. Ultimately, if a constitution is a power-map, then both the separation of powers (especially executive-legislative relations) and devolution inform how that power is exercised. As a corollary, they also inform the extent to which a constitution can successfully prevent the concentration of power within a single figure or office (for the most part, the executive). Both the separation of powers and devolution are about the dispersal of power, and about the *mediation* of power through institutions that are not the central executive.

The other interesting feature about the CDF judgment is the link between meaningful devolution and the political economy. Recall how the first step that the Kenyatta government took towards undermining *majimbo* was simply to choke off funds to the regions, and make their functioning impossible.[96] The most carefully crafted federal or devolved structures can fail if financial control skews too far one way, and allows for the deployment of informal fiscal pressure. 'He who pays the piper calls the tune' is equally true for the relationship between levels of government in a devolved constitution.[97] And while the court did not specifically say so, lurking in the interstices of the judgment is an unmistakable concern about how the manner in which the CDF was implemented would, once again, undermine devolution by distorting the distribution of fiscal control and powers within the scheme of the 2010 Constitution.[98]

The court's judgment did not have an immediate, tangible impact. The specific CDF scheme that it had been considering had been replaced in 2015 by a substantially similar scheme, albeit with one significant difference: under the new scheme, the CDF could be used only for functions falling within the purview of the national government.[99]

96 For a discussion, see *CKRC Final Report*, *supra*, 31; Warris, 'Kenya's fiscal accountability revisited' *supra*.

97 Fiscal control translates often into political and policy control, with policy compliance being made conditional on fiscal transfers. We know this well enough in the international domain.

98 This would not be done directly, in the Kenyatta fashion, but indirectly, in that National Assembly MPs controlling local development projects could increasingly render county governments marginalised or irrelevant.

99 In late 2024, after the completion of this manuscript, the High Court of Kenya struck down the 2015 CDF Act. There was, unfortunately, no time to include an analysis of the 2024 judgment in this book; the judgment, however, largely followed the Supreme Court's reasoning.

The CDF judgment and its reasoning, nonetheless, remain crucial for the project of transformative constitutionalism. As I have argued in this chapter, separation of powers under the 2010 Constitution must be understood in the context of a colonial history where the legislature was explicitly subordinate to the executive, and a post-colonial history where alternative centres of public power – in particular, parliament and the regions – were systematically degraded or eliminated through constitutional amendments. While the 2010 Constitution retained the presidential executive, it sought to restore those alternative centres of power as institutions of accountability and checks and balances: the Assembly, the Senate, and the Counties. And in particular, informed by history, it sought to clarify their functions – and the limits – within the Constitution itself, in order to avoid the function-creep that has marked the rise of the Imperial Presidency throughout the world. It was this history that the Supreme Court drew on when faced with a situation where it was called upon to police the boundaries and limits set up by the Constitution, in the form of a judicially articulated doctrine of functional separation of powers.

A final point: the CDF was not the only instance of the blurring of lines between executive and legislature, and an incentive for the replication of the old structures where the role of parliamentarians was characterised by clientelism and patronage, instead of representation, legislation, and oversight. As I have noted above, despite the restorative and transformative goals of the 2010 Constitution, the National Assembly (and the Senate) continue to suffer from many of the pathologies that marked the Executive-dominated pre-2010 regime. Some of those pathologies (such as the structural weaknesses of political parties) are beyond the capacity of courts to correct. In the CDF Case, however, the Court not only addressed a distortion that it *could* rectify, but also took the opportunity to restate the fundamental role of the legislature in the 2010 Constitutional dispensation, as it should be. There is a value in constitutional courts restating the constitutional position when practice repeatedly departs from it. The clarity with which the Supreme Court did so in the CDF Case, is thus another important facet of the judgment.

### *Addendum: A Comparative Note*

The analysis of the Supreme Court stands out in a comparative perspective. A few years before, the equivalent of the CDF in India – called the MPLADS scheme – had been challenged before the Indian Supreme Court. The arguments that were made before the Supreme Court of India in *Bhim Singh vs Union of India* were strikingly similar to those made before the Supreme Court of Kenya in the CDF case: the separation of powers and federalism. The Indian Supreme Court, however, failed to subject the MPLADS scheme to a similar level of scrutiny. It contented itself by noting that as there was no 'strict' separation of powers, 'each one of the arms at times perform other functions as well' and that 'it is quite logical for the Member of Parliament to carry out developmental activities to the constituencies they represent.'[100] As we have noted above, however, this is only the beginning of the enquiry, not the end of it. It is banal to say that there is no 'strict' separation of powers. The question – as the Supreme Court of Kenya recognised – is what scheme of separation of powers is consistent with the constitutional goal of why separation of powers exists in the first place.

In *Bhim Singh*, the Supreme Court went on to note that the MPs did not exercise direct power over developmental projects; they only made recommendations, which were then acted on by the district authorities.[101] This, however, is an illustration of how it is important for courts – especially in contexts involving power and power relations – to not mistake form for substance. Under the CDF Act, the respective members of Parliament were not involved in directly implementing developmental projects, or personally administering them. What mattered, however, was the overall structural control that MPs exercised over projects: it was at this level that concerns around separation of powers became salient.

And finally, it is striking how the two courts approached the issue of the vertical division of powers between the levels of government. Unlike Kenya, the Indian Constitution does set up a federal structure, albeit one that is 'tilted' towards the centre. For this reason, commentators have often – and misleadingly – referred to India as a 'quasi-federation'. Indeed, it was the language of 'quasi-federalism' that was invoked by the Supreme Court to dismiss the devolution challenge without any serious argument.[102] Interestingly, even as the Supreme Court of Kenya insisted that the Kenyan Constitution is not federal, but unitary with devolved characteristics,[103] it found that once the Constitution set up a devolved scheme of governance, it was the court's role to preserve it – and to guard against its undermining through direct and indirect means. We can therefore see that a constitution with a formally weaker devolved system can nonetheless act as a serious check upon centralised executive power, as long as the purpose of devolution is taken seriously, and the boundaries set up by the Constitution are enforced rigorously. On the other hand, a constitution with a formally stronger federal system entrenched in the Constitution can fail to check centralisation, if concerns of administrative convenience are privileged over constitutional principle. As Githu Muigai notes, the latter was

100 *Bhim Singh vs Union of India*, (2010) 5 SCC 538 (Supreme Court of India).

101 Ibid.

102 Ibid.

103 *The Institute for Social Accountability and Anr vs The National Assembly and Ors* (Supreme Court), *supra*, para 80, relying on *In the Matter of Interim Independent Electoral Commission*, *supra*, and *In the Matter of the Principle of Gender Representation in the National Assembly and Senate*, *supra*.

the dominant approach towards the Constitution in the Kenyan post-colony.[104] In that sense, the Kenyan Supreme Court's judgment presents a true and striking example of 'learning from history'.

## D. The Day After

The CDF case was just one of the many constitutional battles around the structural design of the 2010 Constitution, and the vision of public power – as well as the limits on that power – that it imposes. In July 2023, for example, the High Court handed down an important judgment on recently elected President William Ruto's controversial decision to create an expanded set of public office positions, titled the 'Chief Administrative Secretaries' (CAS).[105] While there was a complex range of technical issues that were considered in the case – not all of which I will deal with here[106] – of relevance for our discussion in this chapter is the question of whether the President was empowered to create these twenty-seven additional positions in the manner in which he had done.[107] The High Court held that the procedure he had followed in doing so was unconstitutional. This was because offices in the public services could only be

[104] Muigai, *Power, Politics & Law*, *supra*.

[105] *Eliud Karanja Matindi and Ors vs The President of the Republic of Kenya and Ors*, [2023] KEHC 19534 (KLR).

[106] For a longer analysis, see Gautam Bhatia, 'Limiting Executive Power, Enabling Public Participation: The Kenyan High Court's CAS Judgment' *Indian Constitutional Law and Philosophy Blog* (7th July 2023), available at <https://indconlawphil.wordpress.com/2023/07/07/limiting-executive-power-enabling-public-participation-the-kenyan-high-courts-cas-judgment/>, visited on 15th September 2024.

[107] The prior history of litigation had established that he was *entitled* to do so, on the recommendation of the Public Service Commission (PSC). In *Okiyah Omtatah and anr vs PSC and 73 ors* [2021] KEHC 464 (KLR), the High Court, while affirming the President's power to create the office of the CAS, had struck down the exercise of that power, on various procedural grounds (including, for example, the fact that the PSC lacked adequate material to come to an independent recommendation, as per its constitutional obligations). Although this decision was stayed by the Court of Appeal, in response, the PSC abolished these posts, and issued a fresh call for twenty-three positions, on the basis that it was complying with the requirements set out by the High Court. A challenge to this process before the Employment and Labour Court was dismissed: *LSK and 2 ors vs AG et al* [2022] KEELRC 13324 (KLR). In the present case, the High Court treated all these issues as having been decided, and falling within the principle of *res judicata*. Thus, the twenty-three CAS positions had been legally created; the question was whether President Ruto's decision to create an additional *twenty-seven positions* was constitutionally valid.

created 'on the recommendation of' the Public Service Commission (PSC), an independent fourth branch institution.[108]

In the present case, the PSC had not filed an affidavit clarifying its role with respect to certain additional CAS positions. For the court, this was fatal to the constitutionality of the expanded CAS positions. It was essential that such posts be created only on the basis of an independent recommendation, and for reasons relevant to the *role* that the CAS was expected to play (and not, for example, for reasons of securing political patronage by expanding public posts and offering them as largesse to political supporters).[109]

Additionally, the PSC was not the only body that was supposed to be involved in the process. As the CAS occupied a position somewhere in between a parliamentary secretary and a principal secretary, much like those positions, it would have to be vetted by Parliament, in accordance with a statute that – additionally – would have to prescribe a cap on the total number of CAS positions. This, too, had been absent in the present case.[110]

As we can see, therefore, the CAS judgment was strongly focused on how, in the creation of public offices, the President could not bypass other constitutional bodies. To do so would, in essence, take Kenya back to the days where Offices of State were handed out as the spoils of political patronage, and became – therefore – an additional and indirect source of the exercise of executive power. As Kramon and Posner note, thus, with respect to the 2010 Constitution:

> Although the constitution does not provide for a prime minister to counterbalance the president, the president's power is nonetheless curtailed, and parliament's strengthened, through new rules governing the presidential appointment of cabinet ministers. Like many African presidents, Kenyatta, Moi, and Kibaki used cabinet appointments

108 Article 132, Constitution of Kenya, 2010. It is worth noting that the battle over the independence of fourth branch institutions – including, and specifically, the powers of removal – was one of the key battles in the lead-up to the constitutional reform movement. Its flashpoint was an unsuccessful attempt to challenge President Moi's decision to fire his deputy Chief of Intelligence, Mwangi Stephen Muriithi, in 1982. Muriithi's counsel, John Khaminwa, made a proto-argument for the independence of fourth branch institutions, arguing that the constitutional power vested in the President to dismiss civil servants 'at his pleasure' could not trump the powers of the independent Public Service Commission. The High Court ruled against Muriithi, and soon after that, both he and John Khaminwa were detained without trial. For an account, see Paul Mwangi, *The Black Bar: Corruption and Political Intrigue within Kenya's Legal Fraternity* (Oakland Media Services 2001) 103–116, available at <https://theverdict.co.ke/wp-content/uploads/2022/07/The-Black-Bar.pdf>, /, visited on 15th September 2024.

109 *Eliud Karanja Matindi vs President, supra*, para 242.

110 Ibid., para 248.

> as instruments of patronage and tools for exerting control over parliament.[111]

Indeed, the High Court evinced a clear understanding of this history when it noted, specifically, that 'we do not think it was the intention of the framers of the Constitution to have 50 CASs deputising 22 Cabinet Secretaries.'[112] Thus, underlying the technical grounds of the decision was the unarticulated major premise that allowing the creation of new public posts for reasons of political patronage was the quickest road back towards the re-centralisation of power that the transformative constitutional project had taken such pains to avoid, in its detailed crafting of the 2010 Constitution.

## D. Conclusion: Restoration and Transformation

In his analysis of legislative development in Africa, Opalo perceptively notes that 'inherited colonial institutions' – such as the legislature – took structurally different forms in the post-colony, based on the context. Thus:

> … while European legislatures were intended to provide checks and balances, pass budgets, and legislate, the dominant functions of postcolonial African legislatures were ascriptive representation of different ethnic groups in the center and the distribution of patronage and targeted benefits (variously described as 'development'). Postcolonial legislators were expected to function as agents of development and were judged by voters on this basis. Thus, clientelism became the fuel of legislative electoral politics and the dominant form of constituency service. This reality enabled African presidents to control the electoral careers of legislators through the rationing of access to patronage and development resources. The end result was a reversal in the fiscal relationship between African legislative and executive branches of government.[113]

This contextual analysis explains why post-colonial Constitutions – and those who administer them – have often evinced an impatience with the separation of powers, seeing it as an inconvenient bottleneck standing in the way of an efficient executive. The fate of the Independence Constitution of Kenya was no exception. The two main impediments to presidential power – the parliament

[111] Kramon and Posner, 'Kenya's New Constitution,' *supra*, 97.

[112] *Eliud Karanja Matindi vs President*, *supra*, para 258.

[113] Opalo, *Legislative Development in Africa*, *supra*, 131 (emphasis supplied). While this chapter has focused on commonwealth Africa, similar themes are evident across the continent. See e.g. J.B. Ojwang, 'Legislative Control of Executive Power in Africa: New Insights' (1986) 19(4) *Verfassung und Recht in Ubersee* 421.

and the regions – were swiftly degraded or dispensed with within a few years of Independence. They were replaced with an executive-bureaucratic constitutional order, which – among other things – reduced and diminished the role of legislators to localised clientelism and service-delivery.

It is in this sense that – as noted above – under the 2010 Constitution, a project of restoration was also a project of transformation. The restoration of parliament as a legislative and deliberative forum, and of the devolved governments, was an essential part of the transformative vision that set itself against the concentration of public power. This vision mandated distribution of public power across institutions, both horizontally (the Presidency and the National Assembly) and vertically (the county governments). And it did so by seeking to constitutionalise that separation of powers in the text and design of the 2010 Constitution, in as clear and concrete terms as possible.

But constitutional texts are always terrains of contestation. No matter how much the detail or specificity, there will always be questioned left unanswered, which will require a return to the first principles. The CDF was one such case. It required the court to go back to the basics, and ask itself *why* the separation of powers mattered to transformative constitutionalism, in order to answer *what* separation of powers was, and whether it was violated by the CDF; and it did so in a context in which – as noted above – the practice around the executive and the legislature continued to be plagued, in some respects, by imbalances of power similar to those of the old regime.

The court's answer, I have argued, was responsive to the colonial and post-colonial history that informed the separation of powers and devolution under the 2010 Constitution. The court understood that, in essence, the CDF belonged to the very constitutional architecture that the 2010 Constitution was meant to transform: what – as we have noted above – Opalo calls 'clientelism … [as] the fuel of electoral politics and the dominant form of constituency service'. While under the CDF 'access to patronage' was no longer in the hands of the executive, and therefore, it did not go as far as "reversing" the fiscal relationship between the legislative and executive branches, it did *blur* that relationship to a great degree.

What is crucial about the CDF judgment, then, is that it marked a judicial pushback against precisely the kind of re-centralisation that is often achieved by a seemingly innocuous blurring of legislative and executive functions (and which has continued to happen even after 2010). Did the CDF, taken by itself, amount to an unravelling of the constitutional scheme, and a return to the 'executive-bureaucratic' regime of the past? Perhaps not. But the Supreme Court was keenly aware that disintegration is often incremental. After all, as a judicial colleague from the United States had once remarked:

> As nightfall does not come at once, neither does oppression. In both instances, there is a twilight when everything remains seemingly

> unchanged. And it is in such twilight that we all must be most aware of change in the air – however slight – lest we become unwitting victims of the darkness.[114]

Thus, the Court was particularly concerned with ensuring that the doctrine of separation of powers was given enough 'bite' so as to ensure that it acted as a check upon any centralising drift within the 2010 Constitution – right at its inception. Once, therefore, we understand the specific colonial and post-colonial trajectories of the legislative-executive relationship and of devolution, we can see how the judgment is an exemplar of transformative constitutionalism.

We see undercurrents of the same idea in subsequent judgments, such as the High Court's CAS Judgment, which were also freighted with the weight of history. And it is equally clear that these disputes will not stop coming to court. For the future, I suggest that the Supreme Court's articulation of the separation of powers in the CDF Case serves as an important and valuable guide for navigating through the choppy waters of executive domination, public power, and transformative constitutionalism.

114 William O. Douglas, *The Douglas Letters: Selections from the Private Papers of Justice William O. Douglas* (Adler & Adler 1987).

4

# Land and Freedom: Socio-Economic Rights and the Mitu-Bell Case

POST-COLONIAL CONSTITUTIONS are often born in riven and unequal societies, marked by histories of violence and dispossession. Transformative constitutions seek to address the burdens of those histories. But constitutions are not inked upon a *tabula rasa*. The new constitutional order is a palimpsest, carrying enduring traces of the social and economic institutions of the past. The success of the transformative project depends on how the constitutional order engages with those institutions.[1]

For all the mutations that it experienced in different parts of the world, colonialism has always cleaved to a certain logic: the logic of material dispossession, often accomplished by imposing capitalist forms of legal property over indigenous systems of community tenure and landholding.[2] Land-grabbing by invoking notions of 'productivity', turning people into tenants on their own land,[3] introducing capitalist agriculture, and forcing precarity as a method of maintaining social control[4] have all been defining features of modern

1 As Karl Marx – a thinker who is rather relevant for the themes of this chapter – observed: 'men make their own history, but they do not make it as they please; they do not make it under self-selected circumstances but under circumstances existing already, given and transmitted from the past.' Karl Marx, *The Eighteenth Brumaire of Louis Bonaparte* (1851–1852), available at <https://www.marxists.org/archive/marx/works/1852/18th-brumaire/>, visited on 15th September 2024.

2 Manji, *The Struggle for Land and Justice in Kenya, supra*; Shivji, *Accumulation in an African Periphery, supra*; Ranajit Guha, *A Rule of Property for Bengal* (Duke University Press 1996).

3 See e.g. H.W.O. Okoth-Ogendo, *Tenants of the Crown: Evolution of Agrarian Law and Institutions in Kenya* (ACTS Press, African Centre for Technology Studies 1991).

4 Reinforced by anti-beggary and vagrancy laws that were enacted across the British colonies, specifically targeted at nomadic individuals or groups who had not yet conformed to a settled way of life, under the euphemism 'having no visible means of sustenance'. In the late 2010s, in a long overdue move, some post-colonial jurisdictions began to strike down these laws. See e.g. the judgment of the constitutional court of Uganda in *Tumwesige Francis v Attorney General* (Constitutional Petition No. 36 of 2018) [2022] UGCC 5 (2nd December 2022); the judgment of the High Court of Jammu and Kashmir in *Suhail Rashid Bhat vs State of Jammu and Kashmir*, PIL 24/2018, judgment dated 25th October, 2019.

colonialism. Furthermore, within the colonial context, patriarchy has invariably intensified dispossession and inequality along gendered lines, overseeing both the visible – and often invisible – subordination of women.[5]

It is therefore scarcely surprising that demands for land justice constituted a core part of twentieth-century independence struggles.[6] Once independence had been accomplished, landlessness and deeply skewed patterns of land ownership were some of the major problems that confronted the framers of post-colonial constitutions.

Liberal constitutions framed in the 'first wave' of decolonisation often chose to avoid directly addressing this issue: that is, they excluded the 'social question' from the purview of constitutionalism.[7] This strategic silence was justified as a choice not to encode any specific ideology into the constitution, and to leave the difficult task of land reform to the legislatures that would follow.[8] But in entrenching an enforceable right to property, these constitutions *did* endorse an economic ideology (in part, as we shall see, the protection of landed or settler interests), and one that would inevitably be wielded as a weapon against legislative efforts at land redistribution.[9]

It was in the 'second wave' of post-colonial constitution-making – in the 1990s onwards – that constitutions began to explicitly address the social question' in response to long-standing demands. The dominant form was an enforceable code of socio-economic rights,[10] such as the right to health, the right to education, and the right to housing, among others.[11] While it

[5] Cora Ann Presley, *Kikuyu Women, the Mau Mau Rebellion, and Social Change in Kenya* (Routledge 1992).

[6] It is hardly a coincidence that the actual name of the "Mau Mau" was the Kenya Land and Freedom Army.

[7] A phrase coined by Hannah Arendt in *On Revolution* (Penguin Books 1963), to refer to questions around material inequality and poverty.

[8] This was the eventual justification provided by B.R. Ambedkar, the chairperson of the Drafting Committee of the Indian Constitution, for removing references to state socialism from the original draft constitution that he himself had prepared.

[9] The first twenty years of the Indian Constitution, for example, saw a see-saw battle between courts and legislatures, over the space that the Constitution offered parliament to enact land reform. Indeed, the judgment in *Kesavananda Bharati* – discussed in Chapter Two – and the famous basic structure doctrine arose out of just such a mundane land dispute.

[10] This is not to suggest that enforceable socio-economic rights were born in the 1990s. The revolutionary French Constitution of 1848 guaranteed a 'right to work' (it did not, as a matter of fact, work), and socio-economic rights have been a staple feature of Latin American constitutionalism since the 1917 Constitution of Mexico. Various constitutions – such as those or Ireland, India, and Uganda – also have non-enforceable 'directive principles' of state or social policy.

[11] See e.g. Sandra Liebenberg, *Socio-Economic Rights Adjudication under a Transformative Constitution* (Juta 2010) for a discussion of South Africa; see also M

may appear that a right, by its very nature, removes a particular good from the realm of markets and commodities, much like their predecessors these constitutions could not ignore the political economy into which they were born.[12] Consequently, the immediate force of these rights was arguably blunted by subjecting them to 'progressive realisation' and budgetary constraints.[13] Nor could these new constitutions overcome the pressures (both internal and external) to retain the old 'property' clauses,[14] which continued to exert a gravitational pull upon the transformative project.

Consider, for example, the right to housing. Ask someone unfamiliar with sophistic legal vocabulary, and they would tell you that a 'right to housing' means a 'right to a home'. But it does not – or at least, it cannot – as long as housing is a commodity on the market. The landless cannot, through court orders, compel the state to build them homes, as that would amount to judicial interference with the budget (and the state will not do so because of the impact on the 'housing market').[15] They cannot stake an enforceable claim to the land they occupy, as the new constitutional order still makes 'legal title' a pre-requisite for recognition of ownership.[16] And when they occupy 'private

---

Sepulveda, 'The Constitutional Court's role in addressing social injustice' in *Social Rights Jurisprudence: Emerging Trends in International and Comparative Law* (M. Langford (ed.), Cambridge University Press 2008), for a discussion of Colombia. For a conceptual discussion, see Sandra Fredman, *Human Rights Transformed* (Oxford University Press 2008).

12 See Gautam Bhatia, 'Horizontal Rights, Political Economy, and the Limits of Constitutional Adjudication' (2023), available at <https://papers.ssrn.com/sol3/papers.cfm?abstract_id=4480401>, visited on 15th May 2024.

13 See, for example, the controversial judgment of the Constitutional Court of South Africa in *Government of the Republic of South Africa vs Grootboom,* 2000 (11) BCLR 1169 (CC).

14 The South African property clause, for example, has been controversial. Critics of South African transformative constitutionalism have highlighted it as an irredeemable bottleneck, and one South African political party – the Economic Freedom Fighters – has made its repeal a policy plank. For a proposed transformative reading of the South African property clause, see Mandisa Shandu and Michael Clark, 'Rethinking Property: Towards a Values-Based Approach to Property Relations in South Africa' (2021) 11(1) *Constitutional Court Review* 1.

15 For the most eloquent articulation of how socio-economic rights run up against the 'mute compulsion' of the market economy, see Amy Kapczyinski, 'The Right to Medicines in an Age of Neoliberalism' (2019) 10(1) *Humanity Journal* 79, and the responses thereto. See also Paola Bergello, 'Courts and social change: Lessons from the struggle to universalise access to HIV treatment in Argentina' (2010–2011) 89 *Texas Law Review* 1611.

16 Subject to a few domain-specific exceptions regarding community land, that many contemporary constitutions contain.

land', their situation is even more precarious, as the owner's constitutional right to property is activated.[17]

Thus, when a judge is called upon to give meaning to the 'right to housing', they find themselves navigating a web of qualifications, caveats, and countervailing considerations, where any attempt to cut through only binds the web tighter. The best-intentioned courts have, thus far, managed only to navigate the edges of the web, untangling some of its harshest strands. They have done this by imposing procedural restrictions upon evictions and overseeing rehabilitation and the provision of alternate accommodation. In other words, they have tried to humanise property law, and – by extension – humanise evictions, without ending them altogether.[18] This is not an entirely transformative solution, but it may be the best that constitutions can do within a political economy of commodities.[19]

This chapter examines the role of the Kenyan judiciary in traversing the contested – yet familiar – terrain of land rights, the right to housing, property rights, and evictions. I begin by noting the salience of land as a site of historical injustice, as well as a terrain for claims *to* justice, both in the colonial period, and under the 1963 Independence Constitution (Section A). I then examine

17 For example, in 2022, the Irish Housing Commission held a set of public consultations on a proposed referendum to introduce a right to housing into the Irish Constitution, where one session was devoted to the question of how any such right could be "balanced" against the right to property. See also A.J. van der Walt, 'Squatting and the Right to Shelter' (1992) 1 *Journal of South African Law* 40.

18 As Robert Cover famously wrote: 'legal interpretation takes place in a field of pain and death.' Robert Cover, 'Violence and the Word' (1986) 95 *The Yale Law Journal* 1601.

19 For an extensive treatment of this issue, in the context of post-apartheid South Africa, see A.J. van der Walt, *Property at the Margins* (Hart 2009). South African jurisprudence is generally acknowledged as one of the leading examples of social rights adjudication in the context of housing, evictions, and property. See e.g. *Port Elizabeth Municipality v Various Occupiers* 2005 (1) SA 217 (CC); *City of Johannesburg v Rand Properties (Pty) Ltd and Others* 2007 (6) SA 417 (SCA); *Occupiers of 51 Olivia Road, Berea Township, and 197 Main Street, Johannesburg v City of Johannesburg and Others* 2008 (3) SA 208 (CC); *Dladla and Another v City of Johannesburg and Others* [2017] ZACC 42 (CC). See the analysis in Sandra Liebenberg, 'Towards a right to alternative accommodation? South Africa's constitutional jurisprudence on evictions' (2005) 2 *Housing and ESC Rights Law Quarterly* 1; For an academic study in a comparative constitutional law context, see Rishika Sahgal, 'Evictions and Participation Rights in India and South Africa' (DPhil Thesis, University of Oxford 2022) available at <https://ora.ox.ac.uk/objects/uuid:5384db59-946f-4275-ab07-7f84273439c7/download_file?file_format=application%2Fpdf&safe_filename=Sahgal_2022_Evictions_and_participation.pdf&type_of_work=Thesis>, visited on 15th September 2024.

how the 2010 Constitution's cluster of land, land rights, and housing provisions attempt to respond both to colonial injustices, as well as the Independence Constitution's entrenchment (both through commission and omission) of those injustices (Section B).

The real test of these provisions – and the constitutional philosophy they articulate – came through two cases that reached the Supreme Court of Kenya in 2020 and 2021: *Mitu-Bell* and *Musembi*. I argue that while they largely hewed to the 'untangling the edges of the web' approach that progressive judiciaries around the world have adopted, there are parts of both judgments that *gesture* towards a more radical, and more transformative, reading (Section C). It remains to be seen whether future judgments can – and will – take up the invitation offered in *Mitu-Bell* and *Musembi*, towards a jurisprudence that seeks not only to untangle the edges, but also bring transformative constitutionalism into the heart of the political economy (Section D).

## A. Dispossession and Commodification

Land – and conflicts over land – have been a flashpoint in Kenya since the formal beginning of colonialism at the end of the nineteenth century. The initial colonial period was marked by dispossession, displacement, and the capture of vast tracts of land by the British colonisers.[20] This was accompanied by the undermining – and eventual destruction – of pre-colonial forms of community land tenure.[21] Through a series of orders and Ordinances passed in 1901–1902 – just six years after Kenya had been made a British Protectorate – the British Commissioner was granted the power to dispose of, sell, or lease 'crown lands' – i.e., all public lands in the Protectorate that were controlled by the Crown 'by virtue of any Treaty, Convention or Agreement'.[22] As early as 1904, the Masaai community had been displaced from their land through a disputed 'treaty' imposed on them.[23] Between 1903 and 1906, '60,000 acres of Kikuyu land were alienated' for the purpose of

20 M.P.K. Sorrenson, *The Origins of European Settlement in Kenya* (OUP 1968).

21 For a judicial discussion of this history, see *In the Matter of the National Land Commission*, [2015] KESC 3 (KLR), para 100.

22 Ibid., para 102.

23 This displacement was further entrenched by another 'treaty' in 1911. See Lotte Hughes, *Moving the Maasai: A Colonial Misadventure* (Palgrave Macmillan 2006); Ben Ole Koissaba, 'Elusive Justice: The Masaai Contestation of Land Appropriation in Kenya: A Historical and Contemporary Perspective' in *Kenya After 50*, *supra*, 188, 193. Such tactics were used elsewhere: see e.g. the discussion by Tembeka Ngcukatobi of the land transfers in the late nineteenth century by the chiefs of the Bapo ba Mogale community to the German Hermannsburg Mission Society, in what is now South Africa, and other such examples. Tembeka Ngcukaitobi, *Land Matters: South Africa's Failed Land Reforms and the Road Ahead* (Penguin Books 2021) 38–40.

European settler agriculture.[24] By 1908, 'the British Government [had] granted exclusive rights of occupancy to people of European descent in an undefined area of highland country assumed to be unoccupied by African tribes.'[25] This process culminated in the enactment of the Crown Lands Ordinance of 1915, which 'brought native land whether occupied or unoccupied within the scope of Crown lands',[26] and – through an interpretation of the colonial court in *Isaka Wainaina wa Gathomo and Anr vs Murito wa Indanagara and Others*[27] – had the effect of turning Kenyans into "tenants of the crown."[28] For Ghai and McAuslan, by this time, "the disinheritance of the Africans from their land was … complete."[29]

With access to land, the settlers also required 'cheap and abundant supply of labour [for the purposes of which] the government proceeded to impose various legislative and financial measures to force Africans into the labour market.'[30] Progressively more repressive legislation – from the Hut and Poll Tax to the Masters and Servants Ordinance, and ultimately, the Resident Native Labourers' Ordinance (RNLO) of 1918, forced these tenants – and their relationship with land – into conditions of economic precarity. The RNLO of 1918 sought to both 'encourage squatting as a source of labour while bringing it under systematic regulation …. "Kaffir farming" was made illegal, squatters' rights as tenants were extinguished, and they were reduced to the status of servants.'[31]

Through a parallel process, meanwhile, the colonial regime also brought in a series of coercive administrative moves to complement these efforts to compel landless Africans 'to work for them in the settler farms and in the newly created sectors of proletarian employment'.[32] Chief amongst these was

24 Tabitha Kanogo, *Squatters and the Roots of the Mau Mau* (James Currey 1987) 9.

25 Oginga Odinga, *Not Yet Uhuru, supra*, 17.

26 Muigai, *Power, Politics & Law, supra*, 83.

27 *Isaka Wainaina vs Murito wa Indagara* (1922–23) Kenya Law Reports Vol. IX 102.

28 Muigai, *Power, Politics & Law, supra*, 83.

29 Ghai and McAuslan, *Public Law and Political Change in Kenya, supra*, 28.

30 Kanogo, *Squatters and the Roots of the Mau Mau, supra*, 8–9. The 'proletarianisation' of Africans by curtailing their 'access to land and farming' was a strategy followed across British colonial domains in Africa. See e.g. Ngcukaitobi, *Land Matters, supra*, 22, 30, discussing the South African example.

31 Berman, *Control and Crisis in Colonial Kenya, supra*, 149. 'Kaffir farming' was effectively a landlord tenant relationship, where European settlers would permit Africans to use land for livestock or agriculture, in return for payment, in cases where the European was an absentee landlord, or lacked the resources to incapable to work the land himself. See Kanogo, *Squatters and the Roots of the Mau Mau, supra*, 15. For a parallel account of the criminalisation of squatting in Transvaal – at around the same time – see Ngcukaitbi, *Land Matters, supra*, 223.

32 Oyaya and Poku, *The Making of the Constitution of Kenya, supra*, 33. See also *The Development of an African Working Class* (R. Sandbrook and R. Cohen (eds.), Longman 1975).

the hated 'pass' – or *kipande* – system,[33] which sought to bring workers under administrative control by imposing penalties both upon the worker (on not producing their pass) and upon their employer (for not demanding it).[34]

This account would be incomplete without a reference to the gendered impact of colonial land policy. As Cora Ann Presley explains, in the pre-colonial period, 'women were the major cultivators … they controlled the disposition of food, determining what was to be consumed, stored, or traded.'[35] The expropriation of land by the British thus led to an intensified proletarianisation of women, many of whom were compelled to migrate to urban settlements and become wage labourers. In addition, the (compelled) change in the nature of agriculture, from subsistence agriculture to cash crops, saw a shift in the labour pattern, where the women who remained in agricultural production were now required to engage in wage labour on coffee estates, thus resulting in a 'loss of control over the productive process'.[36] The histories of land dispossession are thus inextricably linked with the histories of gender inequalities and subordination.

Piecing the fragments of this history together, Tabitha Kanogo summarises early colonial land policy as one that was characterised by dispossession and dislocation (from land), followed by coercion[37] (to create a labour supply

33 The *kipande* was a pass that featured an individual's fingerprints, and employment history, among other things, and had to be produced on demand. Its purpose was to restrict the movement of Africans through the colony. See e.g. Makhan Singh, *History of Kenya's Trade Union Movement* (East African Publishing House 1969) Ch 14. Variants of pass laws existed across British colonies in Africa. See e.g. Ngcukaitobi, *Land Matters*, *supra* 2, 25 noting the use of pass laws for labour control in the 1910s, in the newly formed Union of South Africa.

34 Berman, *Control and Crisis*, *supra*, 147. This regime of law was, of course, racialised and racially differentiated. As Muigai sums up: '[The] genre of [differentiated] laws include regulations, which criminalised wandering about without employment or solicitation; legislation that rendered infringement of labour laws a crime; legislation, which introduced, in effect, a system of pass controls for African males over the age of 15 years; legislation which provided legal sanction to the establishment of African reserves; legislation which institutionalised labour tenancy of African workers thereby creating contractual obligations to the land owners; and legislation which criminalised theft of livestock or agricultural produce, with punishment being extendable to the family of a convict unable to meet the fine.' Muigai, *Power, Politics & Law*, *supra*, 77.

35 Presley, *Kikuyu Women, the Mau Mau Rebellion, and Social Change in Kenya*, *supra*, 4.

36 Ibid., 4–5.

37 This phenomenon – the dispossession of the peasants of their direct access to land through coercive methods, followed by – or even with a view to – proletarianization, and the production of wage-labourers, was first noticed by Karl Marx in his analysis of the enclosure of the commons and the origins of capitalism in England.

for the settler-owned plantations and mixed farming).[38] By the end of the First World War, this had resulted in the creation of an established 'squatter system',[39] which had become integrated into the 'socio-economic structure of European farms and plantations in Kenya'.[40]

The resulting landlessness – and land conflicts – were exacerbated by what Migai Akech calls the colonial construction of 'ethnic citizenship': that is, 'a legacy of the colonial experience, which created "dual citizenship" under which one is first and foremost a citizen of his or her ethnic community, and then a citizen of Kenya.'[41] Berman sums up the entire process as follows:

---

See Karl Marx, *Capital: Volume 1* (Paul North and Paul Reitter (eds.), Paul Reitter (trans.), Princeton University Press 2024) 650–693. The accepted Marxian term for this, so far, has been 'primitive accumulation', while the newest translation uses the term 'original accumulation'. Marx's argument was subsequently developed by Rosa Luxemburg, in the context of early twentieth-century imperialism. Interestingly, Luxemburg's *The Accumulation of Capital* was published in 1913, at the same time that the British were violently separating Kenyans from their land. See Rosa Luxemburg, *The Accumulation of Capital* (1913) (W. Stark (ed.), Agnes Schwarzschild (trans.), Routledge 1951), available at <https://www.marxists.org/archive/luxemburg/1913/accumulation-capital/>, visited on 15th September 2024. For a contemporary gloss of Marx and Luxemburg's analysis on the history of colonialism, see Onur Ulas Ince, 'Primitive Accumulation, New Enclosures, and Global Land Grabs: A Theoretical Intervention' (2014) 79(1) *Rural Sociology* 104, and Robert Nichols, *Theft is Property!: Dispossession and Critical Theory* (Duke University Press 2020). While Nichols' focus is on the settler colonies of the United States, Canada, and New Zealand, his analysis of dispossession and proletarianization bears striking similarities to the situation in Kenya in the first decades of the twentieth century. My thanks to Madhubala P. for pointing me to these references just before the completion of this manuscript.

38 Kanogo, *Squatters and the Roots of the Mau Mau, supra*. Kanogo also describes how an active policy of 'de-stocking' – that is, depriving Africans of their livestock – was used to compel them into dependency upon the labour market. Ibid., Ch. 3.

39 'Squatters' were individuals who lived and worked on farms owned by white settlers, without legal property rights to the land on which they were residing. In return for their work, the settlers allowed them to reside on the land and grow their own food on it.

40 Kanogo, *Squatters and the Roots of the Mau Mau, supra*, 8. Meanwhile, a Maasai representation to the Kenya Land Commission in 1932, raising the historical injustice that had been done to them in 1904 and 1911, met with no success. See Koissaba, 'Elusive Justice', *supra*, 196.

41 Akech, 'Institutional Reform in the New Constitution of Kenya', *supra*. For an illustration, Tabitha Kanogo's account of ethnically and territorially mediated claims to land during the Olenguruone conflict. Kanogo, *Squatters and the Roots of the Mau Mau, supra*, 111.

> First, from the 1920s the growing population density and scarcity of land in the reserves, along with increasing cash crop agriculture, was turning land into a commodity and led the Kikuyu themselves to depict the past and present land patterns according to Western concepts. The process of accumulation and class formation in the reserves, a process expressing growing struggles over the rights of ownership, sale, and purchase of land both within the households of *mbari* and between them and the unrelated *ahoi* households which had made precolonial payments for use rights to portions of *mbari* land … second, the common ideological assumption among colonial administrators that the land use systems necessarily evolved from tribal communalism to modern individual absolute property, and their paternalistic desire to restrict the development of the latter and thereby protect Africans from further loss of land to Europeans by the sale of individual titles, led them to reject or misinterpret evidence of individual rights of land use among *mbari* household heads in the precolonial period and of the contemporary development towards Western forms of property. Moreover, the political difficulty of reversing grants to settlers and restoring the holdings of particular Kikuyu claimants led officials to favour compensation on a communal or 'tribal' basis.[42]

As history records, landlessness was one of the key driving factors of the Mau Mau movement, and a key demand in the struggle for Independence.[43] While the roots of this went back to the founding of the colony, there was a particular intensification of mass evictions and forced dispossession after 1945, as land consolidation (as a way of dealing, *inter alia*, with increasing pressures on land) became a colonial imperative. As Atieno-Odhiambo eloquently notes:

> … the state, but more particularly the settlers, found themselves face to face with their erstwhile guests, the squatters, who also regarded these lands as home and property. The eviction of squatters did not mean 'termination of contract' to the latter. Rather, they experienced being homeless and propertyless in the lands of their birth. Their struggles against this abyss from 1946 onwards must be seen as a struggle about existence, about *mugunda*, land as household and property, and about being.[44]

42 Berman, *Control and Crisis*, *supra*, 94.

43 See, as flagged above, the discussion in Kanogo, *Squatters and the Roots of the Mau Mau*, *supra*, Ch. 3, tracing the origins of the Mau Mau to the conflict over the land settlement scheme at Olenguruone.

44 E.S. Atieno-Odhiambo, 'The Formative Years' in *Decolonization and Independence in Kenya*, *supra*, 25, 28.

While the British responded to the Mau Mau with repression, violence, and large-scale dispossession,[45] they also sought to isolate the revolutionaries and deprive them of popular support through the vehicle of land policy. This involved the commodification of land and the creation of a Kenyan (loyalist) landowning class: that is, 'individualisation was a political tool that came in handy to blunt Africans' demand for land redistribution.'[46]

This was not entirely new: rules of 'individual land ownership' had, for a few decades, contributed to the degradation of indigenous (often communitarian) traditions of land use.[47] But it was the 1950s that saw an acceleration of this process, as the British sought to respond to both the Mau Mau challenge, and to the consequences of their own repressive policies such as the forced repatriation of the Kikuyu back to their 'reserves', which were leading to further pressures upon the land.[48] Through the famous – or notorious – Swynnerton Plan, the British regime oversaw a transition from the old system of settler domination and the formal exclusion of Kenyans from land ownership, to the marketisation of land, with the stated objective of boosting agricultural productivity for the purposes of the world market.[49]

45 Individuals suspected of being a part of the Mau Mau were evicted from the settler farms and 'repatriated' back to the Central Provinces, thus exacerbating the problem of Kikuyu landlessness.

46 Manji, *The Struggle for Land and Justice in Kenya*, *supra*, 39. Berman, *Control and Crisis*, *supra*, 368.

47 See, for example, Jaramogi Oginga Odinga's account of cooperative farming within the Luo communities. Oginga Odinga, *Not Yet Uhuru*, *supra*, 10–11. See also Tabitha Kanogo's description of the *githaka* system among the Kikuyu. Kanogo, *Squatters and the Roots of the Mau Mau*, *supra*, and her account of the Olenguruone scheme, where the colonial government attempted to impose an entirely new system of 'land ownership' at variance with 'Kikuyu practice'. This led to substantial conflict. Ibid., 112–113. Going beyond Kenya, for an account of the 'layered' and 'nested' nature of land rights and land administration in KwaZulu-Natal, see Ben Cousins et al., 'Imithetho yomhlaba yaseMsinga: The living law of land in Msinga, KwaZulu-Natal' PLAAS Research Report 43 (Institute for Poverty, Land and Agrarian Studies, School of Government, Faculty of Economic and Management Sciences, University of the Western Cape 2011), available at <https://repository.uwc.ac.za/xmlui/bitstream/handle/10566/4488/rr_43_imithetho_yomhlaba_yasemsinga_living_law_land_Msinga_2011.pdf?sequence=1&isAllowed=y>, visited on 15th September 2024. The nature of community land tenure was specifically recognised by the North Gauteng High Court in South Africa, in *Baleni and Ors vs Minister of Mineral Resources and Ors* (2019) 2 SA 453 (GP).

48 Caroline Elkins, *Britain's Gulag: The Brutal End of Empire in Kenya* (The Bodley Head 2014) 125–127. For a lived experience account of the policy of 'forced villagisation', see Thiong'o, *In the House of the Interpreter*, *supra*.

49 Manji, *The Struggle for Land and Justice in Kenya*, *supra*, 39. Berman, *Control and Crisis*, *supra*, 369. As the Supreme Court noted in *In the Matter of the National*

With 'funding to the tune of 7.95 million pounds, Swynnerton recognised the challenge of agrarian unrest, but turned it on itself by planning and dividing Africans along class lines: the landed yeomanry on the one hand and the landless would-be labourer/proletariat on the other.'[50] Indeed, as Swynnerton himself stated, the goal was land consolidation and the creation of a 'landed and landless class ... this is a normal step in the evolution of a country.'[51]

Oyaya and Poku note, therefore:

> ... [the] land and agrarian reforms undertaken ... skirted the fundamental constitutional question raised by Africans about the legitimacy of Crown Lands Ordinance and the historical land dispossession and injustices. Instead, they were based on the wrong assumption that the problems in the native reserves were 'due to overpopulation, bad land use, and defective tenure arrangements'.[52]

Thus, the history of land in the colonial period can be summed up by the sequence of *dispossession*, followed by *commodification*: a sequence that created glaring inequalities in patterns of land distribution upon Independence and had the effect – in the words of Atieno-Odhiambo – of a creation of a class of the 'propertied' and the 'propertyless', on the cusp of Independence and beyond.[53] Many years later, the Supreme Court of Kenya would affirm this history – and its relevance for contemporary constitutionalism – in the following way:

> The colonial policy on access to land took certain specific manifestations: the status of radical title-change; indigenous inhabitants lost their claim to all land; an agricultural economy, managed and controlled by the settlers, became dominant; and new political structures emerged, founded upon ownership and control of land. The 'landed gentry' were in control of the machinery of Government; <u>and this was the onset of persistent land problems in Kenya</u>.[54]

---

*Land Commission*, *supra*, at para 104, the Swynnerton Plan was specifically designed to promote individual ownership, to the exclusion of group or community ownership.

50 Atieno-Odhiambo, 'The Formative Years', *supra*, 43.

51 R.J.M. Swynnerton, *A Plan to Intensify the Development of African Agriculture in Kenya* (Nairobi Government Printer 1954) 10, cf. Elkins, *Britain's Gulag*, *supra*, 127. See also the discussion in Nichols, *Theft is Property!*, *supra*, of what the author calls 'recursive dispossession': in essence, after dispossession, the colonising power does grant property rights to the colonised, all the while depriving (a majority of) them of the conditions for the realisation of those rights. Nichols calls this 'a truncated, or "structurally negated" property right, summed up in the memorable phrase, "inclusion [is] conscription."' Ibid., 117, 132.

52 Oyaya and Poku, *The Making of the Constitution of Kenya*, *supra*, 37.

53 Atieno-Odhiambo, 'The Formative Years', *supra*.

54 *In the Matter of the National Land Commission*, *supra*, para 105 (emphasis supplied).

Indeed, at the time of Independence, the problem was particularly acute because, as Ogot observes, when 'the Emergency was lifted, many of the returning detainees and forest fighters either found that their lands had been forfeited and redistributed, or their previous landlessness had been irrevocably confirmed through the land consolidation programmes, which had been fully taken advantage of by pre-Emergency landowners and loyalists.'[55] As Kanogo notes, 'land was all that the landless, impoverished and disgruntled squatters, whose plight had become worse during and after the Mau Mau struggle, really asked of independence, for it was through acquiring land that they gained their security and economic freedom.'[56]

However, even though the freedom movement had been driven by claims for land justice, this did not translate into meaningful transformation at the time of independence.[57] For one, the transfer of power was tightly controlled by the British who, at the Lancaster House negotiations, worked to ensure that there would be no commitments to widespread land redistribution,[58] and that land transfers from the settlers would only be undertaken with due compensation (thus hamstringing any large-scale reform movement).[59] At Lancaster House, the British also rejected claims for the redressal of historical injustices, such as those advanced by the Maasai.[60]

Meanwhile, the nationalists in the KANU party, who were poised to take power when the British departed, and who were aiming for immediate political independence, agreed to the British proposals. This was both out of unwillingness to brook further delay, and out of concern that excessive recalcitrance would see the British hand over power to the rival – more

55 B.A. Ogot, 'The Decisive Years' in *Decolonization and Independence in Kenya*, *supra*, 48, 63–64.

56 Kanogo, *Squatters and the Roots of the Mau Mau*, *supra*, 163 (emphasis supplied).

57 See e.g. the discussion in G. Wasserman, *The Politics of Decolonization: Kenya Europeans and their Land Use, 1960–1965* (Cambridge University Press 1976).

58 This would be a common feature of many of the 'Lancaster House Constitutions' which were negotiated between the British and the representatives of their erstwhile African colonies – in particular, those involving settler societies. Tembeka Ngcukaitobi takes the example of the 1979 Zimbabwean Lancaster House Constitution, which enshrined the right to private property and limited the scope of state takings. Ngcukaitobi, *Land Matters*, *supra*, 4. Zimbabwe's subsequent attempts at land redistribution are their own story, although Ngcukaitobi does note that as late as 2000, a draft property clause proposed by Robert Mugabe's government failed to 'overhaul the Lancaster House agreement – meaning the country's land reform would largely follow a market fundamentalist trajectory.' Ibid. Ngukaitobi also notes that the Namibian Constitution – a decade later – would also follow a similar model, as would – to an extent – the South African Constitution. Ibid., 5–6.

59 Kanogo, *Squatters and the Roots of the Mau Mau*, *supra*, 163.

60 Koissaba, 'Elusive Justice', *supra*, 197.

conservative – KADU party.[61] What therefore followed was a limited resettlement programme, backed by international financial organisations and premised on a willing-buyer-willing-seller model,[62] rather than a programme of *redistribution* and of remedying the problem of landlessness at scale.[63]

Even after Independence was secured, this situation did not change. Rather, it was ideologically entrenched by the new regime.[64] Although the 'radicals [in the government], organised around Vice President Odinga, pushed for an aggressive programme of distribution of settler lands to the landless',[65] the dominant current in the government and in the ruling party, KANU, was in favour of conservation, rather than transformation. In the words of Anderson, the post-colony 'embraced the political blueprint of colonial territoriality in terms of both space and power',[66] including on issues of land.[67] The attitude of the Independence government was summed up by the exchange between President Jomo Kenyatta and his erstwhile fellow-detainee, Bildad Kaggia. When Kaggia wrote a memorandum raising the issue of landlessness amongst the erstwhile freedom fighters, and the eviction of 'squatters' from farms in what had hitherto been the 'White Highlands' if they could not demonstrate occupation for more than four years, Kenyatta's response was to condemn 'illegal squatting' on private property and to praise land consolidation for having raised settlers' incomes.[68] In addition, President Kenyatta notoriously mocked the propertyless Kaggia for being in that position because of not having 'done anything for himself' after Independence.

61 Ibid.

62 For a parallel account of how the post-apartheid South African government adopted the World Bank-promoted 'willing-seller, willing-buyer' model, along with its numerous problems, see Ngcukaitobi, *Land Matters*, *supra*, 118–121.

63 This was known as the 'million-acre scheme'. See Kanogo, *Squatters and the Roots of the Mau Mau*, *supra*, 170. For an analysis of how the Maasai were shut out of access to the scheme, through a combination of deception and coercion, see Koissaba, 'Elusive Justice', *supra*, 200. For a contemporary political defence of the scheme, arguing that the aim was to blend participation in the money economy with retaining communal visions of land access through the setting up of cooperatives, see Tom Mboya, *Freedom and After* (East African Educational Publishers 1986) 170–172.

64 See e.g. Kanyinga Karuti, Lumumba Odenda, and S. Amanor Kojo, 'The Struggle for Sustainable Land Management and Democratic Development in Kenya: A History of Greed and Grievances' in *Land and Sustainable Development in Africa* (Amanor, K.S. and Moyo, S. (eds.), Zed Books 2008) 100.

65 Paul T. Zeleza, 'The Protracted Transition to the Second Republic in Kenya' in *Kenya: The Struggle for a New Constitutional Order*, *supra*, 17, 26.

66 Anderson, '"Yours in the Struggle for Majimbo"', *supra*, 547, 558.

67 See e.g. the Registered Land Act of 1963, passed on the cusp of Independence.

68 Oginga Odinga, *Not Yet Uhuru*, *supra*, 198.

In essence, this summed up the Independence government's view that landlessness was primarily a problem of personal initiative, rather than a structural or institutional issue, to be redressed by state policy. Consequently, the focus of policy was on further reforms of the *tenurial system* (in order to increase efficiency), rather than *land redistribution*. Thus, in 1965, 'the Kenyatta government introduced a land purchase programme, promoting the market as a way to access land rights.'[69] These kinds of policies – which were adopted throughout the East African post-colony[70] – are characterised by McAuslan as the 'traditional' (as opposed to transformational) approach to 'land and land reform … adopting and continuing the colonial approach'.[71]

As Muigai notes, therefore, the Independence Constitution was silent on matters of social justice,[72] including on the issue of land; but more than that, the policies of the post-colonial regime saw that to the old landless from colonialism was added the 'new landless generated by the postcolonial expansion of commodity production'.[73] Manji sums up:

> … [the] approach to land under the new Constitution remained rooted in what Atieno-Odhiambo has described as Kenya's 'ideology of order', which has held political order as the highest priority, and which was not overturned by but in fact survived the democratic transition.[74]

69 Manji, *The Struggle for Land and Justice in Kenya, supra*, 37. In its Final Report, the CKRC specifically critiqued this policy, noting that the assumptions upon which it was based had – over the years – been demonstrated to be misleading. *CKRC Final Report, supra*, 282–283.

70 And beyond: Ngcukaitobi's account of the post-apartheid African National Congress's (ANC) Reconstruction and Development Programme's (RDP) embrace of 'the language of the market' and the vocabulary of productivity and security of tenure bears striking similarities with its counterpart in Kenya, three decades before. See Ngcukaitobi, *Land Matters, supra*, 102.

71 McAuslan characterises the colonial approach in the terms that we have discussed above: one that 'adopts and continues the colonial approach of vesting land in the state, maintains a dual system of land tenure and at the same time adopts an overall policy perspective of moving towards a land market based on registered title to land which implies or … in some cases expressly, provides for the disappearance of customary tenure and, perhaps most important, makes no or little effort to address the inequalities and injustices of the land tenure system inherited at independence and indeed does equally little to prevent its continuance and worsening thereafter.' Patrick McAuslan, *Land Law Reform in Eastern Africa: Traditional or Transformative?* (Routledge 2013) 15.

72 Muigai, *Power, Politics & Law, supra*.

73 Zeleza, 'The Protracted Transition to the Second Republic in Kenya', *supra*, 27.

74 Manji, *The Struggle for Land and Justice in Kenya, supra*, 14. Koissaba also points out that the post-colonial processes around access to land were ethnicized, and mobilising ethnicity became a means of access to land. Koissaba, 'Elusive Justice' *supra*, 199. This carries forward Akech's point about ethnicised access to land during

To this was added the outright capture of land (often illegally) in the late Kenyatta era,[75] and, subsequently, under the regime of President Moi and beyond. The effects of this continue to be felt to the present day, and are still the subject of litigation before the Kenyan courts.[76] As a matter of fact, land-grabbing was fuelled by the same imperative towards the Imperial Presidency that we have discussed in the previous two chapters: the Government Lands Act granted to the President the power to make grants out of un-alienated government land, with the Commissioner acting as the President's delegate.[77] The Commissioner was also given sweeping powers over the alienation of the category of land known as Trust Land, powers that were similarly abused at the behest of the executive.[78] In essence, the executive treated land as a source of patronage, as well as a resource for personal enrichment.[79]

And so, in 2004, after the passing of the Moi era, the Report of the Commission of Enquiry into Irregular and Illegal Allocation of Public Land (the Ndung'u Report) revealed the extent of land-grabbing that had taken place under Moi's rule.[80] As Manji and Cottrell note:

---

the colonial period, *infra*, and demonstrates another instance of colonial continuities on the issue of land.

75 Although the origins of this arguably go back to the beginnings of the Kenyatta regime. See e.g. the discussion of 'Z-Plots' in John Kamau, 'Kenya: When Ministers, Civil Servants Got 100 Acres and Farm House for Free' *Daily Nation* (21st February 2016), available at <https://landportal.org/node/28331>, visited on 15th September 2024.

76 *Dina Management Limited vs County Government of Mombasa and Ors*, Petition 8 of 2021; for an analysis of the judgment, see Ambreena Manji and Jill Cottrell Ghai, 'The Long Shadow of Land Grabbing – Analysing the Decision of the Kenyan Supreme Court in Petition 8 of 2021' *Indian Constitutional Law and Philosophy* (29th June 2023), available at <https://indconlawphil.wordpress.com/2023/06/29/the-long-shadow-of-land-grabbing-analysing-the-decision-of-the-kenya-supreme-court-in-petition-8-of-2021/>, visited on 15th September 2024.

77 See the discussion in *In the Matter of the National Land Commission*, *supra*, para 107; see also the *CKRC Final Report*, *supra*, 259.

78 *In the Matter of the National Land Commission*, *supra*, paras 108–109. The first Trust Land Act was passed in 1939 – as the name suggests – referred to a category of land that was to be held by boards of 'trustees', with input from the Local Native Council. The control referred to in the body of the text above was formalised by the Trust Land Act of 1968. The term 'trust land' no longer exists: after the enactment of the 2010 Constitution, the Trust Land Act was repealed, and the Community Land Act of 2016 was enacted in its place, in order to give effect to Article 63 of the Constitution. Some of these issues are discussed below.

79 For a discussion, see e.g. Kanyinga et al., 'The Struggle for Sustainable Land Management and Democratic Development in Kenya', *supra*, 123.

80 Report of the Commission of Enquiry into Irregular and Illegal Allocation of Public Land, Annexes, Volume 1 (2004), available at <https://www.theelephant.info/documents/the-ndungu-report-annexe-vol-1/>, visited on 15th September 2024. For an

> The Ndung'u report showed that much land that should have been available for the public good – for the building of medical clinics and schools, for prisons, for public parks, roads and other public transport facilities such as railways – had through extensive grabbing instead been transformed into private land. This deprived the public of significant social goods, in order to benefit well-connected individuals and families. The report also revealed the intricate connections between land matters and Kenya's fraught electoral history. The Commission found that illegal allocations of public land increased significantly before or soon after the multiparty general elections of 1992, 1997 and 2002. This was evidence that public land was allocated as political reward and for patronage.[81]

Thus, if the colonial period achieved land concentration and landlessness through by dispossession and commodification, the post-colonial period entrenched this further through land grabbing.

## B. Land in the 2010 Constitution

Post-colonial land policy led to further landlessness, and a rise in squatting by the 1990s – thus bringing land back to the centre of the constitutional reform movement that began with that decade. As Manji notes, therefore, 'the salience of the redistribution versus tenurial reform debate was also reaffirmed by the emergence of rural movements in the 1990s, with struggles to access land through extra-legal means such as occupation or squatting.'[82]

If curtailing the powers of the executive Presidency and bringing the People back into the Constitution was one pillar of the movement, then land justice was the other – equally crucial – pillar. These two pillars were mutually reinforcing. As we have seen, the call to decentralise political power from the hands of the executive was also a call for the 'decentralization of power over the administration of land',[83] given how closely intertwined the two had been during the course of Kenya's post-independence history.

And as the debates at the time of the framing showed, what was at stake was more than untangling the edges of the propertarian web. There was an understanding that 'traditional notions of property do not suffice in transformational contexts, where the foundations of the property regime itself are or should be in question.'[84] As Diepeveen notes, for example, in her exhaustive study of the public hearings of the CKRC:

---

analysis, see Roger Southall, 'The Ngung'u Report: Land and Graft in Kenya' (2005) 32(103) *Review of Political Economy* 142.

81 Manji and Cottrell Ghai, 'The Long Shadow of Land Grabbing', *supra*.

82 Manji, *The Struggle for Land and Justice in Kenya*, *supra*, 46.

83 *In the Matter of the National Land Commission*, *supra*, para 110.

84 Van der Walt, *Property at the Margins*, *supra*, 15.

> The continued relevance of struggles over land was reinforced through discussions of the importance of land, farmers' situation and agriculture as the heart of Kenya's economy. Land as a political grievance for Kikuyu is rooted in the early twentieth century, when frontier land holding units in southern Kikuyuland were allocated to British settlers from 1902/03; from then on, dispossessed Kikuyu migrated to the Rift Valley. The Mau Mau struggle further emphasised the value of land, arguably translating into an internal struggle between Kikuyu, fuelled by dichotomies between landed and landlessness, colonial resistance and appeasement … these references illustrate how, in the public hearings, land continued to be a historical text through which Kikuyu in Central Province understood injustice and inequality.[85]

The land question was central to the Maasai as well, whose dispossession went back to 1904. Indeed, in a detailed memorandum submitted to the CKRC, the Maasai specifically noted how 'the individual land ownership concept is alien to the Maasai community, which held its land collectively on behalf of all its members, irrespective of age or gender.'[86] Locating their dispossession in the imposition of individual property concepts – and thus, in the presumption that an individual could 'cede' land on behalf of the community – the Maasais' claim for constitutional redress, therefore, could not but challenge the logic of political economy at the heart of both the colonial and the post-colonial constitutional orders, when it came to the question of land.[87] In its Final Report, the CKRC specifically noted that one of the key demands that arose out of the public hearings was that 'the Constitution should recognise and respect traditional land tenure and use.'[88]

These issues are reflected in the text and design of the Kenyan Constitution. To start with, unlike its Independence predecessor, the Kenyan Constitution follows the South African model of making socio-economic rights explicitly

85 Diepeveen, '"The Kenyas we don't want"', *supra*, 231.

86 Memoranda to the Constitution of Kenya Review Commission (CKRC), May 2001, cf. Patricia Kameri-Mbote, 'Righting Wrongs: Confronting Land Dispossession in Post-Colonial Contexts' (2009) *East African Law Review* 103. See also Parselelo Kantai, 'In the Grip of the Vampire State: Maasai Land Struggles in Kenyan Politics' (2007) 1(1) *Journal of East African Studies* 107.

87 This narrative is, however, complicated by the fact that, historically, many of the Maasai opted for the sub-division of collectively held group ranches into individual parcels of ownership, in an attempt to protect their interests against internal and external threats of takeover. See Esther Mwangi, 'The Puzzle of Group Ranch Subdivision in Kenya's Maasailand' (2007) 38(5) *Development and Change* 889. For a discussion of the relevant legal text, see The Land (Group Representatives) Act of 1968, and the critique in Koissaba, 'Elusive Justice' *supra*, 201. This history provides a salutary warning that on issues of land, the history is neither linear, nor straightforward.

88 *CKRC Final Report*, *supra*, 98.

enforceable, including the right to housing (subject, of course, to the usual caveats, such as progressive realisation).[89] In *John Kabui Mwai vs Kenya National Examination Council*, the High Court of Kenya explicitly understood the entrenchment of these rights as a part of the project of transformative constitutionalism.[90]

More than that, however, the Constitution has a chapter devoted to 'land and environment',[91] the first part of which explicitly deals with 'land'.[92] The provisions of the chapter directly challenge what Berman calls 'western property rights notions'.[93] Article 61 notes, for example, that 'all land in Kenya belongs to the people of Kenya collectively as a nation, as communities and as individuals.'[94]

Such a prescription, however, would be a pious declaration without institutional support. To this end, the Constitution sets up a National Land Commission as a fourth branch institution[95] with guaranteed independence from the executive, and whose task it is – *inter alia* – to recommend a National

[89] Article 43(1)(b), Constitution of Kenya 2010. There are a few textual difference between the two Constitutions, in that the South African provision guarantees the right of *access* to adequate housing, while the Kenyan provision guarantees the right to *accessible* and adequate housing. The other significant difference is that a provision mirroring the South African Constitution's prohibition upon evictions without a reasoned Court order was twice proposed and twice rejected during the Kenyan constitutional drafting process (first at the stage of the NCC, and then at the stage of the Committee of Experts). See Cottrell Ghai and Ghai, 'The Contribution of the South African Constitution to Kenya's Constitution', *supra*, 252, 263.

[90] *John Kabui Mwai and Ors vs Kenya National Examination Council and Ors*, Petition No. 15 of 2011, decided on 16th September 2011 (High Court); for an early analysis of socio-economic rights under the Kenyan Constitution, see Nicholas Wasonga Orago, 'Socio-Economic Rights and the Potential for Structural Reforms: A Comparative Perspective on the Interpretation of the Socio-Economic Rights in the Constitution of Kenya, 2010' in *Human Rights and Democratic Governance in Kenya*, *supra*, 39.

[91] Chapter V, Constitution of Kenya, 2010.

[92] Chapter V, Part I, Constitution of Kenya, 2010.

[93] Berman, *Control and Crisis*, *supra*, 97.

[94] Article 61, Constitution of Kenya, 2010. This provision must also be understood in the context of a constitutional pushback against ethnic enclaves (as discussed above), and an affirmation that any Kenyan could own land anywhere. We have, therefore, two readings – one individualistic, and one communal – of Article 61, which may – but need not be – sometimes in tension with each other. I thank Professor Ambreena Manji for bringing this point to my notice.

[95] Article 67 read with Article 248(1)(b), Constitution of Kenya, 2010. The role and functions of the NLC – as an independent fourth branch institution – were considered in some detail by the Supreme Court in *In the Matter of the National Land Commission*, *supra*, where the court stressed more on inter-branch cooperation between the NLC,

Land Policy that takes into account principles around equitable access to land.[96] This was, in fact, in pursuance of the recommendations of the Njonjo Commission in the mid-2000s for 'an independent national land institution that it suggested be known as the Kenya National Land Authority which would be entrusted with common (later to be known as community) land'.[97] Notably, all the constitutional drafts through the 2000s had called for a National Land Policy, spurred by the efforts of the Kenya Land Alliance;[98] and indeed, these efforts had born fruit even before the enactment of the 2010 Constitution.[99] In 2009, government and parliament agreed upon a National Land Policy which, *inter alia*, set out a philosophy that promised to move beyond simply looking at land as a productive resource, and also consider issues around livelihood, sustainability, and cultural heritage (the imprint of this upon the 2010 Constitution is evident).[100]

At the same time however, at the level of the text, the transformative character of the 2010 Constitution when it comes to the concepts of land and property is hemmed in by strands of the political economy web. In the same chapter the Constitution also recognises the category of 'private land', setting up a putative clash between that and the ringing – albeit programmatic – declaration that all land belongs to the people of Kenya. There is the ubiquitous property clause, which survived all the drafting negotiation to remain intact in the final text of the Constitution.[101] And there are also the

---

the Ministry, and the county governments. For a critique of the judgment, see Manji, *The Struggle for Land and Justice in Kenya*, *supra*.

96 Article 60(2), Constitution of Kenya, 2010; for post-constitutional attempts by the political elite to dilute the powers of the Commission, see Manji, *The Struggle for Land and Justice in Kenya*, *supra*, Ch. 5. For a contextual and historical account – which this chapter cannot go into – see Catherine Boone, 'Land Conflicts and Distributive Politics in Kenya' (2012) 55(1) *African Studies Review* 75; Catherine Boone et al., 'Land Politics under Kenya's New Constitution: Counties, Devolution, and the National Land Commission' (2016) 16(178) *LSE Working Paper Series*, available at <https://eprints.lse.ac.uk/101817/1/Boone_land_politics_under_kenyas_new_constitution_wp_9.pdf>, visited on 15th September 2024.

97 Manji, *The Struggle for Land and Justice in Kenya*, *supra*, 57.

98 Manji and Cottrell Ghai, 'The Long Shadow of Land Grabbing', *supra*.

99 For the role of the Kenya Land Alliance in the Constitution-making process, see Odenda Lumumba, 'The Role of Civil Society in Land Reforms in Kenya: The Kenya Land Alliance' in *The Gallant Academic: Essays in Honour of HWO Okoth-Ogendo* (Patricia Kameri-Mbote and Collins Odote (eds.), School of Law – University of Nairobi 2017) 171.

100 McAuslan, *Land Law Reform in Eastern Africa*, *supra*, 139.

101 Article 40, Constitution of Kenya, 2010: '... every person has the right, either individually or in association with others, to acquire and own property ... (a) of any description ... and (b) in any part of Kenya.'

missed opportunities, the proposals that were on the table, but did not make it into the text of the Constitution, such as:

> … the land mandates which were accepted by Parliament but did not come to be enshrined in constitutional provisions. These included a direct provision on addressing landlessness, a public purpose requirement for any investments in land, the creation of greater access to land through leasehold routes, new legislation to govern compulsory land acquisition, regulatory powers given to planning authorities to ensure that land is used in the public interest, and the creation of leasehold mechanisms as a way to access land.[102]

Therefore, as Manji observes, distinguishing between 'deep reform' and 'shallow reform':

> The constitutional settlement arrived at in 2010 was the result of significant compromises … In common with South Africa … Kenya embedded a provision protecting private property in the Constitution. On one reading, the existence of a constitutional guarantee of this sort alongside a provision compelling the investigation and resolution of historical land injustices is a contradiction, a good example of Harbeson's observation that the Constitution makes 'possibly conflicting promises to itself.'[103]

It would, therefore, fall to the courts to tease out the consequences flowing from the 'conflicting promises' that the 2010 Constitution made to itself. And it is to the courts that we now turn.

## C. *Mitu-Bell* and *Musembi*

Mitumba Village, located near the Wilson Airport in Nairobi, was home to more than three thousand families. On 15th September, 2011, through a notice published in the newspapers by the Attorney-General, the residents were given one week to vacate the land. They promptly approached the High Court, which

[102] Manji, *The Struggle for Land and Justice in Kenya*, *supra*, 94.

[103] Ibid., 165. These compromises are also reflected in the set of laws that were passed in the immediate aftermath of 2010, to comply with the stipulated transition period. For an extended critique of the post-constitutional statutory framework, with the conclusion that it continues to have 'far too much unregulated power located at the centre', see McAuslan, *Land Law Reform in Eastern Africa*, *supra*, Ch. 11. McAuslan's critique focuses on the hurried way in which these laws were enacted – given the unrealistic timeframes – and the resulting confusion that their implementation will cause. As this chapter does not consider the statutory framework in too much detail, we will not delve further into the substance of McAuslan's critique.

granted them a stay. In an action chillingly reminiscent of the pre-2010 era, the state authorities demolished their homes nonetheless. The stay having become worthless, the residents now came back to the High Court, asking for a declaration that the demolition was illegal and, consequently, that the state was obligated to rehabilitate them in a reasonable, alternative location, and to grant them compensation.

The wrinkle in the case was that the land was public land. The residents did not have legal title to it. Mitumba Village was one of the many settlements whose existence could be traced directly to the political economy choices that we have outlined in the previous two sections: widespread landlessness and inequities in land ownership, leading to squatting and occupation for want of any other option.

The residents prevailed at the High Court, notwithstanding their lack of legal title.[104] Mumbi Ngugi J found the notice of eviction to be defective on both procedural and substantive grounds. Procedurally, the notice had given only seven days to the residents to pack up their lives and move. It fell short of both domestic and international human rights standards. More than that, however, the Kenyan Constitution's commitment to public participation – and centring the People – required meaningful consultations before evictions,[105] regardless of title. Substantively, the constitutional right to housing required

[104] *Mitu-Bell Welfare Society vs Attorney-General and Ors*, Petition No. 164 of 2011, decided on 11th April 2013 (High Court). The judgment is best read alongside *Satrose Ayuma and Ors vs The Registered Trustees of the Kenya Railways Staff Retirement Benefits Scheme*, [2013] KEHC 6003 (KLR), also delivered by the High Court, a few months later; in the latter case, the court also drew on comparative and international jurisprudence to lay down a procedure of bounded deliberation in the case of evictions, where the statutory authority would have to meaningfully engage with the individuals that it was seeking to evict, while ensuring that at no point did the procedure or the offer of alternative accommodation fall below a guaranteed minimal threshold vis-à-vis the rights to shelter and housing.

[105] South African constitutional jurisprudence, in a series of landmark cases, has called this the right to 'meaningful engagement'. For the origins of this jurisprudence, see *Occupiers of 51 Olivia Road, Berea Township and 197 Main Street Johannesburg vs City of Johannesburg and Others*, [2008] ZACC 1 (Constitutional Court of South Africa). See also *Dladla and Anr vs City of Johannesburg and Ors*, [2017] ZACC 42 (Constitutional Court of South Africa). Indeed, South African jurisprudence is particularly relevant, given the similar histories of dispossession and commodification in the colonial/apartheid era, followed by concentration of landholdings after Independence due to the 'market option' that has been followed in both counties (allowing, of course, for differences based on specific histories). We have referred to some of these parallel developments in the footnotes in this chapter; for a comprehensive comparison, Manji's *The Struggle for Land and Justice*, *supra*, and Ngcuaitobi's *Land Matters*, *supra*, can be read together.

the provision of reasonable alternative accommodation before any demolitions could be carried out.[106]

The High Court also returned a finding of other violations: the right to property (the demolition of houses and destruction of belongings), here being turned against the state; the right to non-discrimination (multi-storey buildings, also within the vicinity of the airport, continued to stand); and the rights of children (the local school had been demolished). Noting that mere compensation was not enough of a remedy in a case like this, the High Court turned to another South African innovation: the "structural interdict."[107] A structural interdict is an order of continuous judicial supervision of the case, which requires the State to submit a plan for meaningful engagement with the residents, and the provision of shelter and access to housing.

*Mitu-Bell* was decided by the High Court in 2013, just three years into the new constitutional order. With it, the High Court signalled an intention for Kenyan jurisprudence to join the community of progressive jurisdictions that have constitutionalised the 'untangling the edges of the web' approach that I have referred to above. The High Court's judgment was a model example of the court setting certain procedural and substantive *constraints* upon the state's power to evict the propertyless and to demolish their homes. While leaving the bulldozer of property law untouched, these constraints – when applied by the courts – could work to slow the bulldozer down, or sometimes throw sand in its gears.[108]

The journey, however, would not be a smooth one. The state carried the case in appeal, and the Kenyan Court of Appeal reversed the High Court's judgment.[109] If the High Court's judgment had thrown sand in the gears of the bulldozer, the Court of Appeal not only cleaned out the sand, but applied a fresh dash of oil to the machine. It held that in the absence of any legal right to the land on part of the residents, the State did not owe any constitutional obligations to them. Substantively, the Court of Appeal justified the eviction

[106] The nature of the alternative accommodation is often a product of meaningful engagement, drawing a link between the procedural and the substantive aspects. See e.g. Rishika Sahgal, 'Eviction and Participation Rights in India and South Africa' (DPhil Thesis, University of Oxford, 2022).

[107] In India, this is called the 'continuing mandamus', a term that might be more suitable, as 'interdict' is, in essence, a Roman-Dutch legal concept.

[108] The reference to the bulldozer is not only metaphorical. The Moi era, in particular, was marked by large-scale evictions and demolitions of shanty towns using bulldozers. See, for example, Paul Mwangi's account of the demolitions at Muoroto and Kibagare – just two out of innumerable examples – in Mwangi, *The Black Bar*, *supra*, 168.

[109] *Kenya Airports Authority vs Mitu-Bell Welfare Society and Others*, Civil Appeal No. 218 of 2014, decided on 1st July 2016 (Court of Appeal).

by resorting to that oldest – and easiest – of judicial shibboleths: national security. The right to housing, it further held, could not grant the residents any claims upon the state, as it was a 'progressively realisable' right at best.[110] And in any event, the High Court was not authorised, under the Constitution, to grant a 'structural interdict', and assume supervisory jurisdiction over state authorities: such an approach would violate the separation of powers.[111]

The philosophy animating the Court of Appeal's judgment was summed up in the telling line, when the court noted that 'it is not the role or function of the Courts to re-engineer and redistribute private property rights.'[112] Here, then, was a *conservative* judgment in the classical sense. The court saw its task as *conserving* the existing property regime that had been bequeathed to it, and – in the words of Migai Akech – levelling down the Constitution to make it conform to the property regime, rather than taking upon itself the task of reinterpreting the property regime so as to make it conform to the Constitution.[113]

And so the stage was set for the Supreme Court to decide. In another shift of the pendulum, the Supreme Court set aside the judgment of the Court of Appeal. However, the pendulum did not quite swing back entirely, as the judgment of the High Court was only partially restored. To start with, the Supreme Court found that the Kenyan judiciary did have the authority to issue structural interdicts under Article 23 of the Constitution, but that any such interdict would have to be 'specific, appropriate, clear, effective, and directed at the parties to the suit or any other State agency vested with a constitutional or statutory mandate to enforce the order'.[114] The Supreme Court warned against

110 See the section above, for the sophistry of legal vocabulary.

111 There is an important line of scholarship that argues that classical constitutional doctrines such as the 'separation of powers' need to be fundamentally rethought in the context of transformative constitutionalism, especially where – and to the extent that – these doctrines serve to entrench or perpetuate the very power relations and hierarchies that the constitution is meant to transform. See e.g. Timothy Fish Hodgson, 'The mysteriously appearing and disappearing doctrine of separation of powers: towards a distinctly South African doctrine for a more radically transformative Constitution' (2018) 34(1) *South African Journal on Human Rights* 57.

112 This language is strikingly reminiscent of the notorious nineteenth-century judgment of the United States Supreme Court in *The Civil Rights Cases* 109 U.S. 3 (1883) 22, where the Supreme Court struck down the first attempt at a civil rights law in the United States, noting, *inter alia*, Congress did not have the authority to 'adjust … the social rights of men and races in the community'. There is an intellectual kinship here, across centuries and continents, and across civil/political and socio-economic rights: that is, the idea that the existing structures of power in the society constitute the default normative baseline, and any attempts to alter them must be met with suspicion.

113 Akech, 'Institutional Reform in the New Constitution of Kenya', *supra*.

114 *Mitu-Bell Welfare Society vs The Kenya Airports Authority*, [2021] KESC 34 (KLR), para 122.

general or open-ended structural interdicts that might violate the separation of powers, and found that at least a part of the interdict, as framed by the High Court, had failed to meet this standard.[115]

The Supreme Court than turned to the substantive issues. It found that international law principles were applicable to the case, and in the interpretation of the provisions of the Constitution. Specifically, in the context of this case, the courts could refer to international law guidelines in framing relief.[116] So far, so unsurprising. But then the court came, at last, to the beating heart of the case: the question of the right to housing under the Kenyan Constitution, and its interaction with the property law regime.

Article 43 of the Kenyan Constitution guarantees to every person 'the right to accessible and adequate housing, and to reasonable standards of sanitation'.[117] As I have noted above, there is however a gap between the right to housing, and the right to *a* home, a gap articulated by the words 'progressive realisation'.[118] These words exempt the state from any compulsion to immediately ensure that 'every person' does have a home.[119]

The Supreme Court was entirely aware of this gap. Thus, it commenced its analysis by noting:

> … the right to housing in Kenya is predicated upon one's ability to 'own' land. In other words, unless one has 'title' to land under our land laws, he/she will find it almost impossible to mount a claim of a right to housing, even when faced with the grim possibility of eviction.[120]

115 For a discussion of how the issue of structural interdicts travelled through the three courts, see Martha C. Muzungu, 'Structural interdicts in Kenyan constitutional law' (2022) 1 *Kabarak Law Review* 145.

116 *Mitu-Bell Welfare Society vs The Kenya Airports Authority*, [2021] KESC 34 (KLR), para 142.

117 Article 43, Constitution of Kenya, 2010.

118 Article 21(2), Constitution of Kenya, 2010.

119 While of course progressive realisation does not exempt State policy from judicial review – to be adjudicated on the touchstone of the obligation to respect, protect, promote, and fulfil all rights, including socio-economic rights – it introduces a substantial element of judicial deference. This, it has been seen, provides windows of opportunity to a recalcitrant State to delay and put off fulfilling these obligations to an unforeseeable future. Notably, the Kenyan Constitution does anticipate the most common State objection – budgetary constraints – and tries to cage in the scope of that objection by noting that if the State does claim a lack of resources, it bears the burden of demonstrating that, and also the burden of ensuring that the resources are *prioritised* to serve the interests of the most marginalised.

120 *Mitu-Bell Welfare Society* (Supreme Court), *supra*, para 149. For a theoretical version of this argument, see G.A. Cohen, 'Freedom and Money' in *On the Currency of Egalitarian Justice, and other Essay in Political Philosophy* (G.A. Cohen and Michael Otsuka (eds.), Princeton University Press 2011) 166. The Court did not here consider the situation of *legal* tenants who might be facing eviction.

Here was a striking admission off the bat that the language of socio-economic rights could not – on its own – overcome the 'mute compulsion' of the capitalist political economy,[121] even in a transformative constitution. So, what was the court to do? It went to Article 61 of the Constitution:

> … we are of the considered opinion, that where the landless occupy public land and establish homes thereon, they acquire not title to the land, but a protectable right to housing over the same. Why, one may wonder, should the illegal occupation of public land give rise to the right to shelter, or to any right at all? The retired Constitution did not create a specific category of land known as 'public land'. Instead, the constitution recognized what is referred to as 'un-alienated government land'. The radical title to this land was vested in the president, who through the Commissioner of lands, could alienate it, almost at will. The consequences of this legal regime have been adequately recorded for posterity elsewhere. The 2010 Constitution has radically transformed land tenure in this country by declaring that all land in Kenya belongs the people of Kenya collectively as a nation, communities and individuals. It also now creates a specific category of land known as public land. Therefore, every individual as part of the collectivity of the Kenyan nation has an interest, however indescribable, however unrecognizable, or however transient, in public land.[122]

In other words, from the abstract constitutional principle that all land belongs to 'the People', the Supreme Court crafted the concrete concept of a legal *interest* in land, that existed independent of legal *title* to land.

Sand in the gears of the property law bulldozer.

And what did this interest mean in the context of the case? The court held:

> The right to housing over public land crystallizes by virtue of a long period of occupation by people who have established homes and raised families on the land. This right derives from the principle of equitable access to land under Article 60 (1) (a) of the Constitution. Faced with an eviction on grounds of public interest, such potential evictees have a right to petition the Court for protection. The protection need not necessarily be in the form of an order restraining the State agency from evicting the occupants, given the fact that, the eviction may be entirely justifiable in the public interest. But, under Article 23 (3) of the Constitution, the Court may craft orders aimed at protecting that right, such as compensation, the requirement of adequate notice before

121 Soren Mau, *Mute Compulsion: A Marxist Theory of the Economic Power of Capital* (Verso 2023).

122 *Mitu-Bell Welfare Society* (Supreme Court), *supra*, para 151 (emphasis supplied).

> eviction, the observance of humane conditions during eviction (U.N. Guidelines), the provision of alternative land for settlement, etc.[123]

In other words, the democratic principle of 'all land belongs to the People' vested in every person a legal interest in land, crystallised by possession, that placed fetters on the manner in which the state could displace or evict individuals from land.[124] Note that the central logic of property law remained undisturbed. Legal interest was less than legal title, because unlike legal title, it did not grant to individuals a right of exclusion (of all others), and therefore a presumptive *veto* against their displacement.[125] It did, however, create an intermediate legal category ('legal interest') that everyone was entitled to, and which allowed them to make certain claims on land regardless of title. Thus, as the court concluded:

> The right to housing in its base form (shelter) need not be predicated upon 'title to land'. Indeed, it is the inability of many citizens to acquire private title to land, that condemns them to the indignity of 'informal settlement'. Where the Government fails to provide accessible and adequate housing to all the people, the very least it must do, is to protect the rights and dignity of those in the informal settlements. The Courts are there to ensure that such protection is realized, otherwise these citizens, must forever, wander the corners of their country, in the grim reality of 'the wretched of the earth'.[126]

To this extent, the Supreme Court's judgment restored the High Court's holding, and brought Kenyan jurisprudence back in line with its progressive, global counterpart, as exemplified in international legal instruments, and the constitutional jurisprudence of countries such as South Africa. This, it must be noted, of course, is something short of transformation. For the reasons explained above, humanising the sharp edges of property law by making evictions more difficult to carry out does not 'question the very foundations upon which the current distribution of property rests'.[127]

123 Ibid., para 152 (emphasis supplied).

124 For a discussion on this point, see Victoria Miyandazi, 'Setting the record straight in socio-economic rights adjudication: the *Mitu-Bell Welfare Society* Supreme Court of Kenya judgment' (2022) 6(1) *Kabarak Journal of Law and Ethics* 33.

125 Subject, of course, to principles of eminent domain, which allows the state to take over private property for a set of defined purposes, and with the payment of compensation. The exact nature of the principles of eminent domain vary between jurisdictions.

126 *Mitu-Bell Welfare Society* (Supreme Court), *supra*, para 153 (emphasis supplied).

127 Van der Walt, *Property at the Margins*, *supra*, 16. See e.g., the Prevention of Illegal Eviction from and Unlawful Occupation of Land, Act 19 of 1998 [PIE], South Africa's umbrella legislation for evictions, and the discussion in Van der Walt, *Property at the Margins*, *supra*, 147–161.

However, lurking within the Court's reasoning was a germ of radical possibility. Think back to the outline of the Kenyan Constitution discussed in the previous section, and Ambreena Manji's important insight that the compromises that went into the framing of the land provisions culminated in a document in tension with itself. When the Supreme Court invoked Article 61 to say that *all* land belongs to the Kenyan people, that principle should apply regardless of whether land is 'public' or 'private' (as defined elsewhere in the Constitution). As the legal realists taught us a long time ago, there is no inherent distinction between 'public' and 'private' land. Rather, the distinction is a creation of State legislation (in particular, the property law regime).[128] Indeed, to the extent that the Court interpreted Article 61 to hold that every person had a legal *interest* in land independent of legal title, the distinction between public and private land should not matter, as *title* does not matter.

The remedies that the Supreme Court prescribed against evictions and dispossession, therefore, should apply equally to private land and to public land and, therefore, to 'squatters' on private land.[129] When we think of the histories of dispossession – in both the colonial and the post-colonial period[130] – and in particular, just how the iniquitous patterns of private land ownership that exist today came into being, this proposition probably no longer sounds as off-the-wall as it might on first blush.[131]

Of course, such a holding *would* fundamentally call into question the property law regime, as the foundation of that regime is the property owner's right to exclude all others. And that was why, having unstoppered the bottle with the genie inside, the Supreme Court immediately tried to plug it back in, noting that its holding would apply only to public land, and not to private land.[132]

128 For a sample of the scholarship, see e.g. Robert Hale, 'Force and the State: A Comparison of "Political" and "Economic" Compulsion' (1935) 35 *Columbia Law Review* 149; Morris Cohen, 'The Basis of Contract' (1933) 46 *Harvard Law Review* 553.

129 The CKRC had recommended the requirement of a court order prior to evictions, but this was dropped in the Bomas Draft.

130 It is important to note that one feature of this dispossession was the transfer of populations without consent or participation, often to lands that were fundamentally hostile to the preservation of existing social structures and ways of life. See e.g. the case of the Maasai in Koissaba, 'Elusive Justice', *supra*, discussing how the transfer of population caused disease, economic hardship, a breakdown of social structure. The issue of participation, thus, assumes central importance in a transformative constitutional context.

131 For an interesting analysis of the late-apartheid era South African case of *Kayamandi Town Commission vs Mkhwaso* (1991) 2 SA 630 (C), making broadly the same point albeit in a pre-constitutional context, see Van der Walt, 'Squatting and the Right to Shelter', *supra*, 53.

132 See also Miyandazi, 'Setting the record straight', *supra*, 53, who calls this part of the judgment 'ambiguous'.

But genies in unstoppered bottles are troublesome things. In *Mitu-Bell*, the Supreme Court had been dealing with evictions on public land. A few months later, it was forced to directly confront the issue of evictions and dispossession from *private* land.

In *William Musembi vs The Moi Educational Centre Co Ltd*, the petitioners were residents of two informal settlements within Nairobi County.[133] They claimed to have been occupying the land since 1968, at which time it had been private land. However, in 2013, they were evicted by the Moi Educational Centre, which claimed private ownership of the land. The demolitions and evictions were carried out with the assistance of state officers.

In the High Court, it was Mumbi Ngugi J – once again – who set the ball rolling, finding a violation of the petitioners' rights to dignity, security, and adequate housing, as well as a violation of the constitutional rights of children and elderly persons. Once again, it was the Court of Appeal that reversed, finding that only the rights to dignity and security had been violated, and setting aside Justice Ngugi's order of damages and compensation. The Petitioners appealed to the Supreme Court, creating a near-parallel trajectory to that of *Mitu-Bell*.

With *Mitu-Bell* in the background, the question now was whether – and to what extent – the right to housing could apply in the context of private property; and, in addition, what – if anything – the Constitution had to say, when private parties relied on state forces to carry out evictions. As the court noted:

> … we are tasked with the making of a determination on the rights of the Petitioners against those of the 1st Respondent; to determine whether the State took an active positive role in ensuring that the fundamental rights and freedoms of all the parties concerned in this instant matter were protected and that in so doing, there was no abuse of the rights of the parties and thus, that the State's negative obligation not to abuse or violate these rights and fundamental freedoms was carried out.[134]

As far as state action was concerned, *Mitu-Bell* had already answered the question. Landless people also had a 'protective right to housing' flowing from their legal interest in all land,[135] under Article 61 of the Constitution. To the extent, therefore, that the State was involved (via law enforcement) in evictions, the principles laid down in *Mitu-Bell* applied squarely to the case at hand. And those principles had been blatantly violated: the eviction

133 *William Musembi and Ors vs Moi Educational Centre Co Ltd and Ors*, [2021] KESC 50 (KLR).

134 Ibid., para 54.

135 Ibid., para 61.

had been violently conducted, no notice had been provided, and there was no Court order.[136]

So much for the state. What about the private landowner? The court held:

> … the mandate to ensure the realization and protection of social and economic rights does not extend to the 1st Respondent, a private entity. Even though the 1st Respondent has a negative obligation to ensure that it does not violate the rights of the Petitioners, it is not under any obligation to ensure that those rights are realized, either progressively or immediately.[137]

The conceptual distinction between a negative right of *non-interference* and a positive right of *realisation* structured the court's analysis when it came to the obligations of the Moi Educational Centre. Private respondents, according to the court, were bound to comply with former, but not with the latter.

The distinction between negative and positive obligations has been subjected to extensive scholarly critique, and I will not deal with here. The first thing to note, however, is that whatever the status of the distinction, there is little doubt that an *eviction* does constitute, in the classic negative sense, an 'interference' with the constitutionally guaranteed right to housing. It would therefore follow – although it was not explicitly spelt out in *William Musembi* – that the principles governing evictions, as laid out in *Mitu-Bell* in the context of public land, would apply equally to private land: that is, adequate notice and opportunity, a priority to the needs of children and the elderly, etc.

A slightly more complex question arises when we consider the rights to public participation and reasonable alternative accommodation. Public participation arguably sits at the intersection of negative and positive obligations. At the same time, however, public participation constitutes one of the 'national values and principles of governance' under Article 10 of the Kenyan Constitution. Article 10, in turn, mandates the application of these values to not just state officers, but 'all private persons whenever any of them …

[136] Ibid., para 59. There is an interesting dichotomy here between the Kenyan Supreme Court's analysis, and a landmark judgment of the Supreme Court in *Flagg Bros vs Brooks* 436 U.S. 149 (1978), where the deployment of private forces by a creditor against a debtor's property was held not to violate the Constitution's guarantee of due process. The fact that the legislation in question had delegated the enforcement of debts to private parties was found not to be relevant to the question of whether there was state involvement or not (the dissenting judgment pointed to this delegation as inescapable evidence of State involvement). What might the court's holding in *William Musembi* had been if the private landowner had deployed *private* forces to carry out the eviction?

[137] Ibid., para 64.

applies or interprets this Constitution'.[138] The moment *William Musembi* held, therefore, that Article 43 and the constitutional right to housing was *applicable* in the case of private land and private land-owners, it would follow that any eviction or dispossession was subject to the mandate of Article 10. It would follow, in turn – although *William Musembi* does not explicitly say so – that individuals cannot be evicted from private land without public participation and meaningful engagement.

What of alternative accommodation, surely a positive obligation? It is important here to draw a distinction between an obligation to *provide* alternative accommodation, and an obligation *not to carry out an eviction until alternative accommodation is available.* The former is, no doubt, a positive obligation, and therefore, according to the logic of *William Musembi*, only applicable to the state, and to public land. However, an obligation *not to evict* until alternative accommodation (provided by the state) is available remains in the domain of negative obligations. Much like the requirement of a notice, or of meaningful engagement, it is pre-condition – or a fetter – upon the exercise of the power of eviction.[139]

Indeed, as the discussion in *William Musembi* itself highlighted, evictions are rarely solely 'private actions'. Even where private land is concerned, landowners often have to act in concert with state authorities (either directly, by using the state authorities as the proverbial bulldozer, or by requiring state authorities to forbear from interfering) when it comes to the actual, physical act of demolitions, evictions, and dispossession. This, to repeat, is not new: as we have seen through the course of this chapter, skewed land ownership patterns and landlessness are, themselves, a product of state *and* private action, often working in concert. In one way or another, both *Mitu-Bell* and *Musembi* acknowledged this basic fact. That being the case, it would hardly be far-fetched to argue that where a private landowner proposes to evict landless 'squatters', it follows from the principles laid down in *Mitu-Bell* and *Musembi*, that there is a duty upon the state to provide for alternative accommodation *before* the eviction can go ahead. The state – and state power – is never uninvolved when it comes to issues of land, landlessness, and dispossession.

Could the *William Musembi* court have done more? Undoubtedly, it could. In South Africa, for example, the Constitutional Court similarly began with a distinction between the application of negative and positive socio-economic obligations upon private parties, holding that the latter were categorically

138 Article 10, Constitution of Kenya, 2010.

139 In his analysis of the *Mitu-Bell* judgment, Ian Mwiti Mathenge advances the same argument for how the constitutional principles *should* be applied to a case involving settlers on private land. See Ian Mwiti Mathenge, 'A critique of the Supreme Court's pronouncements on international law and the right to housing in Kenya in *Mitu-Bell Welfare Society*' (2022) 6(1) *Kabarak Journal of Law and Ethics* 1, 28.

excluded.[140] Very soon, however, the court resiled from this position, noting that the question of application would have to be adjudged on a case-by-case basis.[141] Indeed, in that same case, Justice Froneman, in a concurring opinion, specifically observed that the property rights regime served to entrench an existing distribution of property (think back to Atieno-Odhiambo's argument of how colonial policy served to initially create a class of the propertied, and a class of the propertyless), which – in itself – could be the source of constitutional rights violations.[142]

*Mitu-Bell* had gestured towards such an understanding as well, in its reading of Article 61: a reading that, if taken to its logical conclusion, could upend the 'traditional' sacralisation of property regimes. In *William Musembi*, the court had the opportunity to do so, but much like its predecessor judgment in *Mitu-Bell*, the court seemed to shrink from the possible consequences of its judgment. It opted – instead – for a more limited vision of the horizontal application of socio-economic rights in the context of private property regimes.[143]

The invitation, however, remains open.

## D. Conclusion: Glimmers of Transformation

Contemporary property rights are the outcomes of violence and dispossession, orchestrated by the state and executed by private individuals. This is an inescapable truth, common to the (uneven) histories of capitalism across the world; but it is in colonial and post-colonial societies that this truth is most visible, scarred into the physical landscape.

In Kenya, these scars were inflicted twice over: first, by the violent and coercive taking of land, the consequent mass evictions and landlessness, and the superimposition of a market economy upon erased, indigenous systems of community landholding. These were the decades of dispossession and commodification. And secondly, by the Independence Constitution's indifference to reparations, and the independence government's enthusiastic support – and entrenchment – of the market logic underlying property and land transactions, coupled with impunity for state land-grabbing. These were the decades of land concentration through grabbing.

140 *Governing Body of the Juma Musjid Primary School and Ors vs Essay N.O. and Ors*, 2011 (8) BCLR 761 (CC) (Constitutional Court of South Africa). See also the discussion *infra*, in Ch. 5.

141 *Daniels vs Scribante*, 2017 (8) BCLR 949 (CC) (Constitutional Court of South Africa).

142 Ibid., concurring opinion of Froneman J.

143 The court did, however, uphold the High Court's award of damages, which is crucial: all the progressive legal doctrines in the world will, ultimately, be toothless unless they are followed up with concrete enforcement.

The result was a pattern of land-holding and land-ownership, accompanied by large-scale landlessness, that was iniquitous, oppressive, and a major driver of structural inequality and lack of freedom, including – and often especially – along gendered lines. The constitutional reform movement thus placed land justice at the centre of its demands, along with the democratisation of executive power. Indeed, the two demands were complementary and inextricable.

When we think of this history, it becomes clear that if transformative constitutionalism is to mean anything, it must grapple with existing property and land distributions (including their gendered dimensions), which are constituted – and upheld – by legal property regimes. As McAuslan argues, in his study of land law regimes in East African countries, in the post-Independence period:

> Transformation then refers to changes in land law which have as their avowed and deliberate aim the righting of past social and economic injustices and the creation of a system of land law which is designed to ensure that those formerly maltreated or unfairly discriminated against by the land laws are given at the least an equal opportunity and preferably a favourable position in a new land law regime by the redistribution of rights and opportunities to enable them to better their life chances.[144]

This idea of transformation is present in the Kenyan Constitution, through its enforceable right to housing, and – crucially – through the chapter on land, which contains both programmatic (all land belongs to the People) and structural (the National Land Commission) provisions. These provisions should also be read alongside the Constitution's equality and non-discrimination clauses which guarantee substantive gender equality. However, as Ambreena Manji tells us, the Constitution – always the product of a compromise – does not do so unequivocally. Strategic ambiguities and the tensions within the constitutional text make it a terrain of contestation – contestation that is often played out in the courts.

*Mitu-Bell* and *William Musembi* were the two cases that gave the Supreme Court of Kenya a chance to think through issues of land, the political economy, and transformative constitutionalism. Both cases had their beginnings in strongly reasoned judgments by Mumbi Ngugi J at the High Court, before suffering setbacks in the Court of Appeal. In (partially) vindicating Mumbi Ngugi J's judgments, the Supreme Court charted out a path through which landless people, without legal titles to land, could nonetheless claim a certain bouquet of protections from dispossession and evictions, against both public and private parties: requirements of notice, meaningful engagement and public

144 McAuslan, *Land Law Reform in Eastern Africa*, *supra*, 11.

participation, reasonable alternative accommodation, and a prioritisation of the rights of the children and the elderly. The court also affirmed judicial capacity to enforce these protections, through structural interdicts and awards of compensation and damages.

These are important achievements, and cannot be understated. But taken alone, these do not complete the project of transformation, as they remain confined only to untangling the edges of the web of political economy that is, ultimately, responsible for land injustice.

The striking thing about *Mitu-Bell* and *William Musembi*, however, is that both judgments recognise this incompleteness. In *Mitu-Bell*'s invocation of Article 61, we see the beginnings of making the programmatic statement of 'all land to the People' meaningful in practice – a practice that would see genuine interrogation – and possible democratisation – of the existing private property regime. In *William Musembi*, we see the partial extension of this logic *to* a case involving private property, and – according to my reading of the case – an inescapable acknowledgement that evictions from private property are never truly 'private'. They must therefore be subjected to constitutional norms.

And yet, both judgments hesitate, and seek to place fetters upon the full working out of their own, transformative logic. Even as *Mitu-Bell* invokes Article 61, it creates an unpersuasive distinction between public and private land. *William Musembi* blunts the force of this distinction by applying *Mitu-Bell* standards to private land, but creates a further, unpersuasive distinction within the *types* of constitutional standards that can be applied. *Mitu-Bell* and *William Musembi* birth green shoots towards transformative constitutionalism, but in the last analysis, these still 'need more roots/more sap to grow to sunlight/ thirsting for sunlight'.[145]

But *Mitu-Bell* and *William Musembi* do not foreclose these paths – they leave them open.[146] The process of transformative constitutionalism is an ongoing one, and the accumulated burden of a hundred years of property law regimes can hardly be shaken off with one or two judgments. The reasoning in these cases, however, indicates what is possible. It opens up a space for radical transformation, and asks those who come after 'to make the path by walking'.[147]

[145] Christopher Okigbo, 'Siren Limits' in Obi Nwakanma, *Christopher Okigbo, 1930–67: Thirsting for Sunlight* (Boydell and Brewer 2010) 31.

[146] See also, Maurice Oduor, '*Mitu-Bell Welfare Society* redux: a note on the strengths and weaknesses of the Supreme Court judgment' (2022) 6(1) *Kabarak Journal of Law and Ethics* 57, arguing that *Mitu-Bell* established the 'bare minimum', and left the path open for future judgments to build on.

[147] Cf. Antonio Machado, *Border of a Dream: Selected Poems* (Copper Canyon Press 2003) 281.

# 5

# Engaging Private Power: Between the Torrent and the Trickle in *Rose Wangui Mambo*

ON THE eve of Independence, Jaramogi Oginga Odinga, Minister for Home Affairs of what was still the Kenya Colony, issued Ministry Circular No. 2. Innocuously titled 'Membership of Clubs', the circular was addressed to private and non-private clubs. It stated that:

> [The government] wishes to advise all clubs against any discriminatory constitution they might have at present. The government is of the opinion that any constitutions which bar membership solely on grounds of race, colour, or creed, is out of step with the times.[1]

It was unsurprising that Circular No. 2 was one of the first official acts of Kenya's first (broadly) popularly elected government. While colonialism has taken different forms in its journey around the world, one of its common building blocks has always been the maintenance of racial dominance through spatial segregation and exclusion. Look to the history of any anti-colonial freedom movement and you will find it recorded in stark terms, memorialised as a marker of humiliation and subjection.

Under colonialism, spatial segregation was enforced both through laws, and through the action of "private individuals," who owed their power, status, and ability to exclude to their positions within the colonial hierarchy. This is why Ministry Circular No. 2 was categorially addressed to *private* and non-private clubs. Oginga Odinga would later say that his goal was to 'outlaw the <u>social</u> colour bar'.[2] He would also wryly note that 'some [bars, hotels, and clubs] tried to wriggle by claiming that their exclusiveness was based not on colour but on interest, but we were not persuaded'.[3]

1 Circular No. 2 of 1963, 'Membership of Clubs', KNA RZ 4/44, Ministry of Home Affairs Circulars. Extracted in full in Oginga Odinga, *Not Yet Uhuru, supra*, 184. Parklands Sports Club, a private club in Nairobi, traces its history as a multi-racial club to Circular No. 2. See: https://www.parklandssportsclub.org/about-the-club/, visited on 15th September 2024.

2 Oginga Odinga, *Not Yet Uhuru, supra*, 184 (emphasis supplied).

3 Ibid.

However, in highlighting 'race, colour, or creed', Ministry Circular No. 2 was conspicuous by its own exclusion: that of gender. It took fifty years, two constitutions, and a Second Liberation before there arose a chance to remedy that.[4] In 2013, certain women members of the private Limuru County Club filed a constitutional petition challenging a club by-law that prohibited women from participating in the meetings of the Golf Committee. The Petitioners were armed with the constitutional guarantee against non-discrimination on grounds of sex, but also – crucially – with a provision of the 2010 Constitution stipulating that all constitutional rights are enforceable not simply against state action, but against private parties as well.[5]

In *Rose Wangui Mambo vs Limuru County Club*, the High Court of Kenya was called upon to decide whether – and to what extent – the 2010 Constitution is meant to intervene in the 'private sphere' and how – if at all – it is meant to engage *private* power ('horizontality'). The issue remains as relevant as it had been when Oginga Odinga had issued Ministry Circular No. 2 – perhaps even more so, given the rapid growth of various forms of private power over the last few decades. And it is an issue that is at the cutting edge of modern comparative constitutional thinking. In the last five years, the highest courts of Jamaica, South Africa, and India (to name just three) have been confronted with the question of constitutional horizontality: that is, how a constitution – and constitutional norms of equality, free speech, and others – ought to deal with private, non-state power, and with private rights.

This chapter will interrogate this question in the context of Kenyan constitutionalism. It is structured as follows. I begin with a historical overview of the public/private divide, and how State power has been the traditional focus of constitutionalism.[6] I also examine recent efforts – both in constitutional texts and in court judgments – to shift the focus from the state to other *loci* of power, and the limitations of modern constitutional practice in this regard (Section A).

I go on to analyse Article 20 of the Kenyan Constitution. I argue that – as with other parts of the Constitution, discussed previously in this book – the text of Article 20 is potentially transformative both when held up against the colonial period, as well as in comparison with the Independence Constitution, which was a classically *liberal* Constitution on the issue of walling off the private sphere from constitutional intervention (Section B).

Judicial interpretation of Article 20, however, can be divided into two strands. There is a *conservative* strand, which seeks to limit its reach into the private domain, and its ability to interrogate private arrangements of power.

4 The 'Second Liberation' refers to the struggle against the one-party state and for a new constitutional order, which we have discussed at some length through this book.

5 Article 20(1), Constitution of Kenya, 2010.

6 What I have elsewhere referred to as 'default verticality. See Gautam Bhatia, *Horizontal Rights: An Institutional Approach* (Hart 2023).

This conservative strand can be found over the years in certain judgments of the High Court. There is also, however, an opposing strand that takes seriously the question of private power and the potential of the Constitution to democratise private power. The finest exemplar of this strand is the judgment in *Rose Wangui Mambo*. In linking private discrimination to historical and ongoing structures or patterns of domination, and using that as the basis for judicial intervention, I argue that *Rose Wangui Mambo* accorded a transformative interpretation to a transformative constitutional provision (Section C).

Notwithstanding that, however, there remains a continuing hesitation by the courts to build upon the foundation of *Rose Wangui Mambo* (Section D). Thus, the potential transformative futures of horizontality under the Kenyan Constitution remain open. The judgment in *Rose Wangui Mambo* shows one possible path towards those futures (Section E).

## A. The Constitution, the State, and the Public/Private Divide

In 2005, three Kenyan bus companies brought a suit against the Attorney-General and the Minister for Transport. The companies challenged certain road transport rules and regulations which – they argued – had increased their compliance costs to the point of driving them out of business. These regulations, therefore, violated their fundamental right to property.

So far, so familiar. But as a part of their suit, the companies also arraigned their *private creditors*, arguing that any attempt by these creditors to attach company property or wind up their business would also breach their fundamental rights, given that the companies' cash flow problems had been caused by an (allegedly) illegal set of regulations.

This creative attempt to stave off private creditors did not succeed. After an initial *ex parte* stay on enforcement proceedings granted by the first instance judge, when the case came for hearing at the High Court of Kenya, the stay order was swiftly set aside. Justice Nyamu observed that:

> … fundamental rights and freedoms are contained in the Constitution and are principally available against the State because the Constitution's function is to define what constitutes Government and it regulates the relationship between the Government and the governed. On the other hand the rights of individual interests are taken care of in the province of private law and are invariably redressed as such.[7]

[7] *Kenya Bus Services Ltds and Ors vs Attorney-General and Ors*, [Misc Civil Suit No. 413 of 2005, decided on 10th June 2005 (High Court). As recently as 2018, a prominent book on Kenyan constitutional law opened with a similar definition, noting that a constitution 'define[s] the composition and powers or organs of the state and regulates the relations of various state organs to one another and to the private citizen'. See Oyaya and Poku, *The Making of the Constitution of Kenya*, *supra*, 1.

Consequently, 'creditors who are enforcing their rights under *private law*'[8] could not be injuncted from doing so in a constitutional challenge against the state.[9]

In this brief paragraph, Justice Nyamu captured an old – and enduring – intuition about constitutionalism: that a constitution is primarily – if not exclusively – a document about the structures of government, and about the relationship between the 'government and the governed'. Consequently, constitutional rights are enforceable against the state, or its instrumentalities.[10] For regulating relationships between individuals, on the other hand, one must look to private, legislated law.[11]

The origins of this intuition go back to the origins of modern constitutionalism itself, which came into being twinned with the birth of the capitalist state. The eighteenth-century US Constitution – and its Bill of Rights – was exclusively focused on structuring and constraining state power. The reason for this – according to one set of scholars – was that the rising capitalist bourgeoise class (in many ways, the drivers of the late-eighteenth-century revolutions) wanted protection *from* the depredations of an absolutist state, but also, protection *for* their economic activities to continue unimpeded.[12] Thus, the 'structure of constitutional rights was to separate the "public" and the "private" spheres and curtail State power in the public sphere while leaving untouched the "private" spheres of the market and the family.'[13] The intentional result of this, of course, was that structures, hierarchies, and inequalities of power *within* this so-called 'private sphere' were left untouched by constitutional norms.

This dominant view of constitutionalism remained the default view of constitutionalism until the end of the Second World War.[14] A few select exceptions did exist, but in the way of all exceptions, they arguably served to entrench the default. After the US Civil War and the Reconstruction, a fresh set of amendments to the US Constitution included the Thirteenth

8 Ibid.

9 The structure of the case was somewhat similar to a landmark US constitutional case from the 1970s, *Flagg Bros Inc vs Brooks*, 436 U.S. 149 (1978), and with a similar outcome.

10 There is, of course, an equally enduring debate about what constitutes the 'State'.

11 Or, in common law countries, uncodified common law as well – where it still exists!

12 See, e.g., the discussion in Dieter Grimm, *Constitutionalism: Past, Present, and Future* (Oxford University Press 2016).

13 See Bhatia, 'Horizontal Rights, Political Economy, and the Limits of Constitutional Adjudication,' *supra*.

14 But see, however, attempts to reach into the private sphere through the vehicle of socio-economic rights, beginning with the Constitution of Mexico in 1917. These initial attempts were not very successful.

Amendment, which outlawed slavery and involuntary servitude.[15] The Thirteenth Amendment was – and still is – the only provision in the US Constitution that applies horizontally, the product of a very specific set of historical circumstances.[16]

This model – of a specific, horizontal carve-out within a bill of rights that otherwise conforms to the 'structural-liberal'[17] imperatives of confining itself to the state – was also followed by the framers of the Indian Constitution. Responding to a history where rights and human dignity were frequently violated not only by the colonial state machinery, but also by non-state social formations (such as caste) built upon practices of segregation, exclusion, and violence, the Indian framers ensured that the Constitution outlawed the social practices of 'untouchability'[18] and forced labour.[19] The Constitution also prohibited discrimination in access to public accommodations (such as wells and hotels),[20] regardless of who owned them. Once again, however, the practice of limiting horizontality to specific, self-contained enclaves within the bill of rights meant that there has been very little development of horizontality as a *constitutional* principle in India.[21] Even the specific provisions have played very little role in constitutional litigation and adjudication.[22]

15 13th Amendment, Constitution of the United States.

16 Attempts to extend the logic of the 13th Amendment to other contexts – such as abortion – have remained only in the domain of academic argument. See e.g. Andrew Koppelman, 'Originalism, Abortion and the Thirteenth Amendment' (2012) 112 *Columbia Law Review* 1917.

17 Michael W. Dowdle and Michael A. Wilkinson, 'Introduction' in *Constitutionalism beyond Liberalism* (Michael W. Dowdle & Michael A. Wilkinson (eds.), Cambridge University Press 2017) 1.

18 Article 17, Constitution of India.

19 Article 23, Constitution of India.

20 Article 15(2), Constitution of India. Interestingly, a similar provision can be found in Kenya's Independence Constitution. S. 26(7) of the 1963 Constitution read as follows: 'no person shall be treated in a discriminatory manner in respect of access to shops, hotels, lodging-houses, public restaurants, eating houses, beer halls or places of public entertainment or in respect of access to places of public resort maintained wholly or partly out of public funds or dedicated to the use of the general public.' I thank the manuscript's peer reviewer for bringing this to my attention.

21 An expansive view of horizontality was recently articulated by the Indian Supreme Court in *Kaushal Kishor vs Union of India*, SLP No. 34629 of 2017, judgment dated 3rd January 2023. However, the inadequate theorising and internal incoherence in the judgment means that it is unlikely to serve as a philosophical foundation for evolving horizontality doctrine in India.

22 For a 'transformative' reading of horizontal rights under the Indian Constitution, in light of the few judgments that have been handed down, see Bhatia, *Horizontal Rights*, *supra*, Ch. 5; and Gautam Bhatia, *The Transformative Constitution* (HarperCollins 2019).

It was in the second half of the twentieth century that cracks in the edifice began to appear. The rise of the welfare state, and its subsequent retreat, forced the US courts to confront difficult questions of when actions of formally 'private' bodies could be *counted* as State action because of proximity, functional equivalence, state control, or any combination of these features.[23] Parallelly, the German Constitutional Court developed the idea of 'indirect horizontality'. Indirect horizontality stipulated that although constitutional norms were not directly applicable to private *action*, they were applicable to private *law*. Thus, where required, private law (such as, for example, the law of contract) would be reinterpreted so as to ensure that the manner in which it dealt with private action was constitutionally compliant.[24] The doctrine of indirect horizontality was based on the philosophy of the 'total constitution': i.e., that the constitution as an objective order of values that pervaded the entire legal framework, leaving no rules or norms untouched.[25]

While both these approaches continued to operate in the shadow of 'default verticality', a significant advance occurred in the 1990s, during what is broadly referred to as the 'second wave' of constitution-making in the post-colonies. The most striking example of this is the crafting of the South African Constitution. The Interim Constitution of South Africa did not have a horizontal rights provision. One of the questions considered by the South African Constitutional Court in *Du Plessis vs De Klerk*, a case that was brought under the Interim Constitution, was whether constitutional rights could apply horizontally in the absence of a specific, enabling provision.[26] While a majority of the court held that it did not, the judges also recognised that such a conclusion was problematic, especially given the legacy of racism and apartheid that the new Constitution was striving to overcome.[27] Because, as the judges recognised, apartheid was not merely constituted by the state and by laws. It was equally the product of private acts, often (but not always) under the cover of private law (such as the law of contract). And besides, what of the vast inequalities

23 Popularly known as the 'state action doctrine'. See CL Black Jr, 'The Supreme Court, 1966 Term – Foreword: "State Action", Equal Protection, and California's Proposition 14' (1967) 81 *Harvard Law Review* 71.

24 See e.g. BVerfGE 7, 198 (1958) (Lüth) (German Federal Constitutional Court) <https://law.utexas.edu/transnational/foreign-law-translations/german/case.php?id=1369>, visited on 15th September 2024. For a fuller bibliography pertaining to both state action and indirect horizontality, see Bhatia, *Horizontal Rights*, *supra*, Ch. 2–3.

25 Matthias Kumm, 'Who is Afraid of the Total Constitution? Constitutional Rights as Principles and the Constitutionalization of Private Law' (2006) 7(4) *German L J* 341, 355–356, 357.

26 *Du Plessis vs De Klerk*, 1996 (5) BCLR 658 (CC).

27 Ibid., Mahomed DP.

in private power (such as economic or social power) that had been caused by apartheid, and would persist into the future, regardless of alterations in the *legal* structure? Thus, by making the Constitution applicable only to state action, there was a risk that the new constitutional dispensation would simply 'privatise apartheid'[28] instead of overcoming it. As Madala J eloquently noted in dissent:

> The extent of the oppressive measures in South Africa was not confined to government/ individual relations but equally to individual/ individual relations. In its effort to create a new order, our Constitution must have been intended to address these oppressive and undemocratic practices at all levels ... our Constitution starts at the lowest level and attempts to reach the furthest in its endeavours to restructure the dynamics in a previously racist society.[29]

The crafters of the South African Constitution acknowledged this concern, and explicitly wrote horizontal rights into the final version of the Constitution. Section 8(2) of the Constitution was framed in language that would later be adopted by other, newer constitutions. It read:

> A provision of the Bill of Rights binds a natural or a juristic person <u>if, and to the extent that, it is applicable</u>, taking into account <u>the nature of the right</u> and <u>the nature of any duty</u> imposed by the right.[30]

The South African model of horizontality, thus, takes the form of a provision that makes the bill of rights horizontally applicable, but does so in a *qualified* way: not all rights are applicable horizontally in all circumstances, but only where the "nature of the right" makes horizontal application appropriate, and to the 'extent' that it is appropriate. The Constitution does not define applicability or appropriateness. That is left to the courts to work out, on a case-by-case basis.

If the US/Indian model is one of bounded horizontality, then the South African model goes one step further: we can call it bounded *interpretive* horizontality, where the boundaries of horizontal application are not entrenched within the Constitution, but are made the subject of constitutional contestation. It can be immediately seen, however, that the shadow of the state continues to loom. Section 8(2) is hedged in with various textual limitations ('to the extent ... applicable', 'nature of the right', 'nature of the duty'). This wording makes it clear that horizontal application remains something of an exception.

28 Ibid, para 85.

29 Ibid., Madala J, para 163.

30 Section 8(2), Constitution of South Africa, 1996 (emphasis supplied).

South African jurisprudence on Section 8(2) has confirmed this. This jurisprudence has been marked by two features: first, a refusal to lay out a coherent set of principles – or a philosophy – that will determine when a provision of the bill of rights will apply to private relationships.[31] South African cases have tended simply to paraphrase the language of Section 8(2) when adjudicating specific cases,[32] without searching for the underlying normative principle that would explain and justify this language.[33] And secondly, the courts have attempted to limit the scope of horizontality. For example, the Constitutional Court initially held that positive obligations could not apply horizontally,[34] before subsequently walking back on that position.[35] The *scope* of the obligations on private parties has, however, been consistently narrowed by the court.[36]

The qualified nature of the text of Section 8(2), therefore, has been further entrenched by a conservative – if not timid – approach by the South African Constitutional Court. What explains this? The heart of the issue appears to be an unstated concern that too liberal an application of horizontality will open the floodgates to all manner of constitutional claims upon private relationships, in a way that will be difficult to control. All private disputes will become constitutional disputes, shoehorning constitutional norms into the 'private sphere', where they do not belong, and – in the process – undermining private rights and private autonomy.

This concern is starkly reflected in the judgment of the Jamaican Court of Appeal in the famous Tomlinson Case.[37] Tomlinson's Case was a dispute between Maurice Tomlinson, a private individual, and two of the largest privately owned television stations in Jamaica. Tomlinson wanted the television stations to air a Public Service Announcement (PSA) calling for tolerance for same-sex relationships in Jamaica, and was willing to pay the market rate for it. The television stations refused, presumably out of fear of social or political backlash (same-sex relations are illegal in Jamaica, as they are in Kenya). The Jamaican Charter of Rights and Freedoms had a horizontality clause similar in material terms to Section 8(2) of the South African Constitution.

31 Meghan Finn, 'Befriending the Bogeyman: Direct Horizontal Analysis in AB v Pridwin' (2020) 137 *The South African Law Journal* 591.

32 *Khumalo vs Holomisa*, 2002 (8) BCLR 771 (CC).

33 For a recent example, see *AB vs Pridwin Preparatory School*, 2020 (9) BCLR 1029 (CC).

34 *Governing Body of the Juma Musjid Primary School vs Essay N.O.*, 2011 (8) BCLR 761 (CC).

35 *Daniels vs Scribante*, 2017 (8) BCLR 949 (CC).

36 For a more detailed analysis of the judgments, see Bhatia, *Horizontal Rights*, *supra*, Ch. 8.

37 *Maurice Tomlinson v TVJ and Ors* [2020] JMCA Civ 52.

Tomlinson invoked this provision, and argued that this fundamental right to free speech had been violated by powerful private actors, who controlled the infrastructure of communication.

Tomlinson lost his case before the Full Court,[38] and then – on appeal – at the Court of Appeal. Running through the Court of Appeal's judgment was a repeatedly expressed hesitation about 'compelling' a private party to use their property in a certain way, or to 'force' a private party to carry a certain message.[39] The Court of Appeal therefore found that the constitutional balance of rights was tilted in favour of the TV stations. Their right to use their private property as they saw fit trumped Tomlinson's right to freedom of expression, because the only way of enforcing the latter was by violating the core of the former.

Notably, what the Court of Appeal *did not* consider as relevant was the control that private television stations exercise over the means of communication, and – consequently – their disproportionate ability and power – exercised through their property rights over the infrastructure of speech – to shape who gets to effectively 'speak' in a society, and what kinds of messages are communicated. Tomlinson did attempt to raise this point, adverting to the 'commercial institutional strength' of the private television stations. This argument, however, did not carry the day with the Court of Appeal.

Should it have? Let us recall that the goal of horizontal rights – as recognised by the judges in *Du Plessis vs De Klerk* – is to subject private power to constitutional norms. Restricting constitutional rights to the state essentially implies the *conservation* of private hierarchies and structures of power.[40] These private hierarchies are never purely 'private': they are often long-standing and enduring, the result of a historical combination of social or class power and state abstention (or even facilitation).

For example – to return to Ministry Circular No. 2 – the ability of a private club to discriminate is the result of historical *legal* exclusion (clubs being the preserve only of white settlers) and active state policy, that then translates into present-day *economic and social* power, even after 'formal' legal barriers have been removed. A constitutional philosophy of horizontal rights that is to be truly transformative must therefore take such complexities into account. Thus, in Tomlinson's Case, the institutional power enjoyed by private television stations – their legal control over the infrastructure of speech through their property rights, and thus the ability to shape social and cultural norms by gatekeeping access to that infrastructure – should, at least, have informed the Court of Appeal's judgment.

38 The Supreme Court sitting as a Full Court, and in this case, the court of first instance.

39 *Maurice Tomlinson v TVJ and Ors* [2020] JMCA Civ 52, para 158.

40 Subject, of course, to legislative intervention.

However, as we have seen, Tomlinson's Case is just one striking illustration of how, when it comes to comparative constitutional jurisprudence, an ambivalent text, matched by ambivalent decisions, has – so far – failed to realise the transformative potential of horizontality. With this in mind, let us now turn to the Kenyan Constitution.

## B. Horizontality in the Text of the Kenyan Constitution

We have seen, above, two models of constitutional horizontality: bounded and interpretive. A perusal of the 2010 Constitution of Kenya reveals one instance of bounded horizontality. Article 45(3) – whose inspiration can be traced back to the Convention on the Elimination of all Forms of Discrimination Against Women (CEDAW) – states:

> (3) Parties to a marriage are entitled to equal rights at the time of the marriage, during the marriage and at the dissolution of the marriage.[41]

As a social institution, the family has always been the site of some of the most unequal power relations in our society, especially between men and women. It has also been the social institution where constitutional intervention has been most strongly resisted.[42] Consequently, it is hugely significant that the Kenyan Constitution mandates equality within the marital relationship, and equally significant that it does so both during the marriage, *and* upon dissolution. It is well-documented that the economic consequences of *exiting* a marriage are what often force women to *stay* in a marriage, even when it is violent or abusive.

While Article 45(3) flickers with transformative possibilities, its implementation has arguably hit something of a roadblock, after a judicial declaration that the provision *did not* require a default equal distribution of marital assets upon dissolution of the marriage.[43] We shall consider this issue in greater detail in Section D of this chapter.

41 Article 45(3), Constitution of Kenya, 2010.

42 One of the most contentious issues around the framing of the 2010 Constitution was the inclusion of 'kadhi courts', which would apply Islamic personal law to Muslims, and the scope and extent of their jurisdiction. This controversy has continued well into the career of the 2010 Constitution, most recently with the Court of Appeal's decision on the inheritance rights of Muslim children born out of wedlock, delivered in November 2023.

43 *Federation of Women Lawyers v Attorney-General*, Petition No 164B of 2016, decided on 14th May 2018 (High Court). See the discussion in Victoria Miyandazi, *Equality in Kenya's 2010 Constitution* (Hart 2021) 42.

Bounded horizontality is also visible in Article 27, which is the Constitution's non-discrimination provision. After setting out the protected grounds on the bases of which the state may not discriminate against any person under Article 27(4), Article 27(5) adds that 'a person shall not discriminate directly or indirectly against another person on any of the grounds specified or contemplated in clause (4).'[44] This is a remarkable advance, as one of liberal constitutionalism's shibboleths has always been that *private* discrimination is a matter of individual choice and autonomy (at best, subject to regulation through civil rights legislation in some limited and particularly egregious cases), and that it is only *state* discrimination that raises constitutional issues.

As our discussion of Oginga Odinga's Ministry Circular No. 2 showed, however, 'private' discrimination is invariably entrenched within – and has the function of entrenching – patterns of structural domination and exclusion, both past and present, especially in a colonial context. Article 27(5) now provides a constitutional arsenal to address this issue. Of course, its exact scope must, in due course, be interpreted by courts. To use an obvious but helpful example, one would not wish to apply the non-discrimination guarantee to intimate relationships. In the next section, when considering the *Rose Wangui Mambo* case, we will consider how Article 27(5) might be interpreted in a transformative manner.

Beyond Articles 45 and 27, however, it is in Article 20 that the soul of Kenyan constitutional horizontality lies. Article 20(1) states:

> The Bill of Rights applies to all law and binds all State organs and <u>all persons</u>.[45]

Remarkably, and unlike the South African model, Article 20(1) does not hedge in horizontality with qualifications about the nature of the rights and obligations, or the appropriateness of horizontal application. In fact, the bare text of Article 20(1) does not have any qualifications at all. In the same sentence, the Bill of Rights is made applicable, without caveat and without distinction, to state organs *and all persons*.[46]

Unlike bounded or interpretive horizontality, then, Article 20(1) is a model of *unbounded* horizontality. The text appears to suggest that all rights will presumptively apply horizontally, except where the context otherwise requires (for example, the right to vote cannot ordinarily be enforced against a private party).

44 Article 27(5), Constitution of Kenya, 2010.

45 Article 20(1), Constitution of Kenya, 2010 (emphasis supplied).

46 The origins of the text can be found in the CKRC Final Report, which recommended – without qualification – that the Bill of Rights in the new Constitution be '[horizontal] … i.e., apply not just to people in the Government but between people.' *CKRC Final Report, supra*, 126.

The Kenyan Constitution's starting point on transformative constitutionalism and the possibility of constitutional intervention into the 'private sphere' is, therefore, much further down the road than many other constitutions. It is also transformative both with respect to the colonial period, of course (as evidenced by Oginga Odinga's Ministry Circular No. 2), and with respect to the Independence Constitution of 1963, which hewed to the classic liberal constitutionalism that clearly demarcates the public/private divide, and is shaped by default verticality.[47] Thus, as Migai Akech notes, horizontality under the Kenyan Constitution 'debunks the orthodox view in constitutional law, which is that a constitution imposes direct constitutional duties only on government and not on private actors.'[48]

With that in mind, the terrain now shifts to the courts. As we have already seen in our discussion of Article 27(5), the bill of rights cannot be directly transplanted from the context of the state to that of private relationships. Differences do exist, and transformative constitutionalism requires a judicial approach that respects those differences, while also crafting a theory of horizontality that will allow constitutional norms to effectively interrogate institutions and structures of private power and domination. Indeed, the abstract language of Article 20 – as observed by Christina Murray – does give courts considerable leeway in crafting a specifically Kenyan approach to horizontality.[49]

Let us, therefore, turn to how the courts *have* interpreted horizontality under the 2010 Constitution.

47 And, for that reason, was widely accused of helping preserve colonial economic and social hierarchies and power relations.

48 Akech, 'Institutional Reform in the New Constitution of Kenya,' *supra* (emphasis supplied).

49 Murray, 'Kenya's 2010 Constitution', *supra*, 747. Indeed, Brian Sang YK goes a little further, arguing that Article 20(2) – which states that 'every person shall enjoy the rights and fundamental freedoms in the Bill of Rights to the greatest extent consistent with the nature of the right or fundamental freedom' – effectively replicates South Africa's Section 8(2) in substance, and is a textual indicator towards horizontal application being subordinated to vertical application under the Constitution; in essence, a reversion to classic default verticality. See Y.K.B Sang, 'Horizontal Application of Constitutional Rights in Kenya' (2018) 26 *African Journal of International and Comparative Law* 1, 7. See also, Walter Khobe Ochieng, 'The Horizontal Application of the Bill of Rights and the Development of the Law to give effect to Rights and Fundamental Freedoms' (2014) 1(1) *Kabarak Journal of Law and Ethics* 77, 84, for a variant of the argument that Article 20(2) places interpretive limits on Article 20(1). I do not agree: Article 20(2) is not equivalent to Section 8(2), and the phrase 'to the greatest extent possible' does not suggest a limitation upon rights, unlike Section 8(2).

## A Garden of Forking Paths

Article 20(1) of the Constitution of Kenya is a wellspring of transformative potential. Fearing a torrent, however, some of the early judgments of the Kenyan courts have attempted to plug the source – only to risk turning it into an ineffectual trickle.

The tone was set by the judgment of the High Court in *Mwangi Stephen Mureithi vs Hon. Daniel Toroitich Arap Moi.*[50] *Mureithi vs Moi* is a fascinating case because in every way, it straddled the moment of constitutional transformation. The case was filed in 2009 (pre-Constitution), and decided in 2011 (post-Constitution). It sought accountability for acts committed during the era of the one-party state, while on the cusp of the inauguration of a new constitutional order. And it raised a horizontal rights claim under the old, 'retired' Constitution – a claim that had already been repudiated in *Kenya Bus Service Ltd* – even as horizontality was explicitly recognised under the *new* Constitution.

Mwangi Stephen Mureithi was a onetime business partner of ex-President Moi. They had joint holdings in several companies and properties. Mureithi claimed that in 1982, then-President Moi abused his presidential powers in order to have him illegally detained. While Mureithi was in detention, President Moi sold his interests in the companies and properties, caused him tremendous financial loss, and never recompensed him. Now, twenty-seven years later, perhaps infected by the spirit of transformation that was in the air, Mureithi came to court and claimed his long-overdue compensation. He founded his case on a breach of his right to personal liberty, and of the takings/property clause under the old Constitution. The ex-President was arraigned as a Respondent in his personal capacity.

The ex-President naturally resisted the claim, arguing that it was well settled that fundamental rights were only applicable against the state, and not against individuals. Under *Kenya Bus Service Ltd* this was indeed well settled; but then, the constitutional order that birthed *Kenya Bus Service Ltd* was in its dying embers. The pendency of the case saw the formal replacement of the Independence Constitution with the 2010 Constitution. And the judgment's own caption would read: '*In the Matter of: Section 72, 75, and 84(1) of the Constitution of Kenya (Repealed)*'.[51]

The transformative moment is reflected in the judgment of the court.[52] The court began by noting that:

[50] Petition No. 625 of 2009, decided on 6th April 2011 (High Court).

[51] Ibid (emphasis supplied).

[52] There is perhaps some irony in the fact that a few months later, the judge who authored the judgment was declared 'unfit to serve', as part of Kenya's vetting process for judges under the new constitutional order. However, the afterlife of this judgment

> The rigid position that the human rights applies vertically is being overtaken by the emerging trends in the development of human rights law and litigation. We can no longer afford to bury our heads in the sand, for we must appreciate the reality, which is that private individuals and bodies such as clubs and companies wield great power over the individual citizenry, who should as of necessity be protected from such non-State bodies who may for instance discriminate unfairly, or cause other Constitutional breaches.[53]

The transformation of the constitutional order thus saw a transformation in fields of vision. What mattered now was no longer the formal character of the rights-violator (individual or state), but the *nature of the power* they wielded. In a moment of lyricism, the court explicitly located this approach within the new transformative order, calling it a 'new dawn', where rather than 'who the duty holder is … what matters is who should enjoy the rights as enshrined in the Constitution'.[54]

But this origin story was marked by ambivalence, a sign of a court already stuck between the torrent and the trickle. Immediately after engaging in a power-focused analysis, the court signalled a retreat, as if wary of the transformative potential of what it might have unleashed. 'Horizontal application does not and should not cut across the board',[55] the court warned, before retreating still further into the shadow of the old order, by noting that 'horizontal application would not apply as a rule but it would be an exception.'[56] In the case before it, the court found that ex-President Moi was indeed liable to pay compensation; but the ambivalence that accompanied the birth of horizontality in Kenya was to continue colouring its evolution in the years to come.[57]

---

was a vindication of sorts: after it was set aside by the Court of Appeal, in a landmark judgment delivered in 2023, the Supreme Court partially restored the High Court's judgment, including orders for compensation, not executable against the estate of the deceased ex-President Moi.

53 Petition No. 625 of 2009, *supra*. For another decision affirming this position, also in a case filed at the moment of transition (just a few months after the enactment of the 2010 Constitution), see *Satrose Ayuma and Ors vs The Registered Trustees of the Kenya Railways Staff Retirement Benefits Scheme*, [2013] KEHC 6003 (KLR).

54 Petition No. 625 of 2009, *supra*.

55 Ibid.

56 Ibid (emphasis supplied).

57 See, for example, the observations in *Law Society of Kenya vs Betty Sungurua Nyabuto and Ors*, Petition 21 of 2010, decided on 20th January 2012 (High Court), as a classic example: 'The Bill of Rights applies to all persons and binds everybody. However, the nature and extent of a particular right may be limited in scope to apply to the state and not a private individual.'

For example, in yet another case involving a president – this time the then-future President Uhuru Muigai Kenyatta – the High Court rejected his attempts to frame a defamation case against the *Nairobi Star* as a violation of his constitutional rights, and told him to seek his remedies under the law of defamation.[58] But soon after, newspapers were back in the dock, this time defending claims that they had violated certain minors' constitutional right to privacy. In *Jemimah Wambui Ikere vs Standard Group Ltd and Anr*, the High Court reasoned that constitutional claims could not become *substitutes* for private action. In other words, according to the Court, where a remedy under private law already existed, constitutional rights would not apply horizontally.[59] However, having said that, the High Court in *Jemimah Wambui Ikere* did allow the constitutional claim, referring once again to the increasing power of private actors in modern society.[60] This is interesting, as there *do* exist private remedies in case of a breach of privacy, under tort law – albeit of relatively recent vintage, and not yet fully developed in Kenya.[61] The same rationale, however, has appeared in other judgments of the High Court: in specifically acknowledging, for example, that Article 20(1) marks a 'radical departure' from the old constitutional order, but *also* that its application is confined to situations where there is no efficacious alternative remedy available under private law.[62]

Judgments on horizontality under the new constitutional order, therefore, are marked by an interesting internal tension: a recognition that Article 20(1) is transformative in nature, co-existing uneasily with a concern that

[58] *Uhuru Muigai Kenyatta vs Nairobi Star Publications Ltd.,* Petition No. 187 of 2012, decided on 5th April, 2013 (High Court). Notably, indirect horizontality in the United States was born with a defamation case, the famous *New York Times vs Sullivan*, 376 U.S. 254 (1964).

[59] Petition No. 466 of 2012, decided on 18th December 2013 (High Court). This proposition was subsequently reiterated by Lenaola J – who had also adjudicated this case – in *Mike Rubia and Anr vs Dr Moses Mwangi and Ors*, Petition No. 70 of 2012, decided on 26th August 2014 (High Court). The court applied this doctrine in *Stephen Saitoti Kapaiku vs Cocacola Sabco Nairobi Bottlers Ltd*, Petition No. 338 of 2012, decided on 21st June 2013 (High Court), where a claim based on compensation for impurities in soda bottles was held to be misconceived as a constitutional claim, as there was a pre-existing remedy in tort.

[60] Petition No. 466 of 2012, *supra*, para 21.

[61] For a similar analysis in a similar case involving privacy, also decided by Justice Lenaola, see *C.O.M. vs The Standard Group Ltd and Anr*, Petition 192 of 2011, decided on 5th April 2013 (High Court).

[62] *Duncan Muriuki Kaguru v Baobab Beach Resort and Spa Ltd*, Petition No 223 of 2012, decided on 12th June, 2013 (High Court). See also *Abdalla Rhova Hiribae and Ors vs the Attorney General and Ors*, Civil Case No. 14 of 2010, decided on 4th February 2013 (High Court).

transformation might get out of control: between the torrent and the trickle. Thus, in somewhat picturesque terms, the High Court in *Isaac Ngugi vs The Nairobi Hospital and Others* – a case that concerned an individual who was detained by a hospital on the ground of non-payment of bills – compared horizontality to 'a gifted but neglected child with huge potential that is seeking to be released'[63] – just after contributing towards entrenching that very characterisation by limiting horizontality to cases where there existed inadequate enforcement mechanisms for the implementation of a fundamental right![64]

In his analysis of horizontality under the 2010 Constitution, therefore, Brian Sang YK sums it up perfectly when he calls it a 'concept in search of content'.[65] On the one hand, the courts have recognised that Article 20(1) is an integral part of the Constitution's transformative project and a 'radical departure' from the structural liberalism of the Independence Constitution.[66] The courts have also recognised that, at its heart, horizontality is about interrogating power, as it is exercised through structures and institutions in the 'private sphere'. On the other hand, they have sought to give horizontality shape and contours through outlining a set of limitations – primarily, the existence of alternative, efficacious remedies. What is left to be done, however, is the articulation of a *philosophy* of horizontality that knits these diverse strands together, and weaves in Article 20(1) into the transformative web of the 2010 Constitution.

Enter *Rose Wambui Mambo*.

In *Rose Wambui Mambo and Others vs Limuru County Club and Ors*, the constitutional question was stark in its simplicity: 'whether and to what extent … [a court] has jurisdiction to address alleged violations of fundamental rights and freedoms arising from dealings between the private club and its membership.'[67] The Limuru County Club – a private golf club – through a resolution passed by its Board of Directors, amended the club's by-laws to provide that 'the golf committee being a male only affair, only full male members with valid handicaps, and who are fully paid up, will be allowed to participate in the meeting and that lady golfers will attend the meeting as guests.'[68] When the

63 *Isaac Ngugi v The Nairobi Hospital*, Petition No 407 of 2012, decided on 30th September 2013 (High Court), para 24.

64 Ibid. para 23. It was finally held that fundamental rights did apply to this case. In a similar case before the same judge – where the issue was a hotel detaining an individual for non-payment of bills – a similar outcome was reached, albeit without extensive reasoning. See *Sonia Kwamboka Rasugu vs Sandalwood Hotel and Resort Ltd and Anr*, Petition No. 156 of 2011, decided on 26th July 2013 (High Court).

65 Sang, 'Horizontal Application of Constitutional Rights in Kenya', *supra*, 13.

66 For an argument linking transformative constitutionalism with interrogating private power, see Ochieng, 'The Horizontal Application of the Bill of Rights', *supra*.

67 *Rose Wangui Mambo and Ors vs Limuru County Club and Ors, supra*, para 1.

68 Ibid., para 8.

Petitioners – all women golfers, and office-bearers at the club – objected, they were swiftly suspended and removed from positions of authority.

The Petitioners came to court. They argued that their effective disenfranchisement from participation in the affairs of the Golf Committee violated not only the Articles of Association of the club, but also their right to equality and non-discrimination under Article 27 of the Constitution.[69] In this, they were supported by the Attorney-General, who argued that 'chauvinistic' action by private clubs was not immune from constitutional scrutiny.[70] The Respondents, on the other hand – a diverse set that included the club's directors, the Kenya Golf Union, as well as the Kenya Ladies Golf Union – contended, *inter alia*, that this was a 'private issue',[71] and that the court should refrain from interfering in the 'age-old practices in the game of golf and its committees'.[72]

The case came to court on the back of four years of jurisprudence under Article 20(1) of the Constitution, marked – as we have discussed – by a certain ambivalence.[73] This ambivalence was perhaps best summed up in the observations in Isaac Ngugi's Case, which the court referred to in the build-up to its analysis: that, given the transformative nature of the Kenyan Constitution, the court 'would be hesitant to adopt a hard and fast position that would prevent the principles and values of the Constitution being infused into the lives of ordinary Kenyans through application of the Bill of Rights to private relationships where necessary.'[74] In other words, transformation hedged in by a double negative and a requirement of 'necessity'.

Where, then, would it be 'necessary' for the court to infuse the principles and values of the Constitution into the lives of ordinary Kenyans, and into private relationships? In response, the court began by citing a recent Advisory Opinion of the Supreme Court, which had dealt with the issue of the representation of women in elective bodies. In that case, the Supreme Court had taken account of

> … the distinct social imperfection which led to the adoption of Articles 27(8) and 81(b) of the Constitution: that in elective or other public bodies, the participation of women has, for decades, been held at bare nominal levels, on account of discriminatory practices, or gender-indifferent laws, policies and regulations. This presents itself as a

69 Article 27, Constitution of Kenya, 2010.

70 *Rose Wangui Mambo, supra*, para 24.

71 Ibid., para 29.

72 Ibid., para 30.

73 Interestingly, *Rose Wangui Mambo* was decided by a three-judge bench of the High Court. Two of the judges on the bench – Lenaola J and Ngugi J – had, between them, authored most of the horizontal rights judgments that had come before.

74 *Rose Wangui Mambo, supra*, para 64.

> manifestation of historically unequal power relations between men and women in Kenyan society.[75]

It is important to pay close attention to the language of the court. Discrimination was a function not merely of unequal laws, but was constituted by – and constitutive of – the private domain: social 'imperfection', discriminatory *practices* (as opposed to laws, policies, and regulations), and – most crucially – historically unequal 'power relations'. In other words, power relations were mediated through a set of social practices or institutions. It was this unequal *social* power that allowed some to discriminate against, and exclude, others. It was for this reason that the court – in its Advisory Opinion – had used the phrase 'the socialisation of patriarchy'.[76]

The High Court correctly noted that this reasoning was equally applicable to the private sphere.[77] And, having held that horizontal constitutional norms of equality and non-discrimination *were* applicable to the Limuru County Club, it was straightforward enough for the court to then find that the impugned by-law was 'patently discriminatory'.[78] Interestingly, the court also went on to find that the club had violated the Petitioners' constitutional rights to freedom of expression, and a fair administrative procedure (in this case, a fair disciplinary process). Thus, it wasn't simply the right to non-discrimination that the court held to be horizontally applicable – where Article 27(4) specifically provided so – but other constitutional rights as well.

In *Rose Wangui Mambo*, the High Court articulated a transformative vision of horizontality under the Kenyan Constitution. I have, elsewhere, called this the 'institutional approach to horizontality'.[79] The institutional approach draws upon the insight that a bill of rights is, ultimately, about power, and about mitigating or democratising unequal power relations. For a while now, the most visible – and centralised – locus of power in our societies has been the State. That is why constitutional imagination has often been constrained by the State when thinking about bills of rights. Horizontality seeks to liberate constitutionalism from the shackles of the state, through a set of principles that inform us when constitutional rights ought to apply to private relationships, and how to identify those private relationships. The institutional approach does so by arguing that horizontality ought to apply where there exists an

75 Advisory Opinion No. 1 of 2012, Supreme Court of Kenya (emphasis supplied).

76 Ibid., para 47. The court also noted that the 'socialisation of patriarchy' meant that structural inequality in one sphere (in this case, membership in representative bodies) spilled over into inequality in *other* spheres. This is directly relevant for the argument of this chapter.

77 *Rose Wangui Mambo*, *supra*, para 91.

78 Ibid., para 104.

79 Bhatia, *Horizontal Rights*, *supra*.

institution (social, cultural, economic, etc.) – that is, a set of structures, practices, or patterns of behaviour; and, furthermore, where unequal power relations that enable rights violations flow from hierarchies or inequalities created or sanctioned by the said institution.

The institutional approach complements transformative constitutionalism. Both approaches are informed by the fact that historically (as well as in the present), power, violence, inequality, and injustice have invariably been mediated by and through institutions that exist in the 'private sphere': institutions of race, of patriarchy, of property, of the labour market, and so on. And both approaches seek to 'transform' the *status quo* by reaching into the 'private sphere', and bringing constitutional norms and principles to bear upon 'private' relations of power. To put it another way, the institutional approach provides a principle that transformative constitutionalism can use in its quest to democratise the private sphere.

The institutional approach also places limits upon horizontality – limits that the Kenyan courts have been concerned about since the inception of the 2010 Constitution – in order to ensure that there is no uncontrollable 'torrent' of constitutional claims that washes away the existing structure of private law. For the reasons explained above, under the institutional approach, not every exercise of private power is subject to horizontality, but only those where the exercise of power – and the violation of rights – can be traced back to an institutional relationship of inequality or subordination.

And it is here, perhaps, that the High Court in *Rose Wangui Mambo* could have gone a little further. In response to the Limuru County Club's argument that it was in the nature of private clubs to 'discriminate', the court simply reiterated that private parties could not claim immunity from constitutional rights and went on to draw a not entirely convincing distinction between discrimination in terms of *membership* of a club, and discrimination with respect to elective positions *within* the club.[80] But this does leave the question open about how this doctrine might apply to other cases, which are intuitively outside the scope of horizontal application (intimate relationships? home dinners? book clubs?). While the Court did say that there would have to be a 'balancing' of rights, it did not indicate how this balancing might be done.

It is here that a social history of clubs as *institutions* – and their role in both reflecting and entrenching broader social hierarchies – would have helped add principled ballast to the court's opinion.[81] During colonialism, it was private clubs that reinforced spatial segregation and the colour bar. Membership of such clubs has been a historical (and continuing) marker of status. Clubs

80 *Rose Wangui Mambo*, *supra*, 113.

81 See e.g. Dominique Connan, 'Race for Distinction: A Social History of Private Members' Clubs in Colonial Kenya' (PhD Thesis, The European University Institute 2015).

remain spaces where transactions are carried out, deals struck, and professional relationships reaffirmed. Exclusion, thus, is not simply exclusion from an association of like-minded individuals meeting within a private space, but a wider marker of social discrimination, one that is embedded within – and helps strengthen – discrimination in broader society. In the words of the Supreme Court in its gender representation advisory opinion, this is an example of the 'socialisation of patriarchy' where discrimination within one sphere has 'a major negative impact on the social terrain as a whole'.[82] Thus – and to go back to the beginning of this chapter – it was not for nothing that Jaramogi Oginga Odinga saw the de-racialisation of clubs (and other similar spaces) as a primary order of business for the nascent Kenyan democracy.[83]

That analysis – had it been done – might have squared the circle. Even without it, however, the judgment in *Rose Wangui Mambo* laid the foundations for a principled account of horizontality, as an integral feature of the transformative Kenyan Constitution. And it offered an invitation for future courts to build upon this foundation. Time will tell if this invitation is taken up.

## D. The Roads Not (Yet) Taken

Fifteen years on, horizontality under the Kenyan Constitution remains something of a chrysalis, waiting to emerge. While opportunities have been presented to the courts for further evolution of the doctrine, they have not yet been taken up. Most recently, for example, in *Busia Sugar Industry vs Agriculture and Food Authority*, the High Court at Busia did indeed hold that the existence of an alternate remedy in private law could not *defeat* a horizontal rights claim – perhaps the first instance of a categorical judicial rejection the

82 Advisory Opinion No. 1 of 2012, Supreme Court of Kenya, *supra*, para 47.

83 There are some striking similarities with an Indian Supreme Court judgment from 2018, which considered a ban on menstruating-age women from accessing a temple in South India. The Supreme Court found this to be unconstitutional discrimination; in one of the concurring judgments – delivered by Chandrachud J – there was a suggestion of how access to temples wasn't simply about accessing a *private* space, but a marker of equal moral membership of society; exclusion from temples – on the basis of assumptions relating to purity and pollution – was thus embedded within – and constitutive of – broader *social* discrimination. For this reason, the Constitution – and constitutional norms of equality and non-discrimination – were applicable to the issue. While temples are, of course, very different spaces from clubs, the underlying logic remains the same: it is about understanding private action *in the context of* the structures and institutions within which it is located, and to understand how inequalities in the private sphere are shaped by – and shape – those institutions.

At the time of writing, the temple entry judgment is under review by the Supreme Court, and its future is unclear. See *Indian Young Lawyers Association vs State of Kerala*, (2019) 11 SCC 1. See also Bhatia, *The Transformative Constitution*, *supra*, Ch. 5.

position taken in previous High Court judgments discussed above.[84] However, the court restricted its analysis to whether the specific claim at issue – that of legitimate expectation – could be deployed horizontally, and held that it could not.[85] Questions around the principle on the basis of which certain rights could be applied horizontally – and others could not – were therefore left unanswered.

To take another example, in 2023, the Court of Appeal heard a fascinating case at the intersection of horizontality, consumer rights, class discrimination, and the Constitution. The issue revolved around the fact that there was a disparity in nutritional information provided on *glass* Coca-Cola Bottles *vis-à-vis plastic* Coca-Cola Bottles. For the latter – aimed at a more upper-class demographic – more detailed nutritional information, including storage directions and customer service numbers, were provided.[86]

The Court of Appeal upheld the High Court's judgment that had found that this disparity violated the Constitution. At issue were both the Constitution's non-discrimination guarantee (discussed above), as well as Article 46(1), which provides that 'consumers have the right to goods and services of reasonable quality [and] … to the information necessary for them to gain full benefit from goods and services.'[87] While a significant part of the Court of Appeal's judgment dealt with the interplay between Article 46(1) and the Consumer Protection Act,[88] the Court of Appeal also found that there had been discrimination on grounds of purchasing power – that is, class.

While identifying class as a prohibited ground of discrimination, analogous to the listed grounds under Article 27, is a notable development in its own right with transformative possibilities,[89] there is also the issue that this was a

[84] *Busia Sugar Industry Limited v Agriculture and Food Authority & 2 others* [2024] KEHC 1099.

[85] See Gautam Bhatia, 'Addressing Boundary and Transplant Issues in Horizontality: The Judgment of the Kenyan High Court in *Busia Sugar Industry vs Agriculture and Food Authority*' (26th February 2024) *Indian Constitutional Law and Philosophy Blog*, available at <https://indconlawphil.wordpress.com/2024/02/26/addressing-boundary-and-transplant-issues-in-horizontality-the-judgment-of-the-kenyan-high-court-in-busia-sugar-industry-vs-agriculture-and-food-authority/>, visited on 15th September 2024.

[86] See *Nairobi Bottlers Ltd. vs Mark Ndumia Ndung'u*, Civil Appeal No. 99 of 2018, decided on 7th July 2023 (Court of Appeal).

[87] Article 46(1), Constitution of Kenya, 2010.

[88] For an analysis, see Gautam Bhatia, 'Consumer Rights, Discrimination, and the Constitution: The Kenyan Court of Appeals Judgment' (8th July 2023) *The Indian Constitutional Law and Philosophy Blog*, available at <https://indconlawphil.wordpress.com/2023/07/08/consumer-rights-discrimination-and-the-constitution-the-kenyan-court-of-appeals-judgment/>, visited on 15th September 2024.

[89] Given how few constitutions recognise class as a ground of discrimination, expressly or through judicial interpretation.

dispute between private parties. The court's finding of discrimination is thus a finding of horizontality; and what is crucial to note is that this was a case where an alternative remedy *was* available and deployed by the court (that is, statutory remedies under the Consumer Protection Act). The court nonetheless found the non-discriminatory guarantee to be engaged, thus making it clear that the existence of an alternative remedy will not, *ipso facto*, preclude the application of horizontal rights.

Beyond that, however, the court did not explain why – and how – it was applying the anti-discrimination guarantee. This is something of a missed opportunity. The relationship between corporations and consumers – *especially* when it comes to issues such as health and safety – is at the heart of the modern, capitalist political economy. A corporation taking advantage of asymmetric information and power to discriminate against economically vulnerable consumers, in particular, provides fertile ground for the institutional approach. Thus, once the court *had* found that discrimination on grounds of class was constitutionally prohibited, it would have been even more interesting to explain how and when that principle would be applied to *private* discrimination, within the institution of the capitalist market. That analysis remains to be done.[90]

Other than the anti-discrimination provisions, another potential reservoir of transformative horizontality, as noted above, can be found in Article 45 of the Kenyan Constitution. Article 45 is about the 'family'. Recall that Article 45(3), in particular, adopts the bounded horizontality model of the US and Indian Constitutions. It states:

> Parties to a marriage are entitled to equal rights at the time of the marriage, during the marriage and at the dissolution of the marriage.[91]

As Victoria Miyandazi explains, Article 45(3) represents a conscious – if limited – departure from the patriarchal structures and institutions that characterised pre-colonial, colonial, and post-colonial society.[92] Specifically, it was to address 'harmful practices such as … unequal claims to matrimonial property upon divorce'.[93] Early on, the Kenyan courts attempted to accord

[90] For a similar issue, see *Charles Muturi Macharia and Ors vs The Standard Group and Ors*, Petition 13 (E015) of 202 decided on 8th September 2023 (Supreme Court), where the Supreme Court granted damages for the violation of constitutional privacy rights of minor children by private media companies, but did not examine the basis on which it was applying rights horizontally – or even acknowledge that it *was* applying rights horizontally.

[91] Article 45(3), Constitution of Kenya.

[92] Miyandazi, *Equality in Kenya's 2010 Constitution*, *supra*.

[93] Ibid., 42. In its Final Report, the CKRC noted the suggestions emanating from women's groups, namely, that 'value be put on women's work as family care providers

transformative effect to Article 45(3) by holding that, in the absence of a statutory framework, 'equal rights … at the dissolution of marriage' applied directly to marriages, and required a default rule of equal division of marital property upon separation.[94]

The rationale for this is firmly embedded within the institutional approach to horizontality. While the literature on this is detailed and complex,[95] to sum up: the institution of the family – and that of marriage – is gendered in character. One of its defining features is the entrenchment of economic inequality that flows from gendered division of labour into (remunerated) work outside the home, and (unremunerated) domestic work. This inequality often creates a situation where marital property is often formally owned only by the male spouse. This, in turn, bleeds into the stage of the dissolution of the marriage/separation, where it becomes necessary to divide assets.[96] Inequality during separation inevitably tracks back into the nature of the relationship itself, as the very real possibility of economic precarity upon separation (that is, the non-feasibility of exit) affects inequality and exploitation *within* the marriage. Mandating a default rule of equal division – subject, of course, to exceptions based on the particularities of individual cases – is thus an attempt to mitigate this private, institutionally structured inequality.

Soon after, however, with the passage of the Matrimonial Property Act of 2013, the High Court walked back on this position. It held that the law's requirement that courts take into account non-compensated labour (such as domestic work, care work, and emotional labour) during the division of assets at the time of separation was a sufficient safeguard against gendered inequality within marriage.[97] In doing so, however, the court failed to recognise that the equal division rule – as an interpretation of Article 45's horizontal application – was not a rigid commandment, but a *default* position that reflected structural inequalities within marriage. To repeat Sang's characterisation, therefore, Article 45(3) – with all its transformative language of equal rights *within* marriage and the family – remains a 'concept in search of content'.[98]

---

and national builders through formal and informal work', and that 'women should be entitled to their children and property <u>within</u> and outside the marriage.' *CKRC Final Report*, *supra*, 108–109 (emphasis supplied).

94 *Agnes Nanjala William v Jacob Petrus Nicholas Vandergoes*, MSA CA Civil Appeal No 127 of 2011 (UR) (Court of Appeal). This is known as 'community of property' in various jurisdictions.

95 For a longer account of the argument, see Bhatia, *Horizontal Rights*, *supra*, Ch. 7.

96 A problem noted by the CKRC in its Final Report, when considering the application of the extant law, the 1882 Married Women's Property Act, and its intersection with the Constitution. *CKRC Final Report*, *supra*, 280.

97 *Federation of Women Lawyers v Attorney-General*, *supra*.

98 We shall consider a recent judgment – *Ogentoto vs Ogentoto* – that deals with this issue, in the concluding chapter.

## E. Conclusion: Transformative Possibilities

The transformative character of the Kenyan Constitution exists along many dimensions. One crucial dimension – without which the transformative project will remain incomplete – is addressing private structures and hierarchies of power, which were either ignored or (and this often comes to the same thing) sustained and entrenched by previous constitutional orders.

The 2010 Constitution does this in two ways: first, through bounded horizontality provisions, which – for example – explicitly require the anti-discrimination guarantee to be applied to private parties, or explicitly mandate equality within, during, and after a marriage; and secondly, through an unbounded horizontality provision of potentially radical scope. This makes the Bill of Rights applicable *generally* to private relationships, and leaves it to the courts to evolve a philosophy of when – and how – this is to be done.

While the courts' initial approach towards horizontality and private relationships was marked by a degree of ambivalence – stuck between a torrent and a trickle – it is in *Rose Wangui Mambo* that the High Court articulated the beginnings of a transformative approach to horizontality. This approach asks whether private relationships are embedded within historical (or continuing) patterns or *institutions* of inequality, domination, and subordination – especially those that the 2010 Constitution was meant to transform. Is one private party's ability to violate the rights of another a function of their relative, unequal positions within these entrenched and enduring social or economic institutions? Would an application of constitutional rights have the effect of dismantling – or democratising – private institutional power? And, on the other hand, would judicial and constitutional abnegation lead to preserving – or even entrenching – those structures of power? If the answers to each of these questions is 'yes', then the Constitution must be applied to the private relationship at issue. If the answer is 'no', then the parties must look to private law for their remedies.

The potential of the approach in *Rose Wangui Mambo* is immense. We have seen how it could apply to the exercise of private commercial power within the marketplace, or unequal power relations within the marriage and the family. And its purchase is not constrained by national or jurisdictional borders. As we have also seen, through examples such as *Tomlinson*, tackling private relations of power is not limited to contemporary Kenyan constitutional law, but is one of the most urgent issues confronting constitutions – and constitutional courts – worldwide. As the years go by, and private institutional power (especially in the economy) only increases, these issues will become even more urgent. The reasoning in *Rose Wangui Mambo* offers a blueprint – both to Kenyan courts, and courts elsewhere – for how to apply transformative constitutionalism to the private sphere.

With his Ministry Circular No. 2, Jaramogi Oginga Odinga was perhaps on the right track all along.

6

# The Burden of Politics: The 2022 Presidential Election Petition

*The terrible curse about the past is that it starts right now.*[1]

WHEN, IN August 2022, the Supreme Court convened to hear the case of *Raila Odinga and Others vs William Ruto and Others*, the stakes could not have been higher. The 2022 presidential election had finished in a near-dead heat. According to the declared results, William Ruto had edged out Raila Odinga by 50.49% to 48.85%. The elections had been marked by familiar accusations of irregularities, ballot-stuffing, vote-rigging, errors in transmission of results from the polling booths, and – somewhat novel – electoral interference by some mysterious 'Venezuelans' who had apparently been in charge of the software for the voting machines.[2] More spectacularly, when the Chairperson of the Independent Electoral and Boundaries Commission (IEBC), Wafula Chebukati, wanted to declare the results, he found himself facing a rebellion from four of his own fellow-commissioners, who dissociated themselves from the process and held a press conference denouncing him.[3] Chebukati went ahead and declared the results anyway – more grist for the mill of those who believed that William Ruto's electoral victory was irredeemably tainted.

Whichever way the Supreme Court ruled – and under the 2010 Constitution it had to rule, one way or another – it was bound to upset, even enrage, a very large number of people. Not that the Supreme Court was any stranger to

1 Binyavanga Wainaina, *One Day I Will Write About This Place: A Memoir* (Graywolf Press 2012) 59.

2 See e.g. Ian Omondi, 'Masit: Only Chebukati Was Aware of 3 Venezuelans Coming to Kenya with Election Materials' *Citizen Digital* (27th August 2022), available at <https://www.citizen.digital/news/masit-only-chebukati-was-aware-of-3-venezuelans-coming-to-kenya-with-election-materials-n304611>, visited on 15th September 2024.

3 Sharon Mwende, 'Four "rebel" commissioners fault Chebukati for suspending polls' *The Star* (19th August 2022), available at <https://www.the-star.co.ke/news/2022-08-19-four-rebel-commissioners-fault-chebukati-for-suspending-polls/>, visited on 15th September 2024.

such a situation. This was the fourth successive presidential election, after the coming into force of the 2010 Constitution, where the court was being asked to adjudicate a disputed result. Some of the actors were familiar as well. Raila Odinga had been the losing candidate on three of those four occasion – in 2013, 2017,[4] and now in 2022. Wafula Chebukati's conduct (and character) was being arraigned for a third time, after the two elections of 2017. Five of the seven judges who sat in 2022 had been on the bench in 2017, and three of them were survivors from 2013.

In 2013, the Supreme Court had upheld the election of presidential candidate Uhuru Kenyatta, in a decision that had met with widespread criticism.[5] In 2017, the court had set aside the re-election of then-President Kenyatta, finding the election process irredeemably compromised – a decision that had attracted both public praise as well as fierce political backlash.[6] Its subsequent affirmation of the repeat 2017 presidential election had also been met with a mixed reception. And so, at the fourth time of asking, there was little doubt that Supreme Court's power under the Constitution to adjudicate presidential elections was not a power that existed only in name. The Supreme Court *could* – and indeed, *had* – set aside a presidential election, if it so chose.

Not that that made the court's task any easier. We are used to thinking of courts as referees, ensuring that State organs act within the boundaries that the law and the Constitution creates for them. This is a challenging task at the best of times, but it becomes particularly challenging when courts are asked to referee the electoral process. Here, the courts are called upon to maintain a delicate balance. On the one hand, democratic legitimacy flows from elections and electoral outcomes. An unaddressed violation – or a distortion – of the ground rules of the democratic game can have serious downstream impact upon political and institutional legitimacy. In adjudicating these cases, then, a court cannot be too abstentionist, lest it lend judicial credibility to evidently flawed processes.[7]

4 In 2017, after successfully challenging the presidential election, Raila Odinga withdrew from the rerun; the results of the second election were, nonetheless, challenged by other parties.

5 For a summary of the criticism, see Carl Bevelhymer, 'Transformative Constitutionalism and the Adjudication of Elections in Kenya' *FIU Electronic Theses and Dissertations* (2021) 121, available at <https://digitalcommons.fiu.edu/cgi/viewcontent.cgi?article=6105&context=etd>, visited on 15th September 2024.

6 Ibid., 123.

7 See the discussion in Walter Khobe Ochieng, 'Protecting the Integrity of the Electoral Process: The Promise of the *Maina Kiai* Judgement' (2018) 3 *Kabarak Journal of Law and Ethics* 1, making this argument both generally, and in the context of the 2010 Constitution.

On the other hand, over-intervention carries its own risks. Apart from the simple fact that elections at scale are bound to have a certain degree of procedural irregularities, and the setting aside of elections carries serious administrative and other public costs, a court that is seen to be actively *deciding* electoral outcomes is a court that is ripe for political capture.[8] This is specifically true of courts in transitional contexts, or in contexts with a relatively recent history of authoritarianism.[9] In adjudicating high-stakes political contexts, then, courts have to be particularly aware of the institutional context within which they operate, and strive to craft a set of widely acceptable 'neutral principles'[10] for deciding such cases, which nonetheless have enough bite so as to enable judicial invalidation of flawed elections where it is merited. The idea is to decrease the scope of personal discretion,[11] and thereby lessen the prospect that the courts can, in the future, be used as swords against electoral opponents. This, in turn, can provide courts with a measure of insulation against authoritarian takeover.

In this chapter, I shall examine how the Supreme Court of Kenya navigated these challenging issues in the Presidential Election Petition of 2022. I shall begin by considering the history of conflict around Kenyan presidential elections,[12] a history driven by the structure and design of the Independence

8 H. Kwasi Prempeh, 'Comparative Perspectives on Kenya's Post-2013 Election Dispute Resolution Process and Emerging Jurisprudence' in *Balancing the Scales of Electoral Justice: Resolving Disputes from the 2013 Elections in Kenya and the Emerging Jurisprudence* (Collins Odote and Linda Musumba (eds.), International Development Law Organisation 2016) 149, 154.

9 See e.g. the discussions in *Rule By Law: The Politics of Courts in Authoritarian Regimes* (Tom Ginsburg and Tamir Moustafa (eds.), Cambridge University Press 2012), especially the Introduction.

10 The phrase 'neutral principles' comes from Herbert Wechsler, 'Toward Neutral Principles of Constitutional Law' (1959) 73(1) *Harvard Law Review* 1. The quest for 'neutrality' in constitutional law has been critiqued as a chimera at best, and as a mark for upholding *status quo* at worst. That critique is well-taken, and it should be noted that election law is not necessarily immune from these effects of 'neutrality'.

11 For a similar argument applying Wechsler's formulation to the resolution of electoral disputes by the judiciary, see Elisha Zebedee Ongoya, 'Protecting the integrity of the Electoral Process, or, Obfuscating the Electoral Process?' (2018) 3 *Kabarak Journal of Law and Ethics* 11, 13.

12 For a detailed account, see The Independent Review Commission, *Report of the Independent Review Commission on the General Elections held in Kenya on 27th December 2007* [the Kriegler Report], available at <http://kenyalaw.org/kl/fileadmin/CommissionReports/Report-of-the-Independent-Review-Commission-on-the-General-Elections-held-in-Kenya-on-27th-December-2007.pdf>, visited on 15th September 2024. The Kriegler Report was one of the triggers for kick-starting the moribund constitution-making process after the failure of the 2005 referendum.

Constitution. This context is important to understand the 2010 Constitution's attempt to constitutionalise the conduct of disputes over the presidential elections, and to create a pathway towards the resolution of such disputes (Section A). I will then examine the decisions of the Supreme Court in the presidential election challenges of 2013 and 2017 (twice), in order to set the stage for 2022. I will argue that while the court had established its own political legitimacy in deciding such disputes, it was yet to firmly entrench a set of judicial *standards* for deciding presidential election petitions (Section B). The importance of the 2022 Presidential Election Petition lies in how the court did arrive at such standards: in particular, on questions regarding the burden of proof and the standard of proof. What is also important is the 2022 judgment's emphasis on transparency – including transparency in adjudication. This had the effect of opening up the court's own reasoning, and the manner in which it applied these standards, for assessment and critique (Section C). The court's judgment, I will therefore suggest, provides us with an interesting blueprint for how to contain political violence through judicial resolution (Section D).

It may be questioned why the subject of this chapter is the 2022 decision (where the court took the arguably 'easier' step of upholding the election and ratifying the swearing-in of the declared winner) instead of the (first) 2017 decision, where the court took the much more 'difficult' decision of invalidating the election. There are two reasons for this. First, while the importance of the 2017 judgment for the rule of law cannot be underestimated, I focus here on 2022, as that judgment – in my opinion – provides the clearest example of how the Constitution's transformative goal of resolving political conflicts through *constitutionalisation* could work in practice.

Secondly – and perhaps ironically – a court's long-term public credibility as an independent constitutional authority is dependent more on how it reasons when it *upholds* a presidential election, rather than when it invalidates one. It is inevitable that the court's decision, in such a case, will open it up to allegations of timidity, impotence, or capture. But these allegations will have greater bite if the judgment is hasty, or sloppily reasoned. An accretion of such judgments, over time, can lead to a loss of public confidence in the court as a fair and impartial adjudicator of the highest-stakes political disputes, and therefore, an erosion of the constitutional path towards the resolution of such disputes. It is for these reasons, I believe, that the 2022 judgment merits intensive scrutiny, in the context of the overall argument of this book.

## A. The Executive Presidency and Political Conflict

In the previous chapters of this book, we have discussed how, in the first decade of the Independence Constitution, through a set of hyper-amendments, what began as a parliamentary and federal constitutional order was converted into a unitary and presidential system. The concentration of power in the office – and indeed, the person – of the President had deleterious consequences for the separation of powers, the rule of law, and the protection of civil and political rights. However, it also had another consequence: political violence around elections. As Murunga notes, once the Constitution had been 'changed from a document for democratic governance into an instrument of highly concentrated and authoritarian executive power',[13] the structural incentives for election-rigging – and, consequently, conflict – were extremely high (after the *de jure* conversion of Kenya to a one-party state, these conflicts moved to *within* KANU, during the selection of parliamentary candidates).[14]

Moreover, as Kramon and Posner note, even after the return of formal multipartyism with the 1992 elections, 'the centralization of national power in the office of the president'[15] had created a situation where the presidential election, in particular, turned into a winner-takes-all contest, making 'victory at the polls a do-or-die matter'.[16] 'Half the country will feel cut off, whoever wins', the writer Binyavanga Wainaina observed wryly.[17] This structural feature was identified as one of the key driving forces of the post-poll violence in 2007. The nature of the violence was exacerbated by the fact that presidents were seen to be – and often campaigned as – patrons of their respective ethnic communities (or, alternatively, the ethnic coalition that coalesced around them). A presidential election was not simply about gaining political power, but about ethnically mediated distribution of resources and opportunities.[18]

Consequently, the imperative to dismantle the Imperial Presidency in the run-up to the drafting of the Constitution was not merely about stemming the executive abuse of power, but also mitigating the zero-sum character of presidential election contests, in order to avoid more political violence.[19] While that was one side of the coin, the eventual retention of the presidential system in the 2010 Constitution (albeit with more circumscribed powers) made it urgent for the Constitution to have a specific and prescribed method of resolving disputed Presidential elections – especially after the bitter lessons of 2007.

The Constitution's chosen method was the Supreme Court. Article 140(1) stipulates that 'a person may file a petition in the Supreme Court to challenge the election of the President-elect within seven days after the date of the

13 Murunga, Okello, and Sjogren, 'Towards a New Constitutional Order in Kenya: Introduction', *supra*, 1, 3.

14 See Hornsby, *Kenya: A History Since Independence*, *supra*, Ch. 8.

15 Kramon and Posner, 'Kenya's New Constitution', *supra*, 96.

16 Ibid.

17 Wainaina, *One Day I Will Write About This Place*, *supra*, 243.

18 Hornsby, *Kenya: A History Since Independence*, *supra*, Ch. 4. See also Michela Wrong, *It's Our Turn To Eat: The Story of a Kenyan Whistle-Blower* (Harper Perennial 2010).

19 Kramon and Posner, 'Kenya's New Constitution', *supra*.

declaration of the results of the presidential election.'[20] Not only, then, does the Supreme Court bear the burden of adjudicating presidential election disputes, but it bears the *sole* burden of doing so. Article 163(3(a) – which deals with the Supreme Court – is careful to state that the court shall have *exclusive original* jurisdiction to hear and determine disputes relating to the elections to the Office of President arising under Article 140.[21] The Supreme Court is thus the first and final tribunal when it comes to deciding presidential election disputes.

And if this was not enough of a burden, judicial responsibility can neither be delayed nor denied. Article 140(2) states that 'within fourteen days after the filing of a petition under clause (1), the Supreme Court shall hear and determine the petition and its decision shall be final.'[22] In one stroke, Article 140(2) denies to the Supreme Court a range of tools that judiciaries often use to take the sting out of politically fraught situations. The first is delay, or deferral: courts around the world often elect to strategically delay hearing a case if the political climate is too hot at the time, putting off adjudication to a later day, when the situation is calmer, and the court's judgment is unlikely to have an inflammatory effect.[23]

In the case of elections, this strategy is particularly controversial as the issue is so time-sensitive. Nonetheless, courts have held off on ruling on election disputes until even after the elected individual's term of office is complete (making the dispute infructuous).[24] Alternatively – as in the case of the challenge to the Nigerian presidential election in 2023 – they have delayed so long that the incumbent has become entrenched enough in office to be effectively impossible to dislodge, even if the Court were to rule against them. In such situations, judicial decisions affirm a *fait accompli*.[25]

The scheme of Article 140 consciously denies this way out to the Supreme Court. It also precludes the court from deploying other well-worn judicial techniques of 'deciding by not deciding' by invoking rules of legal standing, requiring litigants to approach other forums, or citing procedural technicalities. Article 140 envisions that within fourteen days, the court *will* decide either in favour of ratifying the election or setting it aside: that is, one of the two

20 Article 140(1), Constitution of Kenya, 2010.

21 Article 163(3)(a), Constitution of Kenya, 2010.

22 Article 140(2), Constitution of Kenya, 2010.

23 The Indian Supreme Court is a particularly accomplished master of this game. See e.g. Gautam Bhatia 'Judicial Evasion, Judicial Vagueness, and Judicial Revisionism: A Study of the NCT of Delhi vs Union of India Judgment(s)' in *Constitutional Resilience in South Asia* (Swati Jhaveri, Tarunabh Khaitan and Dinesha Samararatne (eds.), Hart 2023).

24 The Indian judiciary has been frequently known to do this as well.

25 *Peter Gregory Obi and Ors vs Independent National Electoral Commission and Ors*, Petition No. CA/PEPC/03/2023 (Supreme Court of Nigeria).

major presidential candidates will lose, and another will win. The Constitution, thus, places extraordinary faith in the Supreme Court – and an extraordinary burden upon it.

This is not accidental. As John Osogo Ambani notes, one of the pathologies of the old constitutional regime was courts delaying 'in determining election petitions unduly and there [was] a history of some petitions being determined close to the succeeding general elections – at the near close of the contested candidate's term in office'.[26] The specific mandate of Article 140, therefore, needs to be understood in this historical context. As Wangai, Mwangi, and Kilonzo sum up, 'the judicialisation of politics [that is an inevitable effect of Article 140] is not pejorative but rather part of the transformative enterprise engendered in the Constitution.'[27]

## B. 2013 and 2017

The weight of history hung heavy upon the 2013 presidential election petition judgment. That the court was keenly aware of this weight was evident. As it began its analysis, it noted that 'this is the first landmark case bearing on the early steps to consolidate and set in motion the gains of a progressive and unique Constitution.'[28] After all, this was the first election after the violence following the disputed 2007 presidential polls – violence that had been unprecedented in its scope and scale. Apart from everything else, the 2010 Constitution was a response to what had happened in 2007, and the expression of a commitment that such a thing would not be allowed to happen again. It was, therefore, particularly significant that in the first election after the birth of the 2010 Constitution, the very path that it had prescribed for the peaceful resolution of disputed presidential elections was going to be tested; and tested at the instance of Raila Odinga, who had also been at the receiving end in 2007, but had elected not to challenge the result because of a lack of trust in the courts at the time.

26 Ambani, 'The Ghai in our Constitution', *supra*, 173, 183. See also Hon. Justice David Majanja, 'Judiciary's Quest for a Speedy and Just Electoral Dispute Resolution Mechanism: Lessons from Kenya's 2013 Elections' in *Balancing the Scales of Electoral Justice*, *supra*, 19, 20–21. Note, however, that this history of delay did not include presidential election petitions, which, before the 2010 Constitution, never even reached the merits stage.

27 Mukami Wangai, Linus Mwangi, and Josephat Kilonzo, 'Developing Jurisprudence beyond the Horizon: A Critique of the Supreme Court of Kenya Decision in Raila Amolo Odinga and Anr v IEBC and Ors (2017) (2020) 5(1) *Kabarak Journal of Law and Ethics* 69, 77.

28 *Raila Odinga and Ors vs Independent Electoral and Boundaries Commission and Ors*, [2013] KESC 6 (KLR), para 177.

Beyond that, there were other institutions that were put to the test. The Independent Electoral and Boundaries Commission (IEBC) – a child of the 2010 Constitution – was conducting its first presidential election, and its competence and probity were at stake. And then there was the Supreme Court itself: at the apex of a reformed judiciary, an institution that – in the very recent past – was frequently, and justly, accused of being a conveyor belt for transmitting the decisions of the executive.[29] The court was aware of what this moment meant for itself, when it noted that 'it is clear that this Judgment, just as it is important to all Kenyans in political terms, is no less important to the court itself, in terms of the evolution of jurisprudence in the domain of public affairs.'[30] Indeed, perhaps the court was *too* aware of this: later on in the judgment, it repeated the point in even stronger language:

> In this inaugural Supreme Court which is barely two years old, and which is at the centre of the governance processes established under the Constitution of Kenya, 2010, it is the first time the Judges are called upon to declare their perception of their role in a fundamentally political-cum-constitutional process.[31]

How then did the court address itself to the dispute before it? There were three broad contentions raised against the integrity of the election, which had returned Uhuru Kenyatta as the winner, just 8,400 votes above the constitutional threshold of '50%+1' of the votes. *First*, it was argued that there were numerous discrepancies in the IEBC's voting register, and subsequently, in the vote tallying and counting, across the country; *secondly*, that the electronic transmission systems having failed midway, the IEBC had impermissibly resorted to manual transmission of results; and *thirdly*, that if one counted spoiled or invalid ballots among the total number of votes cast, Uhuru Kenyatta had failed to make the '50%+1' threshold.

The challenge, thus, raised disputed issues of both fact and law. So, before the court could begin to analyse the allegations in their specificity, it had to lay out the contours of how it would approach the issues.

The first question that the court had to address was *what*, precisely, a petition challenging an election had to prove. As Berihun Gebeye points out, in his survey of the adjudication of presidential disputes across Africa, courts have split on this question. According to one school of thought, it must be proven *either* that there were material irregularities in the election process, which affected its integrity, *or* that the irregularities (whether material or not) had a demonstrable effect on the outcome ('the disjunctive test'). According to

29 See e.g. Mwangi, *The Black Bar*, *supra*, Ch. 8.

30 *Raila Odinga vs IEBC* (2013), *supra*, para 177.

31 Ibid., para 226.

the other school of thought, however, it must be proven *both* that there were material irregularities, *and* that these irregularities had a demonstrable effect on the outcome: that is, *but for* those irregularities, the winning candidate would not have won ('the conjunctive test').[32] The Supreme Court cited cases that stood for both propositions, and then – without any detailed reasoning – recorded its agreement with the Nigerian position, that is, the conjunctive test: a petitioner would have to show both the existence of material irregularities, *and* that these irregularities affected the validity of the elections.[33]

The next question was *how* these allegations had to be proven. The court was faced with two standards of proof. One was the standard applicable in civil law, which required a claimant to discharge their legal burden of proof on 'the balance of probabilities'. The other was the standard in criminal law, which required 'proof beyond reasonable doubt'. The court adopted what appeared to be an 'intermediate' standard between the two: that is, 'the threshold of proof should, in principle, be above the balance of probability, though not as high as beyond-reasonable-doubt.'[34]

When we place these three propositions together, first, that the petitioner challenging an election bears the burden of proof, secondly, that the petitioner must demonstrate both material irregularities, *and* impact upon the election results, and, thirdly, that these must be proven to a standard beyond the balance of probabilities, it is evident – as Harrington and Manji point out in their critique of the judgment – that it would be almost impossible for a challenge to an election to succeed.[35] And, equally, it would spare the court from too deep or too fine-grained an enquiry into the process by which the election was conducted, and the role played by bodies such as the IEBC. Thus, for example, even though the court found that 'there were many irregularities in the data and information-capture during the registration process',[36] it had not

[32] Berihum Gebeye, 'Judicial Review and Presidential Elections in Africa' in *Judicial Review and Electoral Law in a Global Perspective* (Cristina Fasone, Edmondo Mostacci, and Graziella Romeo (eds.), Hart 2024).

[33] *Raila Odinga vs IEBC* (2013), *supra*, para 196.

[34] Ibid., *supra*, para 203. As Wachira Maina notes, this approach is doubtful, as it involved substituting the word "or" in the Election Act – which set out this test – with the word "and." Wachira Maina, 'Verdict on Kenya's presidential election petition: Five reasons the judgment fails the legal test' *The East African* (20th April 2013), available at <https://www.theeastafrican.co.ke/tea/oped/comment/verdict-on-kenya-s-presidential-election-petition-five-reasons-the-judgment-fails-the-legal-test--1315998>, visited on 15th September 2024.

[35] John Harrington and Ambreena Manji, 'Restoring Leviathan? The Kenyan Supreme Court, constitutional transformation, and the presidential election of 2013' (2015) 9(2) *Journal of East African Studies* 175. For a similar point, see Prempeh, 'Comparative Perspectives on Kenya's Post-2013 Election Dispute Resolution Process', *supra*.

[36] *Raila Odinga vs IEBC* (2013), *supra*, para 256.

been shown that there were *substantial enough* to have affected the credibility of the election process. Indeed, if there is one thing that stands out in the judgment, it is the court's reluctance to grapple with the substance of the allegations, beyond a quick once-over.[37] The legal standards that the court articulated allowed it to accomplish that.

What explains the court's approach in the 2013 presidential election petition? Stacey and Miyandazi argue that the reasons were political. The judiciary – as an institution – still did not enjoy widespread public confidence. Memories of its authoritarian past were still too fresh. On the other hand, the freshly minted IEBC – an institution established under the new Constitution, and whose independence was guaranteed by that Constitution – did enjoy public trust.[38] Consequently, in 2013, the court's institutional credibility was lower than the IEBC's, thus making it difficult for the former to – essentially – sit in judgment over the latter. This explains the court's adoption of a set of deferential legal standards that, ultimately, did not seriously disturb the manner in which the IEBC conducted the presidential election.[39]

Harrington and Manji argue, on the other hand, that the court's judgment reflects a conservative *jurisprudence*, hearkening back to the pre-2010 regime. They point to the court's justification for its ruling on the burden of proof – namely, the presumption that acts conducted by public bodies have been conducted correctly, and in good faith.[40] They also flag the court's repeated focus on the need to avoid 'precipitating a crisis in the operations of the Executive Branch',[41] to argue that the 2013 judgment was a continuation of the old 'law and order' approach to constitutionalism that had characterised the pre-Constitution judiciary.[42] In essence, thus, the judgment failed to properly come to grips with what a transformative constitution required of the court in adjudicating disputed presidential elections.

37 'Sixty per cent of the judgment, by length, is a leisurely rehash of the facts and arguments made by the parties in court. Everything else is given short shrift: Seven paragraphs are spent on reviewing and resolving the issue of the failed technology; another nine paragraphs dispose of the IEBC's discretion to do manual tallies; 11 paragraphs are dedicated to the voters register and, astonishingly for a court given to brevity, 27 paragraphs are set aside to explain why rejected votes must not count in computing presidential percentages." Maina, 'Verdict on Kenya's presidential election petition', *supra*.

38 Richard Stacey and Victoria Miyandazi, 'Constituting and Regulating Democracy: Kenya's Election Commission and the Courts in the 2010s' (2021) 16 *Asian Journal of Comparative Law* 193.

39 Ibid.

40 Harrington and Manji, 'Restoring Leviathan?', *supra*.

41 *Raila Odinga vs IEBC* (2013), *supra*, para 216.

42 Harrington and Manji, 'Restoring Leviathan?', *supra*.

While both accounts are explanatorily persuasive, here, I want to flag another – complementary – impulse that drove the 2013 judgment. Towards the very end of the judgment, the court observed that 'as a basic principle, it should not be for the court to determine who comes to occupy the presidential office.'[43] I suggest that this is the key to understanding the unarticulated major premise of the judgment. The approach adopted by the court makes sense if we consider that it was particularly anxious not to be seen 'tipping' the outcome of the election in one direction or another. But the more the court got into the *substantive* analysis of the factual contentions before it, the more it sifted through evidence for probative value, the more its judgment would – necessarily – look like 'taking a side'. The surest way to avoid such a situation would be to adopt a set of legal standards that would make factual analysis relatively unnecessary, and a judicial approach that was deferential to the decisions of the specialised electoral institution (in this case, the IEBC).

The reason for this – as noted above – is that a court seen to be deeply embedded in *deciding* presidential contests would be a very tempting prize for political capture. This was a particularly urgent concern in 2013, with the Supreme Court having been in existence for only two years. Indeed, the court's emphasis on the 'political' nature of the dispute, as well as its emphasis on the articulation of its own role in such 'political/constitutional disputes', reflects this view.[44]

The problem with the 2013 judgment, however – as its critics pointed out – was that in trying to accomplish this institution-preserving approach, it went too far, reducing its own role to that of a near-passive spectator. The 2010 Constitution's pathway towards resolving disputed presidential elections risked turning into a sham if the only possible adjudicatory outcome was the ratification of the election results.[45]

Furthermore, not only were the standards that the court adopted too deferential, the *manner* in which it came to those standards was problematic in

43 *Raila Odinga vs IEBC* (2013), *supra*, para 299.

44 For a similar reading of the judgment, see Francis Ang'ila Aywa, 'A Critique of the Raila Odinga vs IEBC Decision in Light of the Legal Standards for Presidential Elections in Kenya' in *Balancing the Scales of Electoral Justice*, *supra*, 46, 55.

45 This appeared with particular clarity in election disputes decided in the aftermath of the 2013 judgment, where the Supreme Court rebuffed the Court of Appeal's attempts to craft a less onerous set of standards in challenging electoral processes. See *Gatirau Peter Munya vs Dickson Mwenda Kithinji and Ors*, [2014] KESC 38 (KLR) and *Zacharia Okoth Obado vs Edward Akong'o Oyugi and Ors*, [2014] KESC 22 (KLR). See also, some of the discussions in *New Constitution Same Old Challenges: Reflections on Kenya's 2013 General Elections* (Fred Otieno (ed.), Nairobi/Uraia Trust 2015). See also Muthomi Thiankolu, 'Standards of Review and Resolution of Electoral Disputes in Kenya: A Review of the Jurisdiction of the High Court, the Court of Appeal, and the Supreme Court' in *Balancing the Scales of Electoral Justice*, *supra*, 114.

another way. The court relied upon Section 83 of the Elections Act – which, in turn, incorporated principles of English common law – to articulate its conjunctive test. The correctness of the court's interpretation of Section 83 aside, as Evelyn and Wanyoike point out, the Section itself refers to compliance with the principles laid down *in the Constitution*.[46] In other words, a court faced with an electoral dispute was bound to look at what the Constitution had to say about the norms and standards conducting of elections, and to ask whether the election complied with those standards. In particular, those standards had to be interpreted in light of Kenyan constitutional history, where electoral reform was a big part of what spurred the constitution-making process that finally culminated in the 2010 Constitution.[47]

What the Supreme Court *did do*, however, was the exact opposite. Instead of making the Constitution its normative touchstone, it made Section 83 – read in light of common law and comparative electoral law – its touchstone; rather than ensuring the legal framework was *levelled up* to comply with the Constitution's demands, the Constitution was *levelled down* to meet with the court's autonomous reading of Section 83. This is, of course, the exact opposite of the historically informed transformative reading of the Constitution that we have discussed in this book. It is also why Evelyn and Wanyoike argue that, in essence, the Supreme Court got its analysis back to front.[48]

So the stage was set for a sharp turn, and that is precisely what happened in 2017, when – for a second time – a presidential election was challenged before the Supreme Court; and, for a second time, it was Raila Odinga against President Kenyatta. This time, the result was different.[49]

The most important contributing factor to the outcome was the court's decision to replace the conjunctive test with the disjunctive one, on a plain reading of Section 83 of the Elections Act.[50] This textual reading was also consistent with the constitutional understanding that an election was a *process*

46 Heidi Evelyn and Waikwa Wanyoike, 'A New Dawn Postponed: The Constitutional Threshold for Valid Elections in Kenya and Section 83 of the Elections Act' in *Balancing the Scales of Electoral Justice*, *supra*, 78, 86.

47 Ibid., 93.

48 Ibid., 100.

49 *Raila Odinga and Anr vs Independent Electoral and Boundaries Commission and Ors*, [2017] KESC 42 (KLR).

50 The Court, however, minimised the impact of this departure by performing something of a judicial sleight of hand, noting that the 2013 judgment 'did not render an authoritative interpretation of section 83', but only made a 'tangential reference' to it. Ibid., para 187. For a critique of the 'casual' and 'cavalier' way in which the majority judgment shifted the legal standard from 2013, see Wangai et al., 'Developing Jurisprudence beyond the Horizon', *supra*, 96.

of articulating the will of the people,[51] whose integrity at each stage had to be guaranteed. Thus, it was sufficient for the petitioner to show *either* material irregularities in the conduct of the election, *or* that the election result had been affected by whatever irregularities there were.[52] As the court noted:

> Having analyzed the wording of section 83 of the Elections Act, bearing in mind its legislative history in Kenya and genesis from the Ballot Act and also in light of the need to keep in tune with Kenya's transformative Constitution, it is clear to us that the correct interpretation of the Section is one that ensures that elections are a true reflection of the will of the Kenyan people. Such an election must be one that meets the constitutional standards. An election such as the one at hand, has to be one that is both quantitatively and qualitatively in accordance with the Constitution. It is one where the winner of the presidential contest obtains more than half of all the votes cast in the election; and at least twenty- five per cent of the votes cast in each of more than half of the counties as stipulated in article 138(4) of the Constitution. In addition, the election which gives rise to this result must be held in accordance with the principles of a free and fair elections, which are by secret ballot; free from intimidation; improper influence, or corruption; and administered by an independent body in an impartial, neutral, efficient, accurate and accountable manner as stipulated in article 81.[53]

Therefore, the correct test had to take into account that:

> … no conduct of any election can be perfect. We will also go a step further and add that even though the word substantially is not in our section, we would infer it in the words if it appears in that section. That expression in our view requires that, before vitiating it, the court should, looking at the conduct of the whole election, be satisfied

[51] As the court noted: 'elections are not events, but processes.' *Raila Odinga and Anr vs Independent Electoral and Boundaries Commission and Ors, supra*, para 224.

[52] Interestingly, in the aftermath of the 2013 Judgment, while he was the Presiding Judge of the Court of Appeal at Kisumu – but writing in an extra-curricular capacity – Justice David Maraga had interpreted Section 83 to lay down a disjunctive test, and also indicated some of the qualitative factors, non-compliance with which would void an election. Of course, in 2017, Justice Maraga was the Chief Justice of Kenya. See Justice David K. Maraga, 'Scrutiny in Electoral Disputes: A Kenyan Judicial Perspective' in *Balancing the Scales of Electoral Justice, supra*, 243, 271.

[53] *Raila Odinga and Anr vs Independent Electoral and Boundaries Commission and Ors, supra*, para 212. The court's reading of Section 83 *in light of the Constitution* might have gone some way to address Evelyn and Wanyoike's critique of how the 2013 judgment got the relationship of Section 83 and the Constitution back to front.

> that it substantially breached the principles in the Constitution, the Elections Act and other electoral law. To be voided under the first limb, the election should be what Lord Stephenson called 'a sham or travesty of an election' or what Prof Ekirikubinza refers to as 'a spurious imitation of what elections should be'.[54]

This shift to the disjunctive test was crucial, because ultimately, it was on the basis of demonstrable irregularities that the court ruled that the entire election process had been irredeemably vitiated, and needed a rerun: for example, failure to electronically transmit results from the polling stations to the tallying centre, demonstrable proof that there had been no verification before the declaration of the results,[55] and the existence of multiple forms without the legally stipulated security features.[56] It could not obviously be shown that this had affected the outcome of the election, but as the court noted, it was a serious enough non-compliance with the law to cast doubts on the *integrity* of the process, in the sense of casting doubt on whether the will of the people, expressed through elections, had been made intelligible through the results of those elections:

> But what if the numbers are themselves a product, not of the expression of the free and sovereign will of the people, but of the many unanswered questions with which we are faced? In such a critical process as the election of the President, isn't quality just as important as quantity? In the face of all these troubling questions, would this court, even in the absence of a finding of violations of the Constitution and the law, have confidence to lend legitimacy to this election?[57]

This, naturally, meant that the court did substantively examine the IEBC's conduct, and found it wanting in several respects – a stark distinction from 2013. A particularly clear departure was the court's direction requiring the IEBC to partially allow access to its servers, to both the petitioners and a court-appointed expert committee. The IEBC's refusal to provide relevant information and access[58] allowed the court to draw an adverse inference against its probity, especially as the IEBC refused to provide logs that would have demonstrated whether there was unauthorised access to the servers.[59] In the court's words:

54 Ibid., para 209.
55 Ibid., para 267.
56 Ibid., paras 335, 362.
57 Ibid., para 378.
58 Ibid., para 278.
59 Ibid., para 280.

> It is trite law that failure to comply with a lawful demand, leave alone a specific court order, leaves the court with no option but to draw an adverse inference against the party refusing to comply. In this case, IEBC's contumacious disobedience of this court's order of August 28, 2017 in critical areas leaves us with no option but to accept the petitioners' claims that either IEBC's IT system was infiltrated and compromised and the data therein interfered with or IEBC's officials themselves interfered with the data or simply refused to accept that it had bungled the whole transmission system and were unable to verify the data.[60]

This added to the overall assessment that there were material irregularities that undermined the credibility of the electoral process. On the basis of this holistic assessment, the court declared the election results to be invalid, and ordered a rerun under the provisions of the Constitution:

> … the 2017 presidential election was not conducted in accordance with the principle laid down in the Constitution and the written law on elections in that it was, inter alia, neither transparent nor verifiable. On that ground alone, and on the basis of the interpretation we have given to section 83 of the Elections Act, we have no choice but to nullify it.[61]

The striking difference between the approaches of the 2013 court and the 2017 court are evident. But then, as Stacey and Miyandazi point out, the context was starkly different too. By 2017, the judiciary had had enough time to assert itself and build a reputation for independence and credibility. The IEBC, on the other hand, had been rocked by scandals and had lost public trust.[62] The very reasons that, in 2013, compelled the court to defer, now drove it to intervene.

With the 2017 election decision, the court established that it *could* set aside a presidential election, if to so chose.[63] The sharp divergence in approaches between 2013 and 2017,[64] however, created a degree of ambivalence when it

60 Ibid., para 280.

61 Ibid., para 303.

62 Stacey and Miyandazi, 'Constituting and Regulating Democracy', *supra*.

63 Duncan Okubasu Munabi, 'Judicialisation of "Mega" Politics in Kenya: Contributor to Democratization or Mere Recipe for Backlash?' in *Reflections on the 2017 Elections in Kenya* (James Gondi (ed.), ICJ Kenya 2018) 51, 66.

64 For a detailed examination of the continuities and discontinuities between the 2013 and 2017 decisions, see Bevelhymer, 'Transformative Constitutionalism and the Adjudication of Elections in Kenya', *supra*, Ch. 5.

came to what, precisely, were the principles that the Supreme Court would use in adjudicating a disputed presidential election.[65]

It was an ambivalence that would substantially worsen – very soon.

### *Interlude: the 2017 Rerun Election*

The presidential election rerun was scheduled for 26th October 2017. However, a few weeks before the appointed day, Raila Odinga withdrew from the race, stating that the IEBC had failed to implement the reforms recommended by the court in its judgment – thus making a free and fair election impossible. This turned the poll into an effective no-contest, with Uhuru Kenyatta winning 98% of the vote on a 38% turn-out. Even so, the rerun election was challenged on multiple grounds, by private individuals (*John Harun Mwau and Ors vs IEBC and Ors*).[66] This time, the Supreme Court unanimously upheld the result.

Perhaps understandably, on this occasion, the court did not go too deep into constitutional doctrine. Most of the petitioners' claims were dismissed either because they relied on laws under challenge elsewhere[67] (such as the amendment to section 83 of the Elections Act, which sought to enshrine the conjunctive test into law and add a requirement that an election illegality or irregularity must 'substantially' affect the results of an election);[68] or because – in the opinion of the court – they simply hadn't produced evidence to a standard that would displace the initial, evidentiary burden of proof, and shift it to the IEBC and the other Respondents.[69] This may not be entirely surprising, as it is one thing for a losing candidate – who has access to an entire, nationwide infrastructure of election monitoring, from polling agents to constituency officers – to identify and particularise election irregularities, and quite another for private individuals to do so.[70]

65 For an extended critique arguing that the 2017 judgment suffered both from inconsistency with precedent, as well as a lack of clarity in the legal standards that it articulated, see Wangai et al., 'Developing Jurisprudence beyond the Horizon', *supra*.

66 *John Harun Mwau and Ors vs IEBC and Ors*, Petitions [2017] KESC 54 (KLR).

67 Ibid., para 303.

68 A few months later, the High Court struck down this attempted amendment to Section 83, along with a raft of other amendments to the Elections Act that had been brought in as a response to the Supreme Court's 2017 ruling. See *Katiba Institute and Ors vs The Hon. Attorney General and Ors*, Constitutional Petition No. 548 of 2017, decided on 6th April 2018 (High Court). For a summary of the amendments, see Bevelhymer, 'Transformative Constitutionalism and the Adjudication of Elections in Kenya', *supra*, 363.

69 *John Harun Mwau and Ors vs IEBC and Ors*, *supra*, paras 302, 339, 350, 358, 366, 375, 409.

70 As the court itself noted. Ibid., para 349. Of course, it is an open question whether this would relieve the court of *its* own burden of scrutinising the evidence before it closely, *especially* given the information asymmetry between an ordinary

The petitioners did demonstrate *some* very patent irregularities – such as elections having had to be scrapped in twenty-five constituencies because of violence. The court dealt with this contention by noting that, on the evidence before it, the fault was not that of the police or the IEBC, which had taken all the steps it could to enable voting, but that of unidentified political actors and private persons.[71] In the end, the court broadly reiterated the disjunctive test that it had laid down a few months earlier,[72] and refrained from either developing the law any further, or from developing evidentiary and other adjudicatory practices in presidential disputes. It only held that on facts:

> … the election would be perceived as credible, *in the absence of clear evidence that the bulk of it simply failed;* that *due procedure* was not followed in the conduct of election; that *someone other than IEBC conducted the election*; that the *procedures of vote counting* were not followed; that false results were announced, in place of the true outcome; that the *voters were turned away* from polling stations by IEBC, or by State agencies of power; that the *motions of verification* and announcement of vote-outcome were not complied with. We have stated elsewhere in this judgment that none of these factors were at play or at play in any significant manner.[73]

In view of the fact that this was a rerun election just months after the Supreme Court had – for the first time in its history – invalidated a Presidential election (and come under sustained attack for doing so),[74] and was a non-contested election to boot, the outcome was perhaps inevitable. Judicial bodies – even constitutional courts – have a limited cache of capital for direct confrontations with the political branches at the best of times. Voiding a presidential election where the incumbent had triumphed would exhaust most of that cache under most circumstances.[75]

---

citizen and the IEBC. For a critique of the court's jurisprudence on the issue of burdens of proof in election cases, see Muthomi Thiankolu, 'Role of the Courts in Ensuring Free and Fair Elections in Kenya: A Tale of Fifty-Six Years of Legal Sophistry and Intellectual Dishonesty' (2019) 4(1) *Kabarak Journal of Law and Ethics* 53.

71 *John Harun Mwau and Ors vs IEBC and Ors, supra*, paras 295–297. This reasoning is not entirely convincing, and one wonders if it would have been the same had it been a closely contested election, and twenty-five constituencies not been able to vote because of violence!

72 Ibid., para 373.

73 Ibid., para 407.

74 See e.g. Walter Khobe Ochieng, 'The State of Judicial Independence in Kenya – Reflections from the 2017 Presidential Elections' in *Reflections on the 2017 Elections in Kenya, supra*, 5.

75 Ibid.

However, whatever the *realpolitik* underlying the court's decision, as multiple critics pointed out immediately thereafter, if one actually compared the irregularities that the court had found serious enough to void the election at the first time of asking, with the irregularities that were established with respect to the rerun, there is little doubt that – on an application of the same standards – the rerun election ought to have been invalidated as well. The court avoided doing so by taking the Respondents' explanations for the irregularities at face value on some occasions,[76] and stipulating that the burdens and standards of proof had not been met on others. Yet, this only raised the question of whether the court was retreating into its deferential, 2013 posture once again.

The question grew more urgent as, in the aftermath of the Supreme Court's judgment setting aside the first Presidential election, multiple challenges had been filed challenging the outcomes of other elections that had been conducted alongside the Presidential elections – in particular, certain gubernatorial elections. But petitioners who expected that the taint on the Presidential election would spread to other elections were in for an unpleasant surprise, as the results of those elections were upheld – and often, by invoking standards from the pre-2017 era!

Thus, as Omwanza Ombati noted, while critiquing the court's failure to seriously engage with the substantive issues in the 2017 rerun election, the legal landscape had been left 'in total confusion in relation to democratic consolidation'.[77] The reason for this, Ombati argued, was not just the rerun decision itself. It was also that the Supreme Court's decision on the first 2017 Presidential Election had appeared to mark a jurisprudential shift away from the 2013 court's 'restrictive' approach towards deciding election petitions. However, immediately thereafter, the Election Courts and the Court of Appeal (and, for that matter, the Supreme Court itself) were continuing to apply the restrictive approach, notwithstanding the first 2017 decision.[78]

For this reason, the euphoria around the first 2017 decision subsided swiftly. Its place was taken by a lingering concern. Was the first 2017 decision an anomaly – dictated by a very specific set of circumstances – instead of a genuine shift towards fulfilling the transformative promise of the 2010 Constitution? Were the courts occasioning a reversion to the mean – the mean established in the 2013 judgment? As Lucianna Thuo summed it up:

76 Bevelhymer, 'Transformative Constitutionalism and the Adjudication of Elections in Kenya', *supra*, 294.

77 Omwanza Ombati, 'Jurisprudence on Election-Related Violence in Kenya' in *Reflections on the 2017 Elections in Kenya*, *supra*, 103, 122.

78 Ibid.

> … whereas the Supreme Court may have faltered in the 2013 Raila Odinga Case by not appreciating the constitutional standards for valid elections, then appeared to regain its footing in the 2017 Raila Odinga case by restoring the Constitution to its rightful place as the benchmark for valid elections, it may have inadvertently reverted to the 2013 position in recent cases.[79]

The persistence of these questions meant that when the next election cycle came around – in 2022 – the stakes would, once again, be extremely high: not just for the presidential candidates, but also for the court, for the future prospects of transformative constitutionalism and for the resolution of disputed presidential elections in Kenya.

It is to 2022 that we now turn.

## C. The 2022 Judgment

If the 2013 Presidential election judgment was marked by a sense of history, the 2022 judgment begins on a note of weariness. 'From our history', the court observes in the second sentence of the judgment, 'it is almost inevitable in the course of electoral competition that disputes will arise at all these levels.'[80] 'Election related disputes', the court goes on to note, 'are an intrinsic part of the electoral process.'[81] By 2022, these proceedings were no longer extraordinary, but as regular – and expected – as the presidential election itself.

As in previous years, in 2022, there were a range of challenges to the validity of the presidential election and, once again, the IEBC found itself in the dock. These challenges ranged from accusations that the IEBC servers had been hacked to the breakdown (again!) of technology, and from physical voter suppression to the manipulation of election forms.

Drawing from the 2017 judgment, the court began by setting out the constitutional contours within which the dispute would be adjudicated: that is, on the burdens and standards of proof. It reiterated the 2017 judgment's position that the initial burden was to be borne by the Petitioner, that it had to be established to an 'intermediate' standard of proof ('clear and cogent' evidence), and that the material irregularities had to be such that would affect the outcome *or* the integrity of the election.[82] Indeed, by this time, the latter proposition had

[79] Lucianna Thuo, *Compendium of 2017 Election Petitions* (ICJ Kenya 2019) 282. See also Bevelhymer, 'Transformative Constitutionalism and the Adjudication of Elections in Kenya', *supra*, 301.

[80] *Raila Odinga and Ors vs William Ruto and Ors*, [2022] KESC 54 (KLR), para 1.

[81] Ibid., para 3.

[82] Ibid., paras 32–34. While the court claimed to be following the 2013 judgment, there is a subtle departure that took place in 2017, and which was entrenched in 2022: that the Petitioners need not prove that the material irregularities affected the *outcome*

been accorded constitutional status. In the aftermath of the 2017 judgment, as noted above, Parliament had attempted to restore the 2013 judgment's conjunctive test by amending Section 83. Shortly after, this had been declared unconstitutional by the High Court, on the basis that the conjunctive test was inconsistent with the constitutional requirement that elections be 'free, fair, transparent and credible'.[83]

The proof of the pudding is, of course, in the eating, and the court's application of these standards to the case reveals a few noteworthy features. The first is that – following past precedent – the court explicitly noted that in a proceeding such as this, it could not travel beyond the evidence provided to it by the parties. In analysing the evidence, then, the court hewed closely to the affidavits placed on record by the parties. In many cases, it was able to dismiss a specific allegation because of internal contradictions *within* the Petitioner's affidavits.[84] This was, of course, not new for the court in election cases. However, the reason why this is important deserves to be re-emphasised: in a disputed presidential election, the more a court *foregrounds* itself within the decision, the more it risks weakening the foundations of its own independence. This was – I have argued – the crucial motivating factor behind the way in which the 2013 judgment approached the case. However, unlike the 2013 judgment, one marked difference was that the 2022 judgment *did* examine the evidence closely.[85]

Indeed – and secondly – there was at least one occasion where the court *did* hold that the Petitioners had discharged their initial burden of proof, and that the IEBC was required to explain a material discrepancy – which, the court found, the IEBC successfully managed to do.[86] This concerned the mandatory auditing of the Register of Voters:

---

of the election; it was sufficient to demonstrate that they affected the *integrity* of the election; in other words, the defensible distinction between the inevitable errors that will creep into an activity conducted at such scale, and errors that vitiate the process itself. I deal with this distinction below.

83 *Katiba Institute and Ors vs The Hon. Attorney General and Ors*, *supra*, para 114.

84 See, for example, the discussion on the allegation that Form 34As had been manipulated. *Raila Odinga and Ors vs William Ruto and Ors*, *supra*, paras 59, 97–98, 135, 140–145.

85 See, for example, the detailed consideration of the petitioner's and the respondent's arguments in the context of certain discrepancies in Form 34A. Ibid., paras 151–154.

86 Both Evelyn and Wanyoike, 'A New Dawn Postponed', *supra*, and Prempeh, 'Comparative Perspectives on Kenya's Post-2013 Election Dispute Resolution Process', *supra*, had called for this shifting of the burden of proof in their critiques of the 2013 judgment. But see also Elisha Z. Ongoya, 'Evidentiary Matters in Election Petitions in Kenya: Progress or Backsliding?' in *Balancing the Scales of Electoral Justice*, *supra*, 215.

> The petitioner's submissions as supported by the sworn affidavits regarding the integrity of the Register of Voters, were enough in our view, to shift the evidentiary burden of rebuttal to IEBC. IEBC undertook this burden, by giving a detailed explanation of the remedial measures it had instituted, to address the shortcomings …[87]

These explanations included, for example, various remedial measures in response to certain gaps pointed out by KPMG – the firm that had audited the register of voters. While the court found that the IEBC's explanation was satisfactory, its analysis demonstrated that, as in 2017, neither the placement of the burden of proof on the Petitioner, and nor the intermediate 'standard' of proof, would be insurmountable obstacles.[88]

The third feature of the judgment – although the court did not spell it out in express terms – is the understanding that whether a particular discrepancy or irregularity had to be adjudicated on the touchstone of affecting the *outcome* of the election, or affecting the *integrity* of the election, is context-sensitive. For example, in addressing the issue that there were two KIEMS kits (i.e., the kits from which Form 34A was transmitted) with the same number, the court found that on the balance of evidence before it, the more plausible explanation was a manufacturer's fault, rather than an attempt to falsify election results.[89] *Having found that,* the court went on to note that these irregularities were not of such a magnitude that would have affected the outcome of the election.[90]

While this may, at first blush, once again appear to be a reversion to the 2013 mean, on a closer analysis, the situation is more nuanced. The court's analysis here, I suggest, provides an important – and neutral – guideline for when the *outcome* test is to be employed, and when the *integrity* test is to be applied. If it can be shown that errors or irregularities were innocuous in nature, and a result of human error inevitable in the conduct of something at the scale of a national election, those errors would serve as grounds to set aside the election only if they had impacted the outcome. However, this would not be necessary if the irregularities indicated an undermining of the process itself, as had been the case in 2017.

However, perhaps the most significant feature of the judgment lay in how it approached the challenges to the IEBC's technical competence and

87 *Raila Odinga and Ors vs William Ruto and Ors*, *supra*, para 40.

88 Another interesting distinction between the 2017 and 2022 judgments was that in 2017, voting numbers for presidential candidates and gubernatorial candidates were starkly different. The court held that this shifted the burden of explanation to the IEBC, which it failed to discharge – or even attempt to discharge. In 2022, however, the IEBC had an explanation pertaining to different voting behaviours with respect to voting for the President, and voting for other offices, which the court accepted.

89 Ibid., para 153.

90 Ibid.

probity. One of the bases of criticism of the 2013 judgment's declaration of a presumption of validity for all actions taken by the IEBC – as Harrington and Manji pointed out – was the *asymmetry of information* between the IEBC and the contesting parties.[91] In essence, how the IEBC deployed the technology remained a black box, and it would be very difficult for a contesting party to be able to prove wrongdoing to the extent required under the intermediate standard of proof. In the 2022 judgment – and following precedent established by the 2017 judgment – the court opened the black box by directing – through an interim order – the opening up of the IEBC's servers for scrutiny by the registrar of the court, in the presence of the contesting parties:

> ... pursuant to applications made by the 1st, 3rd and 4th petitioners, the Court on 30th August, 2022, partially granted the applications and ordered an ICT scrutiny, inspection and recount of ballots in specified polling stations under the supervision of the Registrar of the Court.[92]

Unlike in 2017, this time the IEBC did comply with the order. The evidence from the servers, then, was extensively discussed *in* the judgment, bringing the public into the conversation as well. The court began by noting:

> The answer [about the IEBC's control over its technology] is found in the Registrar's Report to the effect that IEBC granted the team, comprising agents of all the petitioners, supervised access to the server for interrogation for the entire duration of the exercise; that IEBC in compliance with the orders of the Court provided its password policy, password matrix, system users and levels of access, workflow... [93]

The importance of this process lies in the fact that in election disputes – above all else – there is a need for judicial reasoning to be *transparent*. Far too often, in the 2013 judgment, the court had simply stated the positions of the parties, and given its conclusion, without explaining *why* it believed that the intermediate standard had not been met (this was especially glaring in the challenges concerning the use of technology). This had prompted Evelyn and Wanyoike to note, for example, in their critique of the 2013 judgment:

> In fact, the seemingly elevated standard of proof that the Supreme Court requires also shields the IEBC from having to explain itself

91 Harrington and Manji, 'Restoring Leviathan?', *supra*. See also Maina, 'Verdict on Kenya's presidential election petition', *supra*: 'Since most of the evidence of wrongdoing will be in the hands of the IEBC – or a similar body – it is extremely difficult to see how a petitioner could ever succeed.'

92 *Raila Odinga vs William Ruto*, *supra*, para 8.

93 Ibid., para 52.

> or disclose all the voting data and electoral process details which also goes against the 2010 Constitution's clear purpose of making the election verifiable and all electoral officials accountable.[94]

The opening up of the servers – and the public analysis of the evidence *in* the judgment – went some way towards remedying that, and providing a degree of transparency such that the court's judgment itself could be audited.[95] Thus, for example, responding to the issue of the IEBC's system having been compromised:

> *Amici* also contended that one of the ways through which IEBC proves its system is not compromised is by providing appropriate server logs that record digital services happening on the computer system. It was their submission that in presenting server logs as digital evidence, which is a critical component in digital forensic science, this places the Court in a position to determine the credibility of the digital evidence before it. This we did, and we reiterate that from the scrutiny exercise, that IEBC provided the logs during the review of the server audit logs where no suspicious activities were discovered, answering this submission in the affirmative.[96]

And, subsequently:

> It is evident that any unauthorized access to the system would leave a trail of logs and none were found. The logs from the scrutiny exercise demonstrated this fact.[97]

When we consider the 2022 presidential election decision as a whole, therefore, what emerges is this: as in 2013, the court was aware that it would have to decide the case before it in a manner that involved the minimal exercise of judicial *discretion*. The most effective way to do that was to develop and articulate a series of legal principles that would govern the court's approach, and minimise the scope for discretion. The crucial difference with 2013, however, was that in that case, the court leaned upon the IEBC, and the presumption of validity of the IEBC's actions, in order to avoid a detailed judicial scrutiny of the petitioner's allegations. This created a kind of 'black box', where the IEBC's methods remained opaque and, as a result, the court's own judgment

94 Evelyn and Wanyoike, 'A New Dawn Postponed', *supra*, 101.

95 An additional pointed to be noted is that in the 2022 judgment, the court went beyond 2017 in ordering for scrutiny of the ballot boxes from disputed polling stations as well. I thank Walter Ochieng for bringing this point to my attention.

96 *Raila Odinga vs William Ruto*, *supra*, para 101.

97 Ibid., para 104.

appeared more an exercise of judicial deference than an exercise of judicial reason. Thus, one of the most damning critiques of the 2013 judgment was simply: 'The Supreme Court [did] not analyse the evidence.'[98]

In 2022, however, the court – as pointed out above – attempted to open the black box, both literally (by subjecting the ICT servers to scrutiny) and metaphorically (by then scrutinising the Registrar's Report). In the process, one valuable gain that was made over 2013 was that the court's own reasoning was more open, and more open to public scrutiny. This was particularly vital, given that the court was *upholding* the election result and *endorsing* the IEBC (in broad terms), rather than – as in 2017 – the reverse. While this is not a defence (or a criticism) of the outcome the court reached (there are many who would argue that the court got it wrong), for the reasons advanced above, the court's process, I believe, marks an important advance towards fulfilling the Constitution's vision of a *constitutional* path towards resolving election disputes.

## D. Conclusion: Threading the Needle

The 2022 Presidential Election judgment is not perfect. The final part of the judgment, for example – where the court looked into the allegations of 'irregularities and illegalities' in the process – is reminiscent of the 2013 judgment and the 2017 rerun judgment, in that the Court set out the contentions of the parties and then declared the allegations not proven, without substantive analysis. Furthermore, the question of whether spoilt or invalid ballots are to be counted in determining whether the leading candidate had attained the required '50%+1' majority came up again in this case. Despite the extended criticism that had been made of the 2013 judgment's decision to not count invalid ballots for this purpose – including criticisms based on the right to vote – the court elected to simply adopt the 2013 judgment on this point, without further analysis.[99]

Indeed, one could argue that at times the court seemed too eager to stress on continuity with both the 2017 judgment and the 2013 judgment, through downplaying – for example – the shift from the conjunctive to the disjunctive test that was first made in 2017, and then affirmed in 2022. This is understandable, as the court would want to present to the public a consistent approach towards adjudicating presidential election disputes. However, given the extensive criticism of the 2013 judgment, it might actually have served the

98 Maina, 'Verdict on Kenya's presidential election petition', *supra*.

99 To be fair, the 2017 judgment had also upheld this interpretation, albeit again, with minimal analysis. In 2017, the Supreme Court noted the critique of the 2013 judgment, noted 'two schools of thought on the issue', and then aligned itself with the 2013 judgment after a rather brief excursion into the law. See *Raila Odinga vs IEBC* (2017), *supra*, para 170.

court to put some daylight between 2013 and 2022 – especially given that it was reaching the same conclusion that it had in 2013.

To many, then, these were reasons to believe that the 2022 judgment remained overly conservative, and did not go far enough; indeed, it marked a regression from 2017. I would suggest, however, that it is equally important to contrast the 2022 judgment with the 2013 judgment, for the reason set out at the beginning of this chapter. It matters *how* a court upholds a presidential election, as much as it matters *whether* it upholds it. And in this context, even if one believes that the court should have set aside the 2022 election, there are nonetheless some important advances that the court made upon its judgment in 2013: in particular, bringing more clarity to the issue of burdens and standards of proof, and also, opening the electoral 'black box' by subjecting both the work of the IEBC, as well as its own analysis of the IEBC's performance, to public scrutiny.

In finding that ever-elusive balance between applying 'neutral' principles of law to adjudicating presidential election disputes on the one hand, and avoiding the perils of excessive deference and a self-attenuation of the judicial role on the other, the court is unlikely to thread the needle through the whole length. But we can perhaps say that in the 2022 judgment, the court went at least some way to realising the 2010 Constitution's transformative goal of resolving presidential election disputes in the courtroom, and through constitutional law, rather than through violence.

# Conclusion

# Between the Bridge and the Horizon

*We live in our times; we cannot live outside them, but ... we can dance just ever so slightly above this finite rhythm that is our lives.*[1]

## A. The Five Axes

IN THE poetry of many cultures, there is an enduring image: of a shore that recedes even as you move towards it. If transformative constitutionalism's metaphor of the bridge expresses confidence that the chasm between the past and the future *will* be bridged, then the language of poetry warns us about the 'essential cruelty of hope'.[2] Transformative constitutionalism may be a bridge, but a bridge to a horizon that is always receding.

The chapters in this book trace the journey of transformative constitutionalism under Kenya's 2010 Constitution, between the bridge and the horizon. These chapters – each dedicated to a constitutional dispute that was brought before the Kenyan courts between 2010 and 2025 – correspond to five axes of transformation.

The first axis is that of constraining the executive and empowering the People. This was at issue in the BBI Case, where an executive-driven attempt to make large-scale changes to the 2010 Constitution was rebuffed by the courts. The ball was set rolling by the High Court, which reached into history to hold that sweeping constitutional change could not be done without a correspondingly deep participation of the People. In doing so, the High Court offered to the world a new – and distinctively Kenyan – articulation of the famous basic structure doctrine. While the Supreme Court disagreed with the High Court on the applicability of the doctrine to the Kenyan context, its own interpretation of the Constitution affirmed – in substance – the document's commitment to public participation in constitutional change. The BBI Bill was ultimately struck down because all three courts – the High Court, the Court of Appeal, and the Supreme Court – agreed that the "popular initiative" was designed to let *the People* speak, and not to have them *spoken for* by

1 Mukoma wa Ngugi, *Unbury Our Dead With Song* (Cassava Republic 2020) 35.

2 Wainana, *One Day I Will Write About This Place*, *supra*, 113.

the executive. The *BBI Case* is thus important not simply because of the innovations in constitutional law doctrine, but also because it demonstrated the judiciary's will and ability to stand up to a *bi-partisan* project of constitutional change, which carried the support of a large segment of the political elite. These are the constitutional furnaces in which an independent judiciary is honed.

The second axis is that of constraining the executive by reviving institutions. Jomo Kenyatta's amendments to the 1963 Constitution were aimed at systematically eliminating or disempowering all institutions that stood between the Presidency and near-imperial power. The two most prominent institutions were parliament and the federal structure (*majimbo*): horizontal and vertical decentralisations of power. Kenyatta succeeded in degrading the first and destroying the second, and constructing an imperial presidency. This was acknowledged to be at the root of many of the problems that engulfed Kenya in the succeeding years, and was at the heart of the constitutional reform movement that began in the 1990s. While political jockeying ensured that the 2010 Constitution retained a presidential system, it came along with an attempt to resurrect other, mediating institutions (albeit in a different form). In the CDF Case, the Supreme Court was faced with a stress-test for those institutions. The Constituency Development Fund implicated the separation of powers, by blurring the line between the legislative and executive functions, and incentivising clientelism and patronage among legislators. It also impacted devolution, by centralizing what were meant to be county functions. The Supreme Court's decision striking down the CDF reaffirmed both principles, in defence of constitutional institutions. The CDF Case is thus a striking example of how, in a post-authoritarian context, classic constitutional principles such as the separation of powers – often accused of fostering undue judicial conservatism – can play a restorative-transformative role.

The third axis is that of socio-economic rights, and the interface between transformative constitutionalism and the political economy. While constraining political power is a crucial element of transformative constitutionalism, the project cannot do without a vision for how a constitution will engage with the entrenched and structural inequalities that are the product both of colonial racialism, and post-colonial capitalism. Modern constitutions attempt to square the circle by entrenching enforceable socio-economic rights within the constitutional document. However, this often runs up against the fact that these rights (to food, to housing, to medicine, among others) refer to goods that are explicitly commodified and subject to the 'mute compulsion' of market logic. In *Mitu-Bell* and *William Musembi*, the Supreme Court was faced with exactly this problem, in the context of evictions from public and private land, and the right to housing. The context could not have been more poignant: 'squatting' and landlessness are the products of original colonial land-grabbing, which were then worsened and entrenched by post-colonial policies. In these cases, the court invoked some of the more radical provisions of the Constitution – such as all land belonging, in principle, to the People – in order to craft a doctrine of procedural and substantive participation that would blunt some of the sharper edges of the sword of private property rights. While other courts – most notably, the South African courts – have developed similar doctrines, the importance of *Mitu-Bell* and *William Musembi* is the potential advancement of this logic into the domain of *private* property, and the transformative potential that that holds.

The fourth axis overlaps with the third: transformative constitutionalism must confront entrenched 'private' power, 'private' hierarchies, and 'private' structures of oppression. In doing so, it must depart from traditional constitutionalism's default focus on the state, and its clean-cut separation of the public and the private spheres. But this is a careful line to tread, one that judiciaries all over the world are grappling with: how do you craft a set of principles that will tell us when a constitution should apply between private parties, and when not? In *Rose Wangui Mambo*, the High Court crafted just such a doctrine, when examining the exclusion of women from positions of responsibility in a private club. The High Court held that the Constitution would apply where the violation of constitutional rights by a private actor could be located within institutional hierarchies or structures of power (in this case, patriarchy; in other cases, race, the market, or other forms of non-state, institutionally mediated social power). This institutional approach is an important contribution towards the global, constitutional debate on horizontal rights, and the scope and limits of their application.

The fifth and final axis takes seriously the title of the *liber amicorum* to Yash Pal Ghai, 'furthering constitutions, birthing peace'. Or, to be more precise, birthing peace *through* furthering constitutions. Article 140 of the 2010 Constitution is an ambitious attempt to constitutionalize the most intractable source of political violence in Kenya: the presidential election. It also places a great burden upon the Supreme Court, the first and final tribunal for this purpose, denying it any wiggle room in negotiating the high-voltage political situation in the immediate aftermath of a disputed election. Arguably, the burden proved too great for a new, and still embattled court, to satisfactorily discharge in 2013; but in 2017 – and then in 2022 – the court worked towards crafting a set of principles for decision, which will serve both when an election is invalidated, and when it is upheld. The analysis in the 2022 decision is particularly important in its interaction between the court, the IEBC, and the People. By requiring the IEBC to open its servers, and then by engaging in a public analysis of its findings, the court – at least partially – tried to open the 'black box' of election disputes and mitigate the asymmetry of information between the institutions and the public.

This book has told the story of transformative constitutionalism in Kenya through the lens of these judgments, and the issues that they have grappled with: issues that, it is crucial to note, are not unique to Kenya, but have risen, in different forms, across the world. The contribution of the Kenyan courts, then, is important not just for transformative constitutionalism *in* Kenya, but for conversations globally. It is important as people in different countries grapple with issues around constraining state power, enabling public participation, enforcing socio-economic rights, breaking down private hierarchies, and containing political violence – and with how constitutions and constitutionalism can help in achieving these goals.

This is not to suggest, of course, that the journey has been smooth. Writing soon after the enactment of the 2010 Constitution, Christina Murray had this to say:

> The Constitution promulgated on 27 August 2010 is not anyone's perfect document. For those who had struggled against Moi's regime, it changes too little. For the governing elite and its supporters, it changes too much. It also leaves considerable space for institutions and their relationships with one another to develop. The courts might be cautious or ambitious; the executive may or may not respect them; Parliament may develop its oversight role energetically or MPs may act opportunistically; the counties might assert authority or be subordinated to the national government, they may be honest and drive development or simply an exercise in decentralizing the problems currently experienced at the national level and so on. <u>More likely, the new system will be a bit of all these things</u>.[3]

A bit of all these things, between the bridge and the horizon. The Constitution's own internal tensions have been reflected in judgments, including the ones that we have studied in this book. For example, in the BBI Case, the Supreme Court could have been clearer about how, exactly, it was embedding public participation into the terms of Article 257, what it would do if it *were to be* faced with a constitutional evisceration, and it could have answered the referendum question in favour of enhanced public participation. The CDF Case was a clear statement of constitutional principle, but it is difficult to ignore the fact that its practical impact is yet to be felt. By the time the court delivered its judgment, the CDF Act had already been replaced; and even after the successor legislation was struck down in 2024 by the High Court (largely on the basis of the Supreme Court's judgment), the strike-down will only take effect from 2026. At the time of writing, there are suggestions of amending the Constitution and entrenching the CDF within the document, to get around the courts' judgments. If – or when – that happens, it would be

3 Murray, 'Kenya's 2010 Constitution', *supra*, 747 (emphasis supplied).

interesting to see how the court responds, and how it interprets its own BBI Judgment in cases when there is a serious claim of constitutional evisceration.

In *Mitu-Bell* and in *William Musembi*, the court gestured towards a transformative understanding of property rights, participation, and housing, but did not fully articulate it. While the judgments flicker with radical possibilities, the actual doctrine they advance is broadly in line with other jurisdictions, and perhaps even slightly more conservative, when compared to South Africa. The transformative project is thus left to a future court. The same is true for *Rose Wangui Mambo*, where the implications of the institutional approach remain to be fully worked out – a task for another day. These observations are offered up not by way of complaint, but perhaps in acknowledgment that transformative constitutionalism is an unfinished project that needs constant renewal. Yet, that very fact lends it a certain transience, or a fragility. Limited gains are always easy to reverse or to turn back. To preserve and advance them needs constant struggle.

And then there are the presidential election judgments, which have dissatisfied many, and not without reason. The court's struggle to preserve the integrity of the election while preserving its own institutional independence has compelled it to make a series of choices that are open to critique. While some of these can be justified under the stresses of the political context, others – such as the refusal to count invalid ballots – are more difficult. Between peace and justice, and a just peace, the court is left to navigate a treacherous path, fraught with challenges.

These five axes are not mutually exclusive. Both the BBI Case and the CDF Case were about containing executive power. The first sought to achieve that by giving a voice to the People, and the second by giving a voice to institutions. *Rose Wangui Mambo* was a case about private institutional power, but so was *William Musembi*, which sought to carry forward the logic of *Mitu-Bell* and impose constitutional obligations in cases of evictions – even from private land. The pathologies of concentrated power that made every presidential election a zero-sum game and compelled the framers of the 2010 Constitution to judicialise presidential election disputes were also responsible for the inequities of land ownership in the post-Independence period. We should therefore think of the five axes as overlapping, constituent elements of an overarching web of transformation, which has, at its heart, a vision of non-concentrated and democratised power. This vision pervades throughout the Constitution, and every time a court is faced with a question of constitutional interpretation, there is an opportunity to renew and affirm that vision, and strengthen the strands of the web.

And finally, the judgments that we have studied are important contributions to a comparative and global conversation. We have studied them in the context of four overlapping frames: first, these judgments engage with constitutionalism as a terrain of power, and of contestation between different visions of power; secondly, they engage with the roles and functions of public institutions common to modern constitutionalism, and also with the intersection between the language of rights and the contemporary political economy; thirdly, they speak to the many histories and many pathologies of commonwealth constitutionalism; and, fourthly, they are part of – and critically interrogate – the tradition of African constitutionalism. Post-2010 Kenyan constitutional jurisprudence, thus, is a flourishing space for many different conversations, of diverse and variegated hues.

## B. Transformation and Beyond

Beyond the five axes and the cases discussed in this book, the Kenyan courts have had other occasions to consider – and develop the project of transformative constitutionalism. In Chapter Five, I discussed how the family – and family structures – are crucial sites of transformative justice, and how the transformative potential of Article 45(3) – guaranteeing equal rights within marriage – has been somewhat blunted, with the rejection of a default rule of a 50% split of assets at the time of dissolution of a marriage. The Matrimonial Property Act of 2013, however, explicitly requires taking into account of non-monetary contributions (such as domestic work and care work) into consideration. Consequently, the next crucial battle is the interpretation of such terms. In 2021, in *MW vs AN*, the High Court at Nakuru handed down an important judgment, stipulating that housework and care-work performed by a wife entitled her to an equal share of the property on dissolution.[4] As Matheka J eloquently spelt out:

> This other part of mothering, housekeeping and taking care of the family is more often than not, not given any value when it comes to sharing matrimonial property. It is easy for the spouse working away from home and sending money to lay claim to the whole property purchased and developed with that money by the spouse staying at home and taking care of the children and the family. That spouse will be heard to say that the other one was not employed so they contributed nothing. <u>That can no longer be a tenable argument as it is a fact that stay at home parents and in particular women because of our cultural connotations do much more work (house wives) due to the nature of the job</u> … hence for a woman in employment who has to balance child bearing and rearing this contribution must be considered. How do we put monetary value to that process where a woman bears the pregnancy, gives birth, and takes care of the babies and where after divorce or separation she takes care of the children single handedly

[4] *MW vs AN*, Matrimonial Cause Number, 20 of 2016, decided on 14th September 2021 (High Court).

> without any help from the father of the children … Should this court take this into consideration when distributing matrimonial property where the husband as in this case is left in the matrimonial home where the wife rents a house to provide shelter for herself and the children? I think it should count, especially where the husband has not supported the raising of the children, has not borne his share of parental responsibility.[5]

And:

> It is time that parties took time to give evidence, sufficient enough to support the value to be placed on the less obvious contribution. It is unfair and unjust for one party to be busy just making their money (the 'seen' income) while the other is doing two or three other jobs in the family whose income is 'unseen' and then claim this other one did nothing. This attitude is so entrenched we still hear women especially who are housewives say: sifanyi kazi (literally I do not do any work) simply because they do not leave the home to go earn money elsewhere.[6]

This is a subtle and sensitive exploration of entrenched inequalities within family structures and a call to ensure that primarily *gendered* tasks – such as house work and care work – are not economically marginalised as they always have been: something that – in turn – has always disempowered and trapped women within oppressive family structures. The High Court's judgment was strikingly similar, in fact, to an earlier judgment of the Constitutional Court of Colombia, which had recognised a widow's legal interest in a home, based on her non-monetary contributions. The court had noted, in particular, how 'invisiblising' domestic work and creating artificial distinctions between 'productive' and 'non-productive work' had the effect of deepening social and gendered inequalities.[7] Many years later, Matheka J took up the same logic and developed it in greater detail within the context of the 2010 Constitution.

Two years after, in *Ogentoto vs Ogentoto*, the Supreme Court adopted a similar formulation, even as it continued to reject a call to establish the 50% rule as a presumptive default position (from which a judge could depart, if circumstances warranted it). It noted the existence of a 'general assumption' that parties to a marriage contribute 'towards the home and the family, in one way or another'.[8] While this recognition is important, the court's judgment

5 Ibid., para 38 (emphasis supplied).

6 Ibid., para 39.

7 *Sentencia Number T-494/1992* (Constitutional Court of Colombia).

8 *Joseph Ombogi Ogentoto vs Martha Bosibiri Ogentoto*, Petition No. 11 of 2020, decided on 27th January 2023 (Supreme Court), para 103.

also reflected an unease with the full working out of this transformative logic, as it noted that equality within marriage did not necessarily entail *redistribution* (of property).[9] It is hard to see, however, how a transition from inequality to equality *would not* entail redistribution in some form! As with *Mitu-Bell*, thus, we can see a hesitation to fully interrogate unequal social structures. In this way, *Ogentoto* shows us both the potential – but also the interpretive and imaginative limits – of transformative constitutionalism, when it is litigated in the courts.

Sticking with the theme of private power structures and equality, in July 2023, the Court of Appeal extended the logic of transformative constitutionalism into the domain of consumer rights.[10] Nairobi Bottlers Ltd was found to violate the Constitution when it provided different nutritional information on glass Coca-Cola bottles and plastic bottles. Other than the fact that Nairobi Bottlers Ltd was a private company – and thus this was a case of horizontal rights, as I briefly discussed in Chapter Five – the decision is significant because the basis of the discrimination was purchasing power of those who bought plastic bottles, vis-à-vis those who bought glass bottles (generalized, of course).[11] In other words, the basis was *class* – a ground that constitutions have been very careful to exclude from their non-discrimination provisions, as doing so would interrogate the structures of political economy in much the same way that I discussed in Chapter Four. The Court of Appeal thus laid the ground for an evolving jurisprudence of subjecting class-based inequalities to the Constitution's non-discrimination clause. Much like *Mitu-Bell*, it will be fascinating to see how much further the courts can take this jurisprudence in the future.

Indeed, discrimination and equality – unsurprisingly – have been litigated frequently under the 2010 Constitution. The Kenyan courts have often faced claims from religious minorities, in relation to "uniform" dress codes or other such rules, which have been framed keeping in mind the default ways of living of the cultural majority. By and large, the Kenyan courts have been responsive to these claims. In *Scoline Anyango Ojung'a vs Healthlink Matcare*, a Seventh-Day Adventist was sacked from her workplace because she asked for a day off on Saturday, in accordance with her religious beliefs. The Employment and Labour Relations Court held this to be unconstitutional, as the employer had failed to provide their employee with the 'reasonable accommodation' that the Constitution's equality and religious freedom

9 For a similar argument, see Marvis Ndubi, 'A commentary on the matrimonial property conundrum in Kenya in JOO vs MBO' (2023) 2 *Kabarak Law Review* 147.

10 *Nairobi Bottlers Ltd. vs Mark Ndumia Ndung'u*, Civil Appeal No. 99 of 2018, decided on 7th July 2023 (Court of Appeal).

11 Ibid.

clauses required.[12] Similar principles were followed by the Court of Appeal in affirming the rights of Jehovah's Witnesses to not attend Catholic Mass at school, and the rights of Muslim students to wear a *hijab*.[13] In all these judgments, what has stood out is the courts' willingness to affirm – unlike in certain other jurisdictions[14] – that social diversity and pluralism does not end at the doorstep of the workplace or the school. Rather, as microcosms of the larger society, the workplace and the school are where diversity and pluralism should be celebrated, instead of being corralled into a culturally dominant understanding of 'uniformity'. Furthermore – and understanding structural imperatives and the absence of genuine choices in such cases – the courts have given short shrift to the 'if you don't like it, go somewhere else' argument, crafting a powerful and persuasive jurisprudence of equality.

However, if there is one domain where the limitations of transformative constitutionalism are starkly visible, it is that of the rights of sexual minorities. In *EG vs Attorney-General*, the High Court declined to strike down a law criminalising same-sex relations. It deployed the familiar – and regressive – logic that what was punished was 'acts' and not individuals, and invoked a moral panic that decriminalisation would 'open the door' towards civil unions and marriage.[15] The court's analysis here was in striking contrast to the subtle and nuanced anti-discrimination jurisprudence that the Kenyan courts have evolved in the context of religious minorities. Here, however, the court refused both to accept indirect and effects-based discrimination, and to accord a purposive interpretation to the open-ended 'grounds' of discrimination set out under Article 27.

A limited redressal arrived in 2023, when a closely divided Supreme Court upheld the rights of LGBTQ+ persons to associate, and struck down the state's refusal to recognise an NGO that championed the rights of queer persons.[16] This brought to an end a decade-long battle for recognition that had passed through the High Court and the Court of Appeal. And even here, the court's

12 *Scoline Anyango Ojung'a vs Healthlink Matcare*, [2023] KEELRC 1607 (KLR).

13 *Mohamed Fugicha vs Methodist Church of Kenya*, [2016] KECA 273 (KLR). The judgment was overturned by the SC on procedural grounds, but effectively revived through an executive circular prohibiting certain kinds of discrimination in schools. For an analysis of the judgment, see Samuel Ngure, 'Accommodation as an expression of the right to equality: A case note on *Fugicha vs Methodist Church of Kenya*' (2022) 6(1) *Kabarak Journal of Law and Ethics* 189. For a discussion of how the judgment advanced a Kenyan understanding of secularism, see Mukami Wangai, 'Religious pluralism in practice: Defining secularism in Kenya's headscarf cases' (2017) 3(1) *Strathmore Law Journal* 177.

14 Such as India.

15 *EG and Ors vs Attorney General and Ors*, Petition No. 150 of 2016, decided on 24th May 2019 (High Court).

16 *NGO Coordination Board vs Eric Gitari and Ors*, [2023] KESC 17 (KLR).

judgment was marked by caution, as it expressly noted that the case was *not* about decriminalisation. At the same time, however, the Supreme Court's finding that 'sexual orientation' could be read into the word 'sex' under Article 27[17] – and thus, sexual orientation was also a protected 'ground' under anti-discrimination law – at the very least opened the door for future decriminalisation. But if one of the core features of transformative constitutionalism is that nobody shall be discriminated against simply on the basis of ascriptive characteristics (race, religion, sex, sexual orientation, and so on), then it must be said that the jurisprudence on sexual minorities – so far – reflects a gap in the judiciary's record.

One cannot, of course, lay the responsibility for this solely at the feet of the judiciary. As with any other constitution, the symphony that is the 2010 Constitution of Kenya has its jarring notes, provisions that seem to be at odds with its emancipatory and transformative vision. John Osogo Ambani traces the evolution of such provisions in the bill of rights to the requirement that a new constitution must be ratified through a referendum, which was introduced in the Njoya Case, and the consequent shadow of majoritarianism, within which certain issues turned particularly contentious. As Ambani notes, in conclusion, taking a few striking examples:

> The strange wording of Article 26(2) and (4) of the 2010 Constitution implying that life begins at conception and that abortion can only be permitted where a trained health professional certifies that the health of the mother is in danger; and the definition of marriage as an institution of persons of opposite sex (under Article 45) will remain constitutional testimonies to the truth of [Yash Pal] Ghai's philosophy that minority rights suffer at the hands of the majorities.[18]

In such a situation, it must be acknowledged that the judiciary's ability to pull against the constitutional current – even if it desires to – is constrained by the gravitational force of the text. Transformative evolution in the interstices is, of course, always possible. Principled adjudication can work towards harmonising the jarring notes, at least to a degree: for example, by seeking to glean the meaning of specific provisions, or to resolve textual ambiguities in light of the Bill of Rights' overarching transformative vision. It remains to be seen whether – and how – that will happen in the future.

17 Ibid.

18 Ambani, 'The Ghai in our Constitution', *supra*, 173, 177. One may think of this as the inevitable dark side of the participatory process. At the same time, however, as a perusal of the CKRC Final Report shows, the restrictive provisions on both abortion and same-sex marriages appear to have had their origins in recommendations of the Technical Working Committees at the National Constitutional Conference. *CKRC Final Report*, *supra*, 380–381, 436–437.

That apart, there are other provisions of the Bill of Rights – and of the Constitution – that the courts have pressed into the service of transformative constitutionalism, in creative and innovative ways. In Constitutional Petition No. E052/2023, the Employment and Labour Relations Court was faced with a familiar problem: a multinational corporation – in this case, Meta – trying to avoid national labour law obligations by outsourcing work to contractors and contractual workers.[19] While the case may appear to be a pure labour law case, the court anchored its analysis within Article 41, which set out a *constitutional* right to fair labour practices. This gave the court constitutional ballast for holding that cleverly drafted contractual arrangements – entered into between deeply unequal parties – could not be used to circumvent labour rights. The court could go – and indeed, did go – behind these arrangements to discern who was exercising *actual* control over the digital workspace, and thereby, the 'principal employer'.[20] To no one's surprise, it was Meta.

The court's remedy is also important, as this case concerned content moderators, and the court specifically recognised the harms to mental health caused by content moderation. In fact, it extracted the affidavits of content-moderators that set out, in stark terms, the nature of the tasks that they had to undertake, and the trauma that they suffered as a result. Meta's attempts to get around this by providing 'wellness counselling' was rightly rejected, and the court directed the provision of appropriate mental health support to the workers. The judgment, therefore, is crucial for at least two reasons: the recognition of mental health obligations of digital employers, but also, the constitutional encasement of labour rights in the era of the online, gig economy. It will be interesting to see if, in the future, the court employs similar logic when the inevitable litigation around the labour rights of platform workers comes up before it.

A second example is the judgment of the Mombasa Court of Appeal in *National Environment Management Authority vs Kelvin Musyoka*.[21] The villagers of Owino-Uhuru had waged a long battle against the poisoning of their environment – and their lungs – by the processing of toxic lead in the vicinity. While it was admitted that the villagers' rights to health and a clean environment had been breached, the question was who bore the liability, between the landowner, the factory owner, the regulatory agencies, and the city council. Recognising that environmental pollution was caused by the connivance of private operators *and* the state, the court noted that 'the state as an economic operator in the process of regulation and development

[19] *Kiana Monique Arendse and Ors vs Meta Platforms Inc and Ors*, [2023] KEELRC 921 (KLR).

[20] Ibid.

[21] *National Environment Management Authority vs Kelvin Musyoka*, [2023] KECA 775 (KLR).

of economic policies is well recognized, and the state and state agencies also engage in economic activities as operators.'[22] Drawing upon Article 69 of the Constitution, which requires the state to engage in preventive and proactive measures with respect to environmental protection, the court found that a failure of regulation – and a failure to erect and maintain regulatory legal *structures* – was a breach of the state's positive obligations under the Constitution.[23] This judgment is, therefore, crucial in its recognition that pollution is embedded within a political economy where both the state and private actors are intimately involved, and for its determination to fashion a structural remedy to deal with the issue (in this case, monetary compensation and reporting requirements for the clean-up).

The judgment is also crucial in that it rejected the argument that pollution was somehow necessary for 'development' and that, therefore, a 'balance' had to be struck between the two. It noted that the Constitution *already* struck that balance in Article 69, through the language of sustainable development. There could be no question, therefore, of any extra-constitutional considerations or justifications. It will be important to see whether – and how – this logic is deployed in future environmental cases.

And what of public – and police – power, the kind of power that had been most abused under the gutted 1963 Constitution? Indeed, as late as 2023, the courts were still dealing with the fall-out from the authoritarian period. Thus, in *Wamwere vs The Attorney-General*, the Supreme Court considered a thirty-year old case of state violence against a group of protesters known as 'the mothers of the political prisoners'.[24] Disagreeing with the High Court and Court of Appeal's holdings that there had been too much delay in bringing the case to court, the Supreme Court highlighted the ongoing need for society to 'confront the wrongdoings from its past'.[25] Transitional justice, thus, could not have a fixed end-date. It was in the very nature of transitions that there would be occurring and recurring attempts at justice, and the retrieval of historical memory in the effort to achieve it.[26] In a striking moment of self-awareness, the court acknowledged the failure of judicial institutions in ensuring that justice in the pre-2010 era, before going on to note:

> To us, a judicial trial serves to send strong expression of formal disapproval of gross abuse of human rights. It also functions to re-commit state institutions and persuade the general citizenry of the importance of human rights in a polity. On the other hand, failure to ensure access

22 Ibid., para 71.

23 Ibid., para 75.

24 *Wamwere and Ors vs Attorney General and Ors*, [2023] KESC 3 (KLR).

25 Ibid., para 40.

26 Ibid.

> to justice could send the wrong signal that judicial imprimatur has been given to these historical wrongs. Such a stance will encourage not deter potential violators of rights. It would also send the signal to the public that they can be complicit in violation of rights without consequences attaching to the perpetration of such atrocities.[27]

Transformative constitutionalism and transitional justice were thus intimately entwined, as they required both a backward-looking view into the past, as well as a forward-looking view that involved a *continuing recommitment* by state institutions towards the goal of transformation. This might be painful, at times: as Mukoma wa Ngugi wrote: 'it hurts to remember, but it is worse to heal.'[28] But it is necessary nonetheless.

A few months later, in *Mwangi Stephen Muriithi vs Hon. Daniel Toroitich Arap Moi*, the Supreme Court had to reach even further back into history: forty years, and to one of President Moi's countless illegal detentions of his political and commercial rivals (by the time the case came to the Supreme Court both parties had – literally – fought each other into the grave).[29] While a narrowly divided Supreme Court dismissed the case on the ground of misjoinder of parties, it did hold that Muriithi's constitutional rights had been violated by his illegal detention. It reaffirmed the inviolability of *habeas corpus* to the justice system (thus, also, ruling out administrative detention – one of the most abused tools of authoritarian leaders[30] – as a constitutionally valid exercise of state power). Notably, the dissenting opinions, which wanted the court to go further, eloquently reiterated the need for courts not to look away from historical injustices, especially when their effects echoed through the halls of memory and into the present.[31]

Of course, ensuring justice for the past has little meaning if its lessons are not internalised in the present. In *Anthony Njenga Mbuti vs Attorney-General*, the High Court was faced with one of those legal constructs that had been a staple of the colonial regime, and then had been gleefully put to use by the post-colonial state.[32] A set of provisions in the criminal code authorised magistrates to demand 'peace bonds' from individuals, upon being informed by the police that the said individuals were '<u>likely</u> to commit a breach of the

27 Ibid., para 56.

28 Mukoma wa Ngugi, *Unbury Our Dead With Song*, *supra*, 40.

29 *Mwangi Stephen Muriithi vs Hon. Daniel Toroitich Arap Moi*, [2023] KESC 61 (KLR). See also *infra*, Ch. 5, for the horizontal rights issue that arose out of this dispute.

30 And of some constitutional democracies. See e.g., Article 22, Constitution of India.

31 *Mwangi Stephen Muriithi vs Hon. Daniel Toroitich Arap Moi*, *supra*.

32 *Anthony Njenga Mbuti and Ors vs Attorney-General and Ors*, [2015] KEHC 6970 (KLR).

peace or disturb the public tranquillity' (or certain variants of this formulation). Failure to execute the bond would lead to imprisonment. The case was brought to court by individuals who had been compelled to execute these bonds (one of them had spent some time in prison after being unable to do so), despite never being accused, charged, or convicted for any offence: but rather, only because the police believed they were likely to commit an offence.

The state defended these provisions by pointing to their hoary roots in English common law, and their continuance in jurisdictions such as Canada.[33] The High Court, however, was having none of it. Pointing, on the one hand, to the constitutional safeguards for those accused of offences and facing trial, Justice Mumbi Ngugi asked how legislation could 'create a class that is somewhere in the void, against whom no evidence has been found, and yet they are subjected to a process which … must be conducted as nearly as the manner in conducting trials in criminal cases, but for whom … no constitutional safeguards are provided?'[34]

The state tried to dodge this question by a simple – but familiar – linguistic trick. People subjected to the 'peace bond', it argued, were neither 'accused' of nor 'arrested' for an offence, but were simply 'suspects'. As such, they were not entitled to constitutional safeguards that were available solely to those accused or arrested.[35]

Transformative constitutionalism does not, however, allow the state to deprive people of their rights simply by classifying them out of it. Thus, Mumbi Ngugi J immediately asked, by way of response: 'Who or what is a suspect? What is his place within our new constitutional dispensation based on human rights, non-discrimination and the rule of law?'[36] In other words, it was existing law that would have to be 'levelled up' to comply with the Constitution, instead of the Constitution being 'levelled down' in order to preserve the existing criminal code. And, as Mumbi Ngugi J recognised, what mattered to the Constitution was not whether an individual was classified as an 'accused' or a 'suspect', but by the manner and form in which coercive state power was being exercised against that individual.

Having framed the issue that way, the outcome was clear. Because of the inherent subjectivity involved in determining the 'likelihood' of a person committing a crime – and subjecting them to state coercion on the basis of

33 Such provisions may also be found in the criminal laws of post-colonial states. See e.g. Section 107 of the Indian Code of Criminal Procedure for a similar provision.

34 *Anthony Njenga Mbuti and Ors vs Attorney-General and Ors, supra*, para 149.

35 This argument has been used successfully by the state in India, where individuals subjected to the state's coercive processes, but not formally labelled 'accused', have been deprived of various constitutional protections, such as the right against self-incrimination – a position that has been sanctioned by the Indian judiciary.

36 Ibid., para 152.

it – the 'peace bonds' provisions were arbitrary, and violated the Constitution. Moreover, they were discriminatory:

> … the peace bond provisions target the poor, those who are perceived to be in the lower echelons of society, and therefore more 'likely' to commit crimes. Almost invariably, the targets are poor young men, who have not been tried and found guilty of any crime.[37]

Thus, notwithstanding their vintage, and how integrated they were into the state's policing practices, the High Court struck down the 'peace bonds' provisions. Here was transformative constitutionalism, as applied to brute, *physical* state power, operating at its finest.[38]

And lest we think that this is only the preserve of constitutional courts, *Directorate of Criminal Investigations vs Calvince Okoth Otieno* is a striking example of transformative constitutionalism in service of personal liberty and against police power, and at the instance of the first line of defence of all constitutional liberties: the magistracy. In *Otieno*, the police arrested certain protesters and asked the court for ten days' custody in order to 'complete their investigation'. The police spiced up their request – as they often do – with claims of a 'larger conspiracy' afoot that had to be nipped in the bud.

Hon M.A. Opondo – the Senior Principal Magistrate – gave this very short shrift. Relying upon prior jurisprudence of the High Court,[39] she began her analysis by noting that 'the acontextual and simplistic pitting of "public order, peace and security" against the personal liberty interests and autonomy of the Applicant … is a dangerous anti-liberty ethos which was rejected by

[37] Ibid., para 162.

[38] There are two other judgments striking down criminal laws that deserve mention, although I will not discuss them in detail here. In 2017, in *Jacqueline Okuta and Anr vs The Hon Attorney-General and Ors*, Petition No. 397 of 2016, decided on 6th February 2017 (High Court), the High Court struck down criminal defamation as unconstitutional. See Gautam Bhatia, 'Notes from a Foreign Field: The High Court of Kenya Strikes Down Criminal Defamation' *Indian Constitutional Law and Philosophy Blog* (8th February 2017), available at <https://indconlawphil.wordpress.com/2017/02/08/notes-from-a-foreign-field-the-high-court-of-kenya-strikes-down-criminal-defamation/>, visited on 15th September 2024. And in 2024, in *Katiba Institute and Ors vs The Director of Public Prosecutions and Ors,* HCCHRPET No E016 of 2023, decided on 18th March 2024 (High Court), the High Court struck down the criminalisation of 'subversive speech'. See Gautam Bhatia, 'Subversive Speech and the Freedom of Expression: the Judgment of the High Court of Kenya' *Indian Constitutional Law and Philosophy Blog* (19th March 2024), available at <https://indconlawphil.wordpress.com/2024/03/19/subversive-speech-and-the-freedom-of-expression-the-judgment-of-the-high-court-of-kenya/>, visited on 15th September 2024.

[39] A copy of the order is on file with the author.

the Constitution of Kenya.'[40] It was dangerous, in particular, because at the stage of remand, where nothing yet has been proven against an individual, this 'ethos' exempts the state from *its* duty of maintaining law and order, and instead, places it upon the shoulders of the accused individuals (by keeping them in further custody).[41]

Applying this doctrine, Hon. Opondo noted that the state's claims of 'conspiracy' rested entirely on unproven and undemonstrated assumptions. She therefore applied the well-known constitutional doctrine of proportionality, and asked whether the state had managed to prove that depriving the accused individuals of their liberty was the *least restrictive* measure available to it. On facts, the state had failed to do so, and therefore, the request for custody was unfounded.

This order is perhaps one of the most striking examples of a genuine commitment to transformative constitutionalism. Detention without trial was one of the most frequently used weapons in the colonial state's armoury, no matter which the colony. Upon Independence, a lot of states – from India to Kenya – adopted it as a part of post-colonial armoury, to be used against their own people (in Kenya, one of Jomo Kenyatta's amendments specifically concerned detention without trial), to the extent where it became entirely normalized. Hon. Opondo's order set the court's face against such normalisation of state power. In essence, it gave life to the oft-quoted platitude that, in a transformative constitutional order, 'one day without liberty is one day too many'.

## C. Conclusion: To Hold Contradictions in Balance

The examples above provide but a flavour of the many and diverse issues that the Kenyan courts have grappled with, in fifteen years of working a transformative constitution. From adjudicating on the validity of a national biometric identification scheme to evolving a jurisprudence of fourth branch institutions, from grappling with how to make public participation a reality to ruling on free speech and criminal defamation, there is enough already for a lifetime's conversation. This book is but one contribution to that conversation.

Above all else, the purpose of this book is to demonstrate that the Constitution is a terrain of contestation. The transformative vision is a vision that is not guaranteed, but must be struggled for. Like any other human creation, the 2010 Constitution is 'crooked timber', a document with its own tensions and contradictions.

40 Ibid.

41 Ibid.

'We don't question each other's contradictions', Binyavanga Wainaina wrote, 'we all have them.'[42] Transformative constitutionalism asks us to hold those contradictions in balance, and move forward nonetheless. The 2010 Constitution of Kenya has had quite the journey so far, in its first fifteen years. And in the coming times, there is no doubt that it is a journey that will continue to surprise, delight, inspire, sometimes disappoint, but always provoke, stimulate, and challenge: upon the bridge, and always towards the horizon.

42 Wainaina, *One Day I Will Write About This Place*, *supra*, 151.

# BIBLIOGRAPHY

## Primary Material

Bethuel A.K. et al., *Report of the Committee of Eminent Persons on the Constitution Review Process* (Government Printer 2006).

Constitution of Kenya Review Commission, *The Final Report of the Constitution of Kenya Review Commission* (2005).

Office of the AU Panel of Eminent Legal Personalities, *Back from the Brink: The 2008 Mediation Process and Reforms in Kenya* (2008), available at <https://www.kofiannanfoundation.org/wp-content/uploads/2014/08/backFromBrink_web.pdf>.

Presidential Task Force on Building Bridges to Unity, *Building Bridges to a United Kenya: from a nation of blood ties to a nation of ideals* (23rd October 2019), available at <https://d2s5ggbxczybtf.cloudfront.net/bbireport.pdf>.

*Report of the Commission of Enquiry into Irregular and Illegal Allocation of Public Land, Annexes, Volume 1* (2004), available at <https://www.theelephant.info/documents/the-ndungu-report-annexe-vol-1/>.

*Report of the Steering Committee on the Implementation of the Building Bridges to a United Kenya Taskforce Report* (October 2020), available at <https://nation.africa/resource/blob/2486392/88e5205129241296af3755acd99809c1/bbi-report-data.pdf>.

The Independent Review Commission, *Report of the Independent Review Commission on the General Elections held in Kenya on 27th December 2007*, <available at http://kenyalaw.org/kl/fileadmin/CommissionReports/Report-of-the-Independent-Review-Commission-on-the-General-Elections-held-in-Kenya-on-27th-December-2007.pdf>.

## Secondary Material

Ackerman B., 'The New Separation of Powers' (2000) 113(3) *The Harvard Law Review* 633.

Adedeji A. (ed.), *Africa within the World: Beyond Dispossession and Dependence* (Zed Books 1994).

Akech M., 'Institutional Reform in the New Constitution of Kenya' *International Centre for Transitional Justice* (October 2010).

Albert R., 'Constitutional Amendment and Dismemberment' (2018) 43(1) *Yale Journal of International Law* 1.

Ambani J.O., 'The Ghai in our Constitution' in *Furthering Constitutions, Birthing Peace: liber amicorum Yash Pal Ghai* (Humphrey Sipalla and J Osogo Ambani (eds.), Strathmore University Press 2021) 173.

Anderson D., '"Yours in the Struggle for Majimbo." Nationalism and the Party Politics of Decolonization in Kenya, 1955–64' (2005) 40(3) *Jounrnal of Contemporary History* 547.

Arato A., *The Adventures of Constituent Power: Beyond Revolutions?* (Cambridge University Press 2017).

Arendt H., *On Revolution* (Penguin Books 1963).

Atieno-Odhiambo E.S., 'The Formative Years' in *Decolonization and Independence in Kenya: 1940–93* (B.A. Ogot and W.R. Ochieng (eds.), James Currey 1995) 25.

Away F.A., 'A Critique of the Raila Odinga vs IEBC Decision in Light of the Legal Standards for Presidential Elections in Kenya' in *Balancing the Scales of Electoral Justice: Resolving Disputes from the 2013 Elections in Kenya and the Emerging Jurisprudence* (Collins Odote and Linda Musumba (eds.), International Development Law Organisation 2016) 46.

Bannon A., 'Designing a Constitution-Drafting Process: Lessons from Kenya' (2007) 116 *The Yale Law Journal* 1824.

Montesquieu, *The Spirit of the Laws* (Colonial Press 1899).

Bergello P., 'Courts and social change: Lessons from the struggle to universalise access to HIV treatment in Argentina' (2010–2011) 89 *Texas Law Review* 1611.

Berman B., *Control and Crisis in Colonial Kenya: the Dialectic of Domination* (Eastern African Studies 1991).

Bevelhymer C., 'Transformative Constitutionalism and the Adjudication of Elections in Kenya' (2021) *FIU Electronic Theses and Dissertations*, available at <https://digitalcommons.fiu.edu/cgi/viewcontent.cgi?article=6105&context=etd>.

Bhatia G., 'Addressing Boundary and Transplant Issues in Horizontality: The Judgment of the Kenyan High Court in *Busia Sugar Industry vs Agriculture and Food Authority*' *Indian Constitutional Law and Philosophy* (26th February 2024), available at <https://indconlawphil.wordpress.com/2024/02/26/addressing-boundary-and-transplant-issues-in-horizontality-the-judgment-of-the-kenyan-high-court-in-busia-sugar-industry-vs-agriculture-and-food-authority/>.

Bhatia G., 'Consumer Rights, Discrimination, and the Constitution: The Kenyan Court of Appeals Judgment' *The Indian Constitutional Law and Philosophy Blog* (8th July 2023), available at <https://indconlawphil.wordpress.com/2023/07/08/consumer-rights-discrimination-and-the-constitution-the-kenyan-court-of-appeals-judgment/>.

Bhatia G., 'Horizontal Rights, Political Economy, and the Limits of Constitutional Adjudication' (2023), available at <https://papers.ssrn.com/sol3/papers.cfm?abstract_id=4480401>.

Bhatia G., 'The Hydra and the Sword: Constitutional Amendments, Political Process, and the BBI Case in Kenya' (2024) *Global Constitutionalism*, forthcoming.

Bhatia G., *Horizontal Rights: An Institutional Approach* (Hart 2023).

Bhatia G., 'Judicial Evasion, Judicial Vagueness, and Judicial Revisionism: A Study of the NCT of Delhi vs Union of India Judgment(s)' in *Constitutional Resilience in South Asia* (Swati Jhaveri, Tarunabh Khaitan and Dinesha Samararatne (eds.), Hart 2023) 235.

Bhatia G., 'Limiting Executive Power, Enabling Public Participation: The Kenyan High Court's CAS Judgment' *Indian Constitutional Law and Philosophy Blog* (7th July 2023), available at <https://indconlawphil.wordpress.com/2023/07/07/limiting-executive-power-enabling-public-participation-the-kenyan-high-courts-cas-judgment/>.

Bhatia G., 'Notes from a Foreign Field: The High Court of Kenya Strikes Down Criminal Defamation' *Indian Constitutional Law and Philosophy Blog* (8th February 2017), available at <https://indconlawphil.wordpress.com/2017/02/08/notes-from-a-foreign-field-the-high-court-of-kenya-strikes-down-criminal-defamation/>.

Bhatia G., 'Subversive Speech and the Freedom of Expression: the Judgment of the High Court of Kenya' *Indian Constitutional Law and Philosophy Blog* (19th March 2024), available at <https://indconlawphil.wordpress.com/2024/03/19/subversive-speech-and-the-freedom-of-expression-the-judgment-of-the-high-court-of-kenya/>.

Bhatia G., *The Transformative Constitution: A Radical Biography in Nine Acts* (HarperCollins India 2019).

Black Jr C.L., 'The Supreme Court, 1966 Term – Foreword: "State Action", Equal Protection, and California's Proposition 14' (1967) 81 *Harvard Law Review* 71.

Boone C., 'Land Conflicts and Distributive Politics in Kenya' (2012) 55(1) *African Studies Review* 75.

Boone C. et al., 'Land Politics under Kenya's New Constitution: Counties, Devolution, and the National Land Commission' *LSE Working Paper Series No. 16–178* (2016), available at <https://eprints.lse.ac.uk/101817/1/Boone_land_politics_under_kenyas_new_constitution_wp_9.pdf>.

Bosire C., 'The Constitutional and Legal Framework of Devolved Government and its Relevance to Development in Kenya' in *Human Rights and Democratic Governance in Kenya: A post-2007 Appraisal* (Morris Kiwinda Mbondeyi et al. (eds.), PULP 2015) 211.

Branch D. and Cheeseman N., 'The politics of control in Kenya: Understanding the bureaucratic-executive state, 1952–78' (2006) 107 *Review of African Political Economy* 11.

Calgaro C., 'Latin American Constitutionalism: Comparative Law Study on Popular Participation for Urban Land Planning' (2023) 15(1) *Rev. Dir. Cid., Rio de Janeiro* 237.

Chitere P. et al., 'Kenya Constitutional Documents: A Comparative Analysis' (2006) *IPAR Working Paper No. 7/2006*, available at <https://www.cmi.no/publications/file/2367-kenya-constitutional-documents.pdf>.

Cohen G.A., 'Freedom and Money' in *On the Currency of Egalitarian Justice, and other Essays in Political Philosophy* (G.A. Cohen and Michael Otsuka (eds.), Princeton University Press 2011) 166.

Cohen M., 'The Basis of Contract' (1933) 46 *Harvard Law Review* 553.

Colón-Rios J.I., *Constituent Power and the Law* (Oxford University Press 2020).

Connan D., 'Race for Distinction: A Social History of Private Members' Clubs in Colonial Kenya' (PhD Thesis, The European University Institute 2015).

Constitutional Court of the Republic of Lithuania, 'On Organising and Calling Referendums: Summary,' available at <https://www.lrkt.lt/en/court-acts/search/170/ta859/summary>.

Cottrell J. and Ghai Y., 'Constitution Making and Democratisation in Kenya (2000–2005)' (2007) 14(1) *Democratisation* 1.

Cousins B. et al., 'Imithetho yomhlaba yaseMsinga: The living law of land in Msinga, KwaZulu-Natal' PLAAS Research Report 43 (Institute for Poverty, Land and Agrarian Studies, School of Government, Faculty of Economic and Management Sciences, University of the Western Cape 2011), available at <https://repository.uwc.ac.za/xmlui/bitstream/handle/10566/4488/rr_43_imithetho_yomhlaba_yasemsinga_living_law_land_Msinga_2011.pdf?sequence=1&isAllowed=y>.

Cover R., 'Violence and the Word' (1986) 95 *The Yale Law Journal* 1601.

D'Arcy M., 'Devolution and County Government' in *The Oxford Handbook of Kenyan Politics* (N. Cheeseman, K. Kanyinga, and G. Lynch (eds.), Oxford University Press 2020) 251.

Dasgupta S., *Legalizing the Revolution: India and the Constitution of the Postcolony* (Cambridge University Press 2024).

Deveaux K., 'UNODC and COPAC Pacific Regional Conference: Constituency Development Funds Conference Discussion Paper and Report' (2022), available at <https://www.unodc.org/roseap/uploads/documents/pacific/2023/CDF_conference_report.pdf>.

de Smith S., *The New Commonwealth and its Constitutions* (Stevens and Sons 1964).

Diepeveen S., '"The Kenyas we don't want": Popular Thought Over Constitutional Review in Kenya, 2002' (2010) 48(2) *The Journal of Modern African Studies* 231.

Douglas W.O., *The Douglas Letters: Selections from the Private Papers of Justice William O. Douglas* (Adler & Adler 1987).

Dowdle M.W. and Wilkinson M.A. (eds.), *Constitutionalism beyond Liberalism* (Cambridge University Press 2017).

Duchacek I.D., *Power Maps: Comparative Politics of Constitutions* (Clio Books 1973)

Elkins C., *Britain's Gulag: The Brutal End of Empire in Kenya* (The Bodley Head 2014).

Evelyn H. and Wanyoike W., 'A New Dawn Postponed: The Constitutional Threshold for Valid Elections in Kenya and Section 83 of the Elections Act' in *Balancing the Scales of Electoral Justice: Resolving Disputes from the 2013 Elections in Kenya and the Emerging Jurisprudence* (Collins Odote and Linda Musumba (eds.), International Development Law Organisation 2016) 78.

Finn M., 'Befriending the Bogeyman: Direct Horizontal Analysis in AB v Pridwin' (2020) 137 *The South African Law Journal* 591.

Fombad C.M., 'The Role of Emerging Hybrid Institutions of Accountability in the Separation of Powers Scheme in Africa' in *Separation of Powers in African Constitutionalism* (Charles M. Fombad (ed.), Oxford University Press 2016) 325.

Fredman S., *Human Rights Transformed* (Oxford University Press 2008).

Gargarella R., *Latin American Constitutionalism 1810—010: The Engine Room of the Constitution* (Oxford University Press 2013).

Gebeye B.A., 'Judicial Review and Presidential Elections in Africa' in *Judicial*

*Review and Electoral Law in a Global Perspective* (Cristina Fasone, Edmondo Mostacci, and Graziella Romeo (eds.), Hart 2024) 175.

Gebeye B.A., *A Theory of African Constitutionalism* (Oxford University Press 2021).

Gertzel C., 'The Provincial Administration in Kenya' (1966) 4(3) *Journal of Commonwealth Political Studies* 201.

Ghai J.C. and Ghai Y., 'The Contribution of the South African Constitution to Kenya's Constitution' in *Constitutional Triumphs, Constitutional Disappointments: A Critical Assessment of the 1996 South African Constitution's Local and International Influence* (Rosalind Dixon and Theunis Roux (eds.), Cambridge University Press 2018) 252.

Ghai Y. and Cottrell J., 'The State and Constitutionalism in Postcolonial Societies in Africa' in *Law's Ethical, Global and Theoretical Contexts: Essays in Honour of William Twining* (Upendra Baxi, Christopher McCrudden, and Abdul Paliwala (eds.), Cambridge University Press 2015) 165.

Ghai Y.P. and McAuslan J.P., *Public Law and Political Change in Kenya: A Study of the Legal Framework of Government from Colonial Times to the Present* (Oxford University Press 1970).

Ghai Y.P., 'Chimeras of Constitutionalism: State, Economy, and Society in Africa' Unpublished Paper, University of Pretoria, available at <https://www.up.ac.za/media/shared/Legacy/sitefiles/file/47/15338/chimera_of_constitutionalism_ygl.pdf>.

Ghai Y.P., 'Constitutions and constitutionalism: the fate of the 2010 Constitution' in *Kenya: The Struggle for a New Constitutional Order* (Godwin R. Murunga, Duncan Okello, and Anders Sjögren (eds.), Zed Books 2014) 119.

Ginsburg T. and Moustafa T. (eds.), *Rule by Law: The Politics of Courts in Authoritarian Regimes* (Cambridge University Press 2012).

Grimm D., *Constitutionalism: Past, Present, and Future* (Oxford University Press 2016).

Guha R., *A Rule of Property for Bengal* (Duke University Press 1996).

Hale R., 'Force and the State: A Comparison of "Political" and "Economic" Compulsion' (1935) 35 *Columbia Law Review* 149.

Harrington J. and Manji A., 'Restoring Leviathan? The Kenyan Supreme Court, constitutional transformation, and the presidential election of 2013' (2015) 9(2) *Journal of East African Studies* 175.

Hassan M., 'Continuity Despite Change: Kenya's New Constitution and Executive Power' (2015) 22(4) *Democratization* 587.

Hassan M., 'Federalism and Devolution' in *The Routledge Handbook of Democratization in Africa* (Gabrielle Lynch and Peter VonDoepp (eds.), Routledge 2020) 91.

Herrera J.C., 'Judicial Dialogue and Transformative Constitutionalism in Latin America: the Case of Indigenous Peoples and Afro-descendants' (2019) 43 *Revista Derecho del Estado* 191.

Hodgson T.F., 'The mysteriously appearing and disappearing doctrine of separation of powers: towards a distinctly South African doctrine for a more radically transformative Constitution' (2018) 34(1) *South African Journal on Human Rights* 57.

Hornsby C., *Kenya: A History Since Independence* (I.B. Tauris 2012).

Hughes L., *Moving the Maasai: A Colonial Misadventure* (Palgrave Macmillan 2006).

Ihonvbere J.O., 'Politics of Constitutional Reform and Democratisation in Africa' in *Dynamics and Policy Implications of the Global Reforms at the end of the Second Millennium* (Takumbi Lumumba-Kasongo (ed.), Brill 2000) 9.

Ince O.U., 'Primitive Accumulation, New Enclosures, and Global Land Grabs: A Theoretical Intervention' (2014) 79(1) *Rural Sociology* 104.

Islam N., *Waiting for the People: The Idea of Democracy in Indian Anticolonial Thought* (Harvard University Press 2024).

Kamau J., 'Kenya: When Ministers, Civil Servants Got 100 Acres and Farm House for Free' *Daily Nation* (21st February 2016), available at <https://landportal.org/node/28331>.

Kameri-Mbote P., 'Righting Wrongs: Confronting Land Dispossession in Post-Colonial Contexts' (2009) *East African Law Review* 103.

Kanogo T., *Squatters and the Roots of the Mau Mau* (James Currey 1987).

Kantai P., 'In the Grip of the Vampire State: Maasai Land Struggles in Kenyan Politics' (2007) 1(1) *Journal of East African Studies* 107.

Kapczyinski A., 'The Right to Medicines in an Age of Neoliberalism' (2019) 10(1) *Humanity Journal* 79.

Karuti K., Odenda L., and Kojo S.A., 'The Struggle for Sustainable Land Management and Democratic Development in Kenya: A History of Greed and Grievances' in *Land and Sustainable Development in Africa* (K.S. Amanor and S. Moyo (eds.), Zed Books 2008) 100.

Khaitan T., 'Guarantor Institutions' (2021) *The Asian Journal of Comparative Law* 1.

Khobe W.O., 'Presidential Veto in the Law-Making process: The Case of Kenya's Amendatory Recommendations' (2023) 67(1) *Journal of African Law* 79.

Kithinji M.M., Koster M.M., and Rotich J.P., 'Introduction' in *Kenya After 50: Reconfiguring Education, Gender, and Policy* (Michael Mwenda Kithinji, Mickie Mwanzia Koster, and Jerono P. Rotich (eds.), Palgrave Macmillan 2016) 1.

Klare K.E., 'Legal Culture and Transformative Constitutionalism' (1998) 14(1) *South African Journal on Human Rights* 146.

Koissaba B.O., 'Elusive Justice: The Masaai Contestation of Land Appropriation in Kenya: A Historical and Contemporary Perspective' in *Kenya After 50: Reconfiguring Historical, Political, and Policy Milestones* (Michael Mwenda Kithinji, Mickie Mwanzia Koster, and Jerono P. Rotich (eds.), Palgrave MacMillan 2016) 188.

Koppelman A., 'Originalism, Abortion and the Thirteenth Amendment' (2012) 112 *Columbia Law Review* 1917.

Kramon E. and Posner D.N., 'Kenya's New Constitution' (2011) 22(2) *Journal of Democracy* 89.

Kumm M., 'Who is Afraid of the Total Constitution? Constitutional Rights as Principles and the Constitutionalization of Private Law' (2006) 7(4) *German L J* 341.

Landau D. and Dixon R., 'Restorative Constitutionalism' (2024) 81(2) *Washington and Lee Review* 455.

Landau D. and Dixon R., 'Tiered Constitutional Design' (2018) 86 *George Washington Law Review* 438.

Liebenberg S., 'Towards a right to alternative accommodation? South Africa's constitutional jurisprudence on evictions' (2005) 2 *Housing and ESC Rights Law Quarterly* 1

Liebenberg S., *Socio-Economic Rights Adjudication under a Transformative Constitution* (Juta 2010)

Locke J., *Two Treatises of Government* (Peter Laslett (ed.), Cambridge University Press 1970).

Lumumba O., 'The Role of Civil Society in Land Reforms in Kenya: The Kenya Land Alliance' in *The Gallant Academic: Essays in Honour of HWO Okoth-Ogendo* (Patricia Kameri-Mbote and Collins Odote (eds.), School of Law – University of Nairobi 2017) 171.

Luxemburg R., *The Accumulation of Capital* (1913) (Dr. W. Stark (ed.), Agnes Schwarzschild (trans.), Routledge 1951), available at <https://www.marxists.org/archive/luxemburg/1913/accumulation-capital/>.

Lynch G., 'The Fruits of Perception: "Ethnic Politics" and the Case of Kenya's Constitutional Referendum' (2006) 65(2) *African Studies* 233.

Machado A., *Border of a Dream: Selected Poems* (Copper Canyon Press 2003).

Madison J., 'The Federalist No. 47' *The New York Packet* (1st February 1788), available at <https://avalon.law.yale.edu/18th_century/fed47.asp>.

Maina W., 'Verdict on Kenya's presidential election petition: Five reasons the judgment fails the legal test' *The East African* (20th April 2013), available at <https://www.theeastafrican.co.ke/tea/oped/comment/verdict-on-kenya-s-presidential-election-petition-five-reasons-the-judgment-fails-the-legal-test--1315998>.

Majanja D., 'Judiciary's Quest for a Speedy and Just Electoral Dispute Resolution Mechanism: Lessons from Kenya's 2013 Elections' in *Balancing the Scales of Electoral Justice: Resolving Disputes from the 2013 Elections in Kenya and the Emerging Jurisprudence* (Collins Odote and Linda Musumba (eds.), International Development Law Organisation 2016) 19.

Manji A., *The Struggle for Land and Justice in Kenya* (James Currey 2021).

Manji A. and Ghai J.C., 'The Long Shadow of Land Grabbing – Analysing the Decision of the Kenyan Supreme Court in Petition 8 of 2021' *Indian Constitutional Law and Philosophy Blog* (29th June 2023), available at <https://indconlawphil.wordpress.com/2023/06/29/the-long-shadow-of-land-grabbing-analysing-the-decision-of-the-kenya-supreme-court-in-petition-8-of-2021/>.

Maraga, D.K., 'Scrutiny in Electoral Disputes: A Kenyan Judicial Perspective' in *Balancing the Scales of Electoral Justice: Resolving Disputes from the 2013 Elections in Kenya and the Emerging Jurisprudence* (Collins Odote and Linda Musumba (eds.), International Development Law Organisation 2016) 243.

Marx K. and Engels F., *Capital: Volume 1* (Paul North and Paul Reitter (eds.), Paul Reitter (trans.), Princeton University Press 2024).

Marx K., *The Eighteenth Brumaire of Louis Bonaparte* (1851–1852), available at <https://www.marxists.org/archive/marx/works/1852/18th-brumaire/>.

Mathenge I.M., 'A critique of the Supreme Court's pronouncements on international law and the right to housing in Kenya in *Mitu-Bell Welfare Society*' (2022) 6(1) *Kabarak Journal of Law and Ethics* 1.

Mati J.M., 'Antinomies in the Struggle for the Transformation of the Kenyan Constitution (1990–2010)' (2013) 31(2) *Journal of Contemporary African Studies* 235.

Mau S., *Mute Compulsion: A Marxist Theory of the Economic Power of Capital* (Verso 2023).

Maxon R., 'Constitution-Making in Contemporary Kenya: Lessons from the 20th Century' (2009) 1(1) *Kenya Studies Review* 11.

Maxon R.M., 'The Demise and Rise of *Majimbo* in Independent Kenya' in *Kenya After 50: Reconfiguring Historical, Political, and Policy Milestones* (Michael Mwenda Kithinji, Mickie Mwanzia Koster, and Jerono P. Rotich (eds.), Palgrave MacMillan 2016) 19.

Mazrui A.A., *The Africans: A Triple Heritage* (Little Brown & Co. 1986).

Mboya T., *Freedom and After* (East African Educational Publishers 1963).

Mbugua P.K., 'Why BBI Will Not Promote Peace or Prevent Violence' *The Elephant* (20th November 2020), available at <https://www.theelephant.info/analysis/2020/11/20/why-bbi-will-not-promote-peace-or-prevent-violence/>.

McAuslan P., *Land Law Reform in Eastern Africa: Traditional or Transformative?* (Routledge 2013).

Miyandazi V., *Equality in Kenya's 2010 Constitution* (Hart 2021).

Miyandazi V., 'Setting the record straight in socio-economic rights adjudication: the *Mitu-Bell Welfare Society* Supreme Court of Kenya judgment' (2022) 6(1) *Kabarak Journal of Law and Ethics* 33.

Muhula R. and Ndegwa S., 'Instrumentalism and constitution-making in Kenya' in *Kenya: The Struggle for a New Constitutional Order* (Godwin R. Murunga, Duncan Okello, and Anders Sjögren (eds.), Zed Books 2014) 79.

Muigai G., *Power, Politics & Law: Dynamics of Constitutional Change in Kenya, 1887–2022* (Kabarak University Press 2022).

Munabi D.O., 'Judicialisation of "Mega" Politics in Kenya: Contributor to Democratization or Mere Recipe for Backlash?' in *Reflections on the 2017 Elections in Kenya* (James Gondi (ed.), ICJ Kenya 2018) 51.

Mureinik E., 'A Bridge to Where? Introducing the Interim Bill of Rights' (1994) 10(1) *South African Journal on Human Rights* 31.

Murray C., 'Kenya's 2010 Constitution' (2013) 61 *Neue Folge Band Jahrbuch des offentlichen Rechts* 747.

Murray C., 'Making and Remaking Kenya's Constitution' in *Constitution Makers on Constitution Making* (Tom Ginsburg and Sumit Bisarya (eds.), Cambridge University Press 2022) 37.

Murunga G.R., 'Elite Compromises and the Content of the 2010 Constitution' in *Kenya: The Struggle for a New Constitutional Order* (Godwin R. Murunga, Duncan Okello, and Anders Sjögren (eds.), Zed Books 2014) 144.

Murunga G.R., Okello D., and Sjögren A., 'Towards a New Constitutional Order in Kenya: Introduction" in *Kenya: The Struggle for a New Constitutional Order* (Godwin R. Murunga, Duncan Okello, and Anders Sjögren (eds.), Zed Books 2014) 1.

Musila J. and Wamere G., 'The Vulnerable Guardian Angel: Kenya's Parliament in the Post-2010 Constitution' in *Ten Years On: Assessing the Achievements of the Constitution of Kenya 2010* (Yash Pal Ghai, Emily Kinama, and Jill Cottrell Ghai (eds.), Katiba Institute 2021) 19.

Mutua M., 'Justice under Siege: The Rule of Law and Judicial Subservience in Kenya' (2001) 23 *Human Rights Quarterly* 96.

Mutua M., *Kenya's Quest for Democracy: Taming Leviathan* (Lynne Rienner Publishers 2008).

Mutunga W., *Constitution Making from the Middle: Civil Society and Transition Politics in Kenya, 1992–1997* (SAREAT 1999).

Muzungu M.C., 'Structural interdicts in Kenyan constitutional law' (2022) 1 *Kabarak Law Review* 145.

Mwangi E., 'The Puzzle of Group Ranch Subdivision in Kenya's Maasailand' (2007) 38(5) *Development and Change* 889.

Mwangi P., *The Black Bar: Corruption and Political Intrigue within Kenya's Legal Fraternity* (Oakland Media Services 2001), available at <https://theverdict.co.ke/wp-content/uploads/2022/07/The-Black-Bar.pdf>.

Mwende S., 'Four "rebel" commissioners fault Chebukati for suspending polls' *The Star* (19th August 2022), available at <https://www.the-star.co.ke/news/2022-08-19-four-rebel-commissioners-fault-chebukati-for-suspending-polls/>.

Ndubi M., 'A commentary on the matrimonial property conundrum in Kenya in JOO vs MBO' (2023) 2 *Kabarak Law Review* 147.

Ngcukaitobi T., *Land Matters: South Africa's Failed Land Reforms and the Road Ahead* (Penguin Books 2021).

Ngira D.O., 'Some Passing Reflections on the Building Bridges Initiative' (2020) 5(1) *Kabarak Journal of Law and Ethics* 279.

Ngure S., 'Accommodation as an expression of the right to equality: A case note on *Fugicha vs Methodist Church of Kenya*' (2022) 6(1) *Kabarak Journal of Law and Ethics* 189.

Nichols R., *Theft is Property!: Dispossession and Critical Theory* (Duke University Press 2020).

Njau R., 'The Scar: a Tragedy' (1963) 8 *Transition* 23.

Nwabueze B.O., *Presidentialism in Commonwealth Africa* (St Martin's Press 1974).

Obi Nwakanma, *Christopher Okigbo, 1930–67: Thirsting for Sunlight* (Boydell and Brewer 2010).

Nyong'o P.A., 'State and Society in Kenya: The Disintegration of the Nationalist Coalitions and the Rise of Presidential Authoritarianism 1963–78' (1989) 88(351) *African Affairs* 229.

Ochieng W.K., 'Protecting the Integrity of the Electoral Process: The Promise of the *Maina Kiai* Judgement' (2018) 3 *Kabarak Journal of Law and Ethics* 1.

Ochieng W.K., 'The Horizontal Application of the Bill of Rights and the Development of the Law to give effect to Rights and Fundamental Freedoms' (2014) 1(1) *Kabarak Journal of Law and Ethics* 77.

Ochieng W.K., 'The Independence, Accountability, and Effectiveness of Constitutional Commissions and Independent Offices in Kenya' (2019) 4(1) *Kabarak Journal of Law and Ethics* 135.

Ochieng W.K., 'The State of Judicial Independence in Kenya – Reflections from the 2017 Presidential Elections' in *Reflections on the 2017 Elections in Kenya* (James Gondi (ed.), ICJ Kenya 2018) 5.

Odinga J.O., *Not Yet Uhuru* (Hienemann 1969).

Oduor M., '*Mitu-Bell Welfare Society* redux: a note on the strengths and weaknesses of the Supreme Court judgment' (2022) 6(1) *Kabarak Journal of Law and Ethics* 57.

Oduor O., *Things They Lost* (Scribner 2022).

Ogot B.A. and Ochieng W.R., *Decolonization and Independence in Kenya, 1940–93* (James Currey 1995).

Ogot B.A., 'The Decisive Years' in *Decolonization and Independence in Kenya, 1940-93* (James Currey 1995) 48.

Ojwang J.B., 'Legislative Control of Executive Power in Africa: New Insights' (1986) 19(4) *Verfassung und Recht in Ubersee* 421.

Ojwang J.B., 'The Nature and Scope of the Executive Power in English and French-Speaking Africa: A Comparative Perspective' (1980) 13 *Verfassung und Recht in Ubersee* 319.

Okoth-Ogendo H.W.O., 'Constitutions without Constitutionalism: an African Political Paradox' in *Constitutionalism and Democracy: Transitions in the Contemporary World* (Douglas Greenberg, Melanie B Oliviero, and Stanley N. Katz (eds.), The American Council of Learned Societies 1993) 65.

Okoth-Ogendo H.W.O., 'The Politics of Constitutional Change Since Independence, 1963-69' (1972) 71(282) *African Affairs* 9.

Okoth-Ogendo H.W.O., *Tenants of the Crown: Evolution of Agrarian Law and Institutions in Kenya* (ACTS Press, African Centre for Technology Studies 1991).

Ombati O., 'Jurisprudence on Election-Related Violence in Kenya' in *Reflections on the 2017 Elections in Kenya* (James Gondi (ed.), ICJ Kenya 2018) 103.

Omondi I., 'Masit: Only Chebukati Was Aware of 3 Venezuelans Coming to Kenya with Election Materials' *Citizen Digital* (27th August 2022), available at <https://www.citizen.digital/news/masit-only-chebukati-was-aware-of-3-venezuelans-coming-to-kenya-with-election-materials-n304611>.

Ongoya E.Z., 'Protecting the integrity of the Electoral Process, or, Obfuscating the Electoral Process?' (2018) 3 *Kabarak Journal of Law and Ethics* 11.

Opalo K.O., *Legislative Development in Africa: Politics and Postcolonial Legacies* (Cambridge University Press 2019).

Orago N.W., 'Socio-Economic Rights and the Potential for Structural Reforms: A Comparative Perspective on the Interpretation of the Socio-Economic Rights in the Constitution of Kenya, 2010' in *Human Rights and Democratic Governance in Kenya: A post-2007 Appraisal* (Morris Kiwinda Mbondeyi et al. (eds.), PULP 2015) 39.

Otieno F. (ed.), *New Constitution Same Old Challenges: Reflections on Kenya's 2013 General Elections* (Nairobi/Uraia Trust 2015).

Owino S., 'MPs shocker for Ruto, Raila over Nadco Report' *The Nation* (12th October 2024), available at <https://nation.africa/kenya/news/politics/mps-shocker-for-ruto-raila-over-nadco-report-4792790#story>.

Owuor Y.A., *The Dragonfly Sea* (Knopf 2019).

Oyaya C.O. and Poku N.K., *The Making of the Constitution of Kenya: A Century of Struggle and the Future of Constitutionalism* (Routledge 2018).

Oyugi W.O. and Ochieng J.O., 'The Politics of the Provincial Administration' in *The Oxford Handbook of Kenyan Politics* (Nic Cheeseman, Karuti Kanyinga, and Gabrielle Lynch (eds.), OUP 2020) 221.

Prempeh H.K., 'Comparative Perspectives on Kenya's Post-2013 Election Dispute Resolution Process and Emerging Jurisprudence' in *Balancing the Scales of Electoral Justice: Resolving Disputes from the 2013 Elections in Kenya and the Emerging Jurisprudence* (Collins Odote and Linda Musumba (eds.), International Development Law Organisation 2016) 149.

Presley C.A., *Kikuyu Women, the Mau Mau Rebellion, and Social Change in Kenya* (Routledge 1992).

Riofrancos T., *Resource Radicals: From Petro-Nationalism to Post-Extractivism in Ecuador* (Duke University Press 2020).

Roznai Y., *Unconstitutional Constitutional Amendments: The Limits of Amendment Powers* (OUP 2017).

Sahgal R., 'Evictions and Participation Rights in India and South Africa' (DPhil Thesis, University of Oxford 2022).

Sandbrook R. and Cohen R. (eds.), *The Development of an African Working Class* (Longman 1975).

Sang Y.K.B., 'Horizontal Application of Constitutional Rights in Kenya' (2018) 26 *African Journal of International and Comparative Law* 1.

Schlesinger Jr A.M., *The Imperial Presidency* (Houghton Mifflin 1973).

Sepulveda M., 'The Constitutional Court's Role in Addressing Social Injustice' in *Social Rights Jurisprudence: Emerging Trends in international and comparative law* (M Langford (ed.), Cambridge University Press 2008) 144.

Shandu M. and Clark M., 'Rethinking Property: Towards a Values-Based Approach to Property Relations in South Africa' (2021) 11(1) *Constitutional Court Review* 1.

Shivji I.G., *Accumulation in an African Periphery: A Theoretical Framework* (Mkuki na Nyota Publishers 2009).

Signe L., 'Executive Power and Horizontal Accountability' in *The Routledge Handbook of Democratization in Africa* (Gabrielle Lynch and Peter VonDoepp (eds.), Routledge 2020) 117.

Sihanya B., 'Reconstructing the Kenyan Constitution and State, 1963–2010: Lessons from German and American Constitutionalism' (2010) 6(1) *Law Society of Kenya Journal* 1.

Singh M., *History of Kenya's Trade Union Movement* (East African Publishing House 1969).

Sorrenson M.P.K., *The Origins of European Settlement in Kenya* (Oxford University Press 1968).

Southall R., 'The Ngung'u Report: Land and Graft in Kenya' (2005) 32(103) *Review of Political Economy* 142.

Stacey R. and Miyandazi V., 'Constituting and Regulating Democracy: Kenya's Election Commission and the Courts in the 2010s' (2021) 16 *Asian Journal of Comparative Law* 193.

Swynnerton R.J.M., *A Plan to Intensify the Development of African Agriculture in Kenya* (Nairobi Government Printer 1954).

Tamarkin M., 'The Roots of Political Stability in Kenya' (1978) 77(308) *African Affairs* 297.

Thiankolu M., 'Role of the Courts in Ensuring Free and Fair Elections in Kenya: A Tale of Fifty-Six Years of Legal Sophistry and Intellectual Dishonesty' (2019) 4(1) *Kabarak Journal of Law and Ethics* 53.

Thiankolu M., 'Standards of Review and Resolution of Electoral Disputes in Kenya: A Review of the Jurisdiction of the High Court, the Court of Appeal, and the Supreme Court' in *Balancing the Scales of Electoral Justice: Resolving Disputes from the 2013 Elections in Kenya and the Emerging Jurisprudence* (Collins Odote and Linda Musumba (eds.), International Development Law Organisation 2016) 114.

Thuo L., *Compendium of 2017 Election Petitions* (ICJ Kenya 2019).

Tierney S., *Constitutional Referendums: The Theory and Practice of Republican Deliberation* (Oxford University Press 2012).

Tillin L., 'Building a National Economy: Origins of Centralised Federalism in India' (2021) 51(2) *The Journal of Federalism* 161.

van der Walt A.J., 'Squatting and the Right to Shelter' (1992) 1 *Journal of South African Law* 40.

van der Walt A.J., *Property at the Margins* (Hart 2009).

Velasco-Rivera M. and Colón-Rios J., 'On the legal implications of a "permanent" constituent power' (2023) 12(2) *Global Constitutionalism* 269.

Verdugo S., 'Is it time to abandon the theory of constituent power?' (2023) 21(1) *International Journal of Constitutional Law* 14.

wa Ngugi M., *Unbury Our Dead With Song* (Cassava Republic 2020).

wa Thiong'o N., *In the House of the Interpreter* (Vintage Books 2013).

Wainaina B., *How to Write About Africa* (Hamish Hamilton 2022).

Wainaina B., *One Day I Will Write About This Place: A Memoir* (Graywolf Press 2012).

Waldron J., 'Separation of Powers in Thought and Practice' (2013) 54(2) *Boston College Law Review* 433.

Waluchow W. and Kyritsis D., 'Constitutionalism' in *The Stanford Encyclopaedia of Philosophy* (May 2023), available at https://plato.stanford.edu/entries/constitutionalism/.

Wangai M., 'Religious pluralism in practice: Defining secularism in Kenya's headscarf cases' (2017) 3(1) *Strathmore Law Journal* 177.

Wangai M., Mwangi L., and Kilonzo J., 'Developing Jurisprudence beyond the Horizon: A Critique of the Supreme Court of Kenya Decision in Raila Amolo Odinga and Anr v IEBC and Ors (2017)' (2020) 5(1) *Kabarak Journal of Law and Ethics* 69.

Wanjala S. (ed.), *Essays on Land Law: The Reform Debate in Kenya* (University of Nairobi Press 2000).

Warris A., 'Kenya's fiscal accountability revisited: A review of the historical erosion of the country's fiscal Constitution from 1962 to 2010' in *Human Rights and Democratic Governance in Kenya: A post-2007 Appraisal* (Morris Kiwinda Mbondenyi et al (eds.), PULP 2015) 301.

Wasserman G., *The Politics of Decolonization: Kenya Europeans and their Land Use, 1960–1965* (Cambridge University Press 1976).

Wechsler H., 'Toward Neutral Principles of Constitutional Law' (1959) 73(1) *Harvard Law Review* 1.

Whitaker B.E. and Giersh J., 'Voting on a Constitution: Implications for Democracy in Kenya' (2009) 27(1) *Journal of Contemporary African Studies* 1.

Wolff J., 'New Constitutions and the Transformation of Democracy in Bolivia and Ecuador' in *New Constitutionalism in Latin America: Promises and Practices* (Almot Schilling-Vacaflor and Detlef Nolte (eds.), Routledge 2012) 183.

Wrong M., *It's Our Turn To Eat: The Story of a Kenyan Whistle-Blower* (Harper Perennial 2010).

Zeleza P.T., 'The Protracted Transition to the Second Republic in Kenya' in *Kenya: The Struggle for a New Constitutional Order* (Godwin R. Murunga, Duncan Okello, and Anders Sjögren (eds.), Zed Books 2014) 17.

# INDEX

Printed and bound by CPI Group (UK) Ltd, Croydon, CR0 4YY

13/09/2026

14961005-0004